ADDICTED TO ROMANCE

By the same author

An Immodest Violet: The Life of Violet Hunt

ADDICTED TO ROMANCE

The Life and Adventures of Elinor Glyn

JOAN HARDWICK

ANDRE DEUTSCH

First published in Great Britain in 1994 by
André Deutsch Limited
106 Great Russell Street
London WC1B 3LJ

Cataloguing-in-Publication data for this title
is available from the British Library

ISBN 0 233 98866 1

Typeset by Falcon Graphic Art Ltd
Wallington, Surrey
Printed in Great Britain by
St Edmundsbury Press, Bury St Edmonds, Suffolk

For Keith

CONTENTS

LIST OF ILLUSTRATIONS

Unless otherwise indicated all photographs are used by the kind permission of Christopher Davson and Elspeth Chowdhary Best.

ACKNOWLEDGEMENTS

Elinor Glyn's own family have been most kind and co-operative in letting me see her papers, answering my questions and allowing me to use photographs in their possession. I wish to thank particularly Christopher Davson, Elspeth Chowdhary Best, Lady Susan Glyn and Sir Anthony Glyn. The latter's biography of his grandmother, *Elinor Glyn*, is still, and will long remain, an indispensable account for anyone interested in Elinor Glyn and the period in which she lived.

Many boxes of papers, books, magazines, photographs and even clothes relevant to this biography were stored in the attics above the stables at Carlton Curlieu Hall. My thanks go to Lady Clarissa Palmer for allowing me to spend time working at her home and for her helpful comments on the Glyn family.

Early in my research I received help and kind advice from the archival staff at *The News of The World*, the newspaper to which Elinor was attached as a war correspondent.

An earlier biography of Elinor Glyn and her sister Lucy, *The It Girls*, by Meredith Etherington-Smith and Jeremy Pilcher proved most useful.

My thanks to Gerald Duckworth & Co. Ltd., Elinor's first publishers, for allowing me to quote from her works. I am also grateful to Weidenfeld & Nicolson for permission to quote from Nigel Nicolson's *Mary Curzon*.

Many people have given me assistance in collecting photographic material. I should like to thank in particular Lord and Lady Ravensdale, Tom Rosenthal and Bev Dietrich, the curator of Guelph Civic Museum.

Despite increasingly reduced budgets and attendant pressures the staff of the library of the University of British Columbia have, as always, been extremely helpful.

There are few copies of Elinor Glyn's books available for sale these days. Where have they all gone? I would, therefore, like to thank Pamela Lewis for her assiduous search for books in England and Cheryl Cooper for actually finding for me a much prized copy of *Three Weeks*.

Esther Whitby encouraged my work from the outset. Her successor as my editor, Clare Chambers, has offered many valuable suggestions which have undoubtedly improved the book.

My family has been wonderfully supportive. From afar Rose and Charles Bellhouse have taken a close interest in the book's progress. My son, Benjamin Alldritt, has been a willing research assistant spending many hours in the library and on the computer looking up obscure information.

But the person who has shared most closely with me my research on Elinor Glyn and to whom I owe most is my husband Keith Alldritt. He has driven me to out of the way places, helped me to track down houses in Paris and Versailles and shared with me his extensive knowledge of the Edwardian period. Most valuably of all he took time out from his own writing to read and make careful comments on the first draft of this biography. The help and support he has given me has been invaluable.

PROLOGUE

> On looking back at my life, I see that the dominant interest, in fact the fundamental impulse behind every action, has been the desire for romance.

So wrote Elinor Glyn in her autobiography *Romantic Adventure* written in 1936 when she was seventy-seven. She had just recovered from a serious illness and was looking back to what had shaped her life to that point.

There is a photograph of her taken in that year by Cecil Beaton. She sits on a sofa with her two handsome cats. She is dressed in a rich, long, flowing dark robe with fur-trimmed sleeves. The darkness of her dress is calculatedly offset by a shining necklace. Her luxuriant hair is coiled in braids around her head. She is the focus of her room with its profusion of antique furniture, ornaments, framed photographs, flower arrangements in huge vases, books, portraits on the wall. And on the floor are three tiger skins.

It is a curious photograph. Elinor does not look like the seventy-seven-year-old woman we know her to have been. Her clothes and her surroundings in no way suggest that the date of the photograph is 1936. The room appears to be in a large aristocratic house. It is the kind of room frequently described in Elinor Glyn's novels.

It is, in fact, a very carefully constructed scene belying many realities. The principal actress in this scene is Elinor Glyn herself, quite consciously playing the role of the *grande dame*.

During the course of her life she had created many such scenes designed to provide a suitable ambience for the person she felt herself to be at any given time. As a child she had imagined for herself the setting of a palace or a castle. As a young married woman she had created a romantic boudoir filled with pink silk roses. In Paris she had painted her house in colours which she believed influenced her mood and her mind. In Hollywood she had transformed her hotel rooms with silks and satins and chinoiserie furniture and wallpaper to offset what she saw as the vulgarity of her larger surroundings.

But it was in her spacious room in her apartment in Connaught Place in Mayfair overlooking Hyde Park that she had created for herself the image she wanted to be remembered for. The room looks French rather than English because Elinor wanted to suggest that relationship to the French aristocracy of which she was so proud. There are the two cats to remind us of her early portrait as 'Le Chat Nellie'. There are the books, from which she drew sustenance all her life, within easy reach. The sofa she sits on demands that upright carriage on which she always insisted. But offsetting this severity are the flowers and the silk cushions.

Yet dominating this sophisticated and civilised room, vying even with Elinor herself for attention, are the three tiger skins. This was the animal that from the time of her first visit to Paris had an almost totemic significance for Elinor, and each of the skins visible in the room represents an important and memorable phase in her life.

The image is compelling. We forget or do not realise that we are not seeing a youngish woman of noble birth sitting in one of the rooms of her inherited stately home.

So determined was Elinor on the scene she had created that perhaps she failed to realise that the reality behind the construction is even more impressive and interesting than the fiction. For this elderly woman was not a princess in disguise, as she had hoped as a child. She had, in fact, been born to middle-class Canadian parents and she had achieved her long-desired image not as the result of an accident of birth, nor even a successful marriage, but through hard work, determination and, above all, imagination.

1 AN UNPROPITIOUS BEGINNING

Childhood was not a subject that greatly interested Elinor Glyn. There are few children in her novels, and in her autobiography she does not dwell on her own childhood. Although she spent the first eight years of her life in Canada, she never wrote about it at length and she never returned to the place where she had grown up.

Despite this apparent lack of interest in her early years, the influences of her childhood are everywhere apparent in her work. Her sister Lucy went so far as to say that the fact that the two of them had turned out to be so talented in their different ways and that they had led such remarkable lives was entirely due to the nature of their parents' marriage. In her autobiography *Discretions and Indiscretions* she writes:

> If I were asked now what I consider to be the greatest asset that any human being can bring into life I should reply, 'a great zest for living' and this was bequeathed to me by my parents, as it was to my sister, Elinor Glyn, their only other child, together with a great love of beauty. It was a fitting heritage of their romance.

Unlike her two daughters, Elinor Sutherland was not only happily married; she also loved having children. She had been blissfully happy when early in 1864 she discovered that she was pregnant for the second time. Her lively and beautiful child Lucy Christiana was only eight months old at the time. But the young mother liked the idea of having a large family such as she herself had been part of. She had youth, energy and good spirits and, above all, she had a husband with whom she was passionately in love. He was doing well in his career as an engineer, and the future looked bright as contract after contract guaranteed him work for the foreseeable future.

Elinor Saunders had met her husband Douglas Sutherland almost four years earlier at her parents' farm, Woodlands, in Guelph,

Ontario. Her attractive looks and shy manners had already brought her suitors from among the sons of neighbouring farmers. Her parents and she herself had expected her to marry one of them eventually and to settle down and raise a family in Guelph or close by.

Then one spring morning a new young man had appeared at her parents' regular open-house. He was tall and handsome and completely different in manner from the young men she was accustomed to. Douglas Sutherland had emigrated from Scotland to Canada hoping to do well in the young country where his talents as an engineer would surely be appreciated. His early success and his sense of coming from a distinguished Scottish family (he was sure he was descended from the Dukes of Sutherland) gave him an attractive air of self-confidence. Elinor Saunders fell in love at once and had no hesitation in accepting Sutherland's proposal when it came a week later. Colonel and Mrs Saunders were more hesitant than their daughter. They thought that perhaps Elinor was too young to know her own mind, that she had had insufficient opportunities to meet other young men, and that she had not known Douglas Sutherland long enough to make such a lasting commitment to him. And, although they liked the young Scot and admired his intelligence and willingness to work hard, they were concerned about the kind of future he offered their daughter.

However, they were impressed by the determination that Elinor showed in the matter of her marriage. They knew that, despite her shyness, she possessed a good deal of common sense and that she was usually willing to do whatever her parents thought best. And, after all, they did believe in love matches rather than arranged marriages. The longer they knew Douglas Sutherland the more they appreciated his strength of character. It was already apparent that he had a great influence over their daughter and that he exercised it for the good. No one could seriously doubt that he would be a responsible and loving husband and that Elinor would be a devoted wife. As for the fact that his work would inevitably involve a good deal of travel, it was only how they had begun their own married life.

They gave their consent and in January of 1861 the marriage took place.

The Sutherlands began married life in a small house in Guelph. They were extremely happy together. They both loved music and reading and were delighted with each other's company. But the first of their misfortunes came quickly. Their new house burnt to the ground and they lost most of their possessions including their wedding gifts. There was little time to mourn this loss, however, as Douglas Sutherland was offered a new contract. In the circumstances this offer of work seemed most timely and he accepted it with alacrity, even though the new job meant that they had to leave Guelph and begin again in New York City.

It was a wrench for Elinor to leave the small Canadian town where she had been born and the large family in which she had grown up and to find herself suddenly alone with her husband in a large and alien city in a foreign country. But her courage and good sense did not desert her and before long she found herself enjoying the bustle of New York. The handsome young newlyweds were popular and were soon leading a busy social life and making many friends. Elinor was content with her new life and would have been happy to stay in New York, but when the Civil War broke out, it once again became necessary to move. The future for the Scots engineer no longer looked so promising. When he was offered a job in Brazil he decided that he must accept it despite the hardships he could foresee in undertaking work in South America. He offered Elinor the opportunity of returning home to her family until he had completed his new contract. But she would not hear of being parted from her husband so soon after their marriage and she insisted on going with him to Brazil.

The journey to Rio de Janeiro was quite unlike anything Elinor had known before in her life. The rough seas made her so ill that when at last they reached their destination she was in no condition to travel any further. She had no choice but to stay in Rio de Janeiro at the British ambassador's residence until she was fit enough to face the further rigours of a journey inland. She was very much aware that in her weakened state she would have been a burden to her husband.

As soon as she was well enough Elinor set off to join him. She immediately appreciated why he had insisted that she must be fully well before she left Rio. She had not expected to find the journey inland easy or pleasant but she had not anticipated the total lack of comfort which awaited her when she reached the railway line where Douglas Sutherland was working.

All her life she remembered the horror of the miserable ruined shack in which she tried in vain to make a home. It was worse than anything her mother had encountered in her pioneering days in Canada. For, to her horror, the fastidious Elinor was not even able to keep their shack clean. It was only with the greatest difficulty that she was able to keep herself clean, as there was little water and, of course, no sanitation.

Her early life in Guelph had lacked many comforts but she had not had to face there the terrifying insects and snakes and worst of all the ever present rats. She could barely sleep at night for fear of them, and it seemed like a nightmare when she discovered that they had actually devoured her wedding shawl.

The terrible months she spent in Brazil did not diminish her love for Douglas. She never blamed him for taking her into such a miserable situation. In fact it was while they were in Brazil that their first child was conceived. Fortunately Douglas Sutherland was able to complete his contract and take his wife to Britain to a house in St John's Wood in London in time for baby Lucy's birth.

It was in this same house that Elinor became pregnant a second time. The couple's happiness was slightly clouded by the fact that Douglas had by then accepted work in Italy where he was to assist in the building of a new viaduct near Turin. Elinor's dearest wish was to go to Italy with him. But she was persuaded that it would be better for Lucy and the new baby if, until the child was born, she were go to and stay with an aunt who lived in Jersey. She could then join her husband taking both children with her.

On 17 October 1864 Elinor Sutherland's second daughter was born. She was named Elinor after her mother. A month later, just as Elinor was beginning to think of joining her husband in Turin, she had an urgent letter from the company he was working for. She learnt, with dismay, that having come safely through all the perils of Brazil, he had contracted typhus fever in Italy and was desperately ill.

With little hesitation Elinor decided that she must leave her two baby daughters in the care of her aunt while she travelled as fast as she could to her husband. It was no false alarm. Douglas Sutherland was even more ill than she had feared. Unable to speak Italian she felt that she could not nurse him properly in Turin. She determined to take him back to England where she felt sure she could restore him to health.

The journey back to London was in its way even more of a nightmare than the sea crossing to Brazil. Douglas Sutherland was clearly failing and was delirious most of the time. How great was her relief when she reached London. But it was not to last. Despite her devoted nursing it was not possible to save her husband. Douglas Sutherland died in London on 30 January, hardly aware that his second daughter had been born.

Elinor's situation could scarcely have been worse. She was still recovering from giving birth. She had travelled to Italy alone, tortured by anxiety. She had returned almost immediately with the frightening responsibility of a very sick man. And now at twenty-three she had lost the husband she loved so much and was left with two very small children.

One of Douglas Sutherland's requests to her as he became sure that he was dying was that Elinor should try to stay in England and bring up their children there. At the time his wish seemed reasonable. He had been working with a partner on an invention for the uncoupling of railway trucks and carriages. He had every reason to believe that once this device was patented it would bring in a substantial income in royalties. He died believing that his wife was financially secure.

His judgement about the invention was accurate; his judgement of his partner was less good. After Sutherland's death this man laid total claim to the royalties from their joint venture. In her traumatised state Elinor had no idea how to enforce her claim to a half. It was as much as she could do to arrange for her husband's burial at All Souls, Kensal Green, and to retrieve her daughters from Jersey and take them to London.

However much she wanted to carry out her husband's wishes she found herself unable to do so. She had very little money and no prospect of more. There was no way that a woman of her class with two small children could think of earning a living. Her anxious family was urgent in its desire that she should return to Canada. In her situation the temptation of being looked after once more was too strong to resist.

On 10 August 1865, recognising that no other reasonable choice was open to her, Elinor, with her two daughters, left England by steamer. They reached Toronto on 25 August and then travelled by train to Guelph. For Elinor it was a sad end to all her high hopes when she had left with her husband only four years earlier.

Though no one could have known it at the time, it was a different story for the young Elinor. For she was about to come under the influence of a powerful woman whose forcefully expressed views were to play a large part in forming her character and shaping her life.

2 PIONEERING GRANDPARENTS

Thomas Saunders, young Elinor's grandfather, was of mixed English and French descent while his wife Lucy had an Irish background. They had begun their married life in a manner not unlike that of their daughter and Douglas Sutherland. They too had travelled – their first child being born in India and the second in France.

In the early 1830s they were attracted by the clever publicity of John Galt and the Canada Company. The Company advertised farm land at reasonable prices in the area around the newly created township of Guelph in Ontario, Canada. It was an inviting proposition for a young couple willing to start life in a new country. Although they had only sufficient money to make the necessary down-payment on a plot of land and little else besides, they decided to take their chances, and left France for Canada.

Their first shock and disappointment when they arrived at Guelph was the appearance of the 'city' they had been lured to. For at that time the so-called city existed more on paper than in reality. In 1830 it consisted of thirty log houses, thirty shanties, a large frame tavern in the process of being built, one store, and the walls for several other proposed stone buildings. The Saunderses quickly realised that they were pioneering rather than joining an established community.

The first years in Canada were harder than anything they had imagined when they had left their home in France. They were dogged by bad luck. The house they built to shelter the family burnt to the ground shortly after it was finished, and they had to begin all over again. They had managed to plant their first crops knowing that their only source of income would be from whatever they could grow. But the crops failed and they had little capital to tide them over another year. It was small comfort to know that they were far from alone in facing these difficulties. Many of the first settlers in Guelph had spent all they had on buying their land. Like the Saunderses they had not realised how primitive and difficult life in Guelph would be. When the crops failed many families were not only without money to buy the equipment to farm more efficiently the next year, but they were also without the means to buy the necessities of life. Worst of all, many of the pioneering families were not able to pay the instalments on their mortgages. They had to sell their farms at a considerable loss and return to their families in Europe. They cursed the way in which the Canada Company had misled them, leaving them poorer than when they had started.

The Saunderses were slightly better off than many of their neighbours. Family members in London hearing of their plight offered money to see them through the first difficult years. Family in France helped by sending gifts of clothes and small luxuries. Determined to make a success of their venture the Saunderses and their ever increasing family stayed in Guelph.

Despite all their hard work and courage it was some years before they began to feel that they were making any progress. The sheer isolation of the Guelph community, which the Saunderses had not understood when they read the Canada Company's tempting publicity, made everything so much harder. The town itself had few amenities. It did not even boast a mill. In the winter it was possible to journey to more developed communities such as Hamilton and Dundas by sleigh. But once the snow began to melt the relatively short journey became a major undertaking. The unmade roads which connected Guelph with other places became almost impassable because of thick mud and the number of alarmingly deep pot-holes. Thomas Saunders would set out with one of his sons and another man, knowing that the journey might take two days each way. The cart would jolt and lurch and it was not unusual to be thrown out of the cart into the mud. Much later in 1866 Thomas Saunders wrote about these early days in the *Guelph Weekly Mercury*. It was surely an understatement when he described these necessary journeys as being of 'toil rather than of pleasure'. Looking back, he could describe all the hardships as the price to be paid for the privilege of being a pioneer. It is unlikely that he felt quite the same way at the time.

It was a strange life as well as a hard one that the Saunders family led in Canada. During the long daylight hours of summer everyone worked hard to achieve the bare necessities of life. They laboured on the farm growing their own food, hoping to harvest enough to sell the surplus for cash, and made their own candles and soap because there was nowhere to buy such things. Comforts of any kind were few.

But in the evenings, especially in the long dark winters, they would try to recreate in their log cabin in the wilds something of the civilised European life they had left behind them. Good teachers were hard to find in that community of farmers, but the Saunderses were prepared to employ less than satisfactory ones rather than none in order to ensure that their children would grow up with at least some education in literature and languages. Thomas and especially Lucy always looked to the day when they would not have to work so hard and when the family would be able to realise fully its aspirations to gentility and culture. A reminder of the very different kind of life they had once led and an inspiration in their aim to achieve it once more in Canada was the annual gift of a barrel of goods sent by the family in France.

The silk stockings, corsets and Parisian dresses sent by Thomas's parents might have seemed extraordinarily inappropriate for a family struggling to run a farm in Guelph. And, of course, they were of no use during the day. But it was a different matter in the evenings when the family gathered together in their log cabin, changed into these unlikely clothes to share their evening meal together and to recreate the atmosphere of another time and place.

It was on such evenings that carefully selected books, many sent from France, were read aloud, and the parents tried to instil into their young Canadian family the values they had learnt in other places and circumstances.

Like so many immigrants Thomas and Lucy Saunders clung to the values and attitudes prevalent in France at the time of their departure from Europe. They lived in a time warp with little sense of how things might have developed and changed in the country they had left. What they continued to expect of their children in their isolation bore little resemblance to what they might have expected had they remained in England or France. Much later in her life their granddaughter became very much aware of this discrepancy and put it to good use in her first novel.

Gradually, and much more slowly than had been hoped and expected, the town of Guelph began to grow and prosper. Both Thomas Saunders and his son of the same name were active in the affairs of their community, serving on building committees and helping to organise a local militia. Thomas and Lucy's own prosperity grew with that of the town. They were eventually wealthy enough to be able to sell their original farm, Woodlands, and retire in 1860 to an estate called Summerhill just outside the township, taking their family with them.

When the widowed Elinor Sutherland returned to Guelph, although she had only been away for four years, she found it had greatly changed. The opening of the railway line from Toronto had brought increased prosperity which was visible in the number of new houses and public buildings.

The family, however, had changed very little. Mother, father, brothers and sisters and their children welcomed Elinor and her children warmly. They were delighted with the two new additions and impressed by the fact that on the voyage over the young Elinor had learnt to walk and already worn out her first pair of shoes. It was not long before the newcomers were completely absorbed into the larger family.

3 FIRST IMPRESSIONS

The years spent in Canada had a profound influence on Elinor Glyn's life. She said herself that the time at Summerhill 'developed my character, moulded my tastes and coloured my point of view for life'.[1]

These are large claims to make for that period from the age of one to six and yet Elinor's subsequent life and especially her books suggest that she did not exaggerate.

Her mother's influence was not great at this time. Having steeled herself to take her husband back to London from Italy, to face up to his death, make the arrangements for his funeral, collect her daughters from Jersey and then to get herself and her two active and demanding children to Canada, Elinor Sutherland was exhausted physically and emotionally. For the first time she could sit back and survey her situation and its implications and for the first time she could afford to grieve. She no longer had to look after her children single-handedly; there were other members of the family only too ready to help. She no longer had to worry about money or maintaining an establishment. The qualities that had sustained her through the last difficult years were no longer called upon. Understandably she fell back into the role of one of the youngest daughters dependent upon her parents. She fell into a stupor, and for some time she did little else but sit by the fire and mourn her lost love. Others quickly became more important figures in her daughters' lives.

The baby of the Saunders family, the unmarried Henrietta, 'a deliciously romantic creature' undertook the day-to-day care of the little girls. She lavished love and attention on the two fatherless children. But Lucy soon tired of this. She was a tomboy, and preferred the more robust and active company of her young cousins. Elinor, however, responded to her aunt with affection. Henrietta was especially happy to have the children to care for because she had been disappointed in love. Elinor was far too young to understand this but she seems to have sensed her aunt's melancholy from the way in which she would console herself. It was Henrietta's habit to read aloud from Tennyson's *Idylls of the King*, the first of which had been published in 1856. Like her American contemporary Edith Wharton, the young Elinor revelled in the poems about lovelorn maidens and knights in shining armour doing gallant deeds for love and honour. When she was left alone to play, she would create fantasies based on the stories of knights and ladies and unrequited love. She claimed in later life that it was at this time that she learnt great quantities of poetry by heart including 'Guinevere' and 'Elaine'. The influence of this poetry encountered so young can be seen clearly in her writing as an adult. For not only are the *Idylls* frequently mentioned in her novels and essays, they provide that romantic sense of the relationships between men and women which she never really discarded.

The most important member of the household was Lucy Saunders, Elinor and Lucy's grandmother for whom Lucy had been named. Lucy Saunders was in her sixties at the time. She is described by Anthony Glyn, who is quoting his grandmother Elinor Glyn, as 'a frightening woman, proud, aloof, autocratic, with dramatic manners and a withering tongue'.[2] She had the massive confidence of someone who had not only overcome hardships and brought up a large family in difficult circumstances, but who had achieved prosperity and status in the community in which she lived. When her new grandchildren first arrived in her home she was interested in shaping their characters just as she had shaped those of her own children.

She had not, however, taken into account the very different circumstances she had to deal with. She or her husband had been constantly present in the lives of their children as they grew up. The hard life these children had led in the context of a large and closely knit family had done much to determine the kind of adults they grew into.

Life at Summerhill in the late 1860s was very different from what it had been at Woodlands in the 1820s. It was a comfortable life in the new house, 'a gracious colonial building with a columned portico set in a pleasant park', and it did not offer natural hardships.[3] Lucy Saunders had to invent ways of teaching her grandchildren the discipline which would enable them to be outwardly calm even in the most trying circumstances.

One method she used was to have the children brought to her room twice a day: on each occasion for the first five minutes she made them sit absolutely still and in silence. The five minutes seemed interminable to the little girls. Lucy hated these times and began to hate her grandmother for imposing them upon her. As soon as she was allowed she would rush from her grandmother's room and join in the more lively and congenial activities of her cousins.

Two incidents remained in Elinor's mind as being typical of her grandmother's strict training and her insistence that it was vulgar to show emotion in public.

Elinor hated caterpillars. When one day a furry green creature dropped on her from a tree she screamed with horror. Her grandmother heard of this incident and made a point of dropping another caterpillar onto Elinor and making her sit still while it crawled over her.

Then she discovered that Elinor was afraid of the dark. She told the little girl in no uncertain terms that this was a contemptible fear that she would not tolerate in a grandchild of hers. Elinor never did overcome this fear but she learnt not to show it to anyone.

While Lucy kept out of her grandmother's way as far as possible, and often had to beg her more indulgent grandfather to intervene when she was in disgrace, Elinor responded to the old woman's challenge. She learnt from her a self-discipline which enabled her to appear composed in public whatever emotions raged within. All her heroines are distinguished by their ability to sit still and by the fact that they are not afraid of being silent rather than indulging in idle nervous chatter. It must be said that the adult Elinor's self-control in private was not so complete!

There were compensations for the dull times in her grandmother's rooms. Lucy Saunders approved of Elinor more than of her other Sutherland grandchild. She saw in her something of herself. She would tell the little girl vivid stories of what life had been like in those first pioneering days in Canada. She made a great impression with her tales, and when, in *Romantic Adventure*, Elinor looked back at the history of her maternal grandparents she spoke of them admiringly as 'a gallant old pair of settlers'. She saw in their lives 'the very essence of romance'.

Her sense of the romance of their lives had much to do with those other tales her grandmother told her. Lucy Saunders herself was not French but of Irish extraction. But she took as much pride as he did, if not more, in her husband's French background. She had all the fanaticism of a convert about her husband's country. The France she told Elinor about was the France of the Bourbons. She fired her imagination with the glories of the Sun King and his wonderful château of Versailles. She told her about the rigid etiquette and the grand formality of the court in that glorious setting. She described the Hall of Mirrors with its antechambers, the room of peace and the room of war. She impressed upon the wondering child how in her own small way she tried to maintain the values of that marvellous society; that her disciplining of her grandchildren was to that end. She made a bitter comparison between the way the Sun King had cared for those of his subjects who had colonised Quebec, even ensuring personally that they were sent supplies they needed, and the cynical way the Canada Company had abandoned the families it had taken money from.

Then she told her the story of Marie Antoinette, and how she had used the Petit Trianon to escape from the formalities of court, and how she had later decided to play at being a country girl at Le Hameau. She went on to tell her granddaughter that the revolution had shamefully swept away all that the Bourbons stood for. She had stories of the courage of French aristocrats facing the fury of the mob and even the guillotine.

Elinor accepted all that her grandmother told her. She became a passionate believer in the *ancien régime*. Even her early visits to France did nothing to shake her conviction that the revolution in France had been entirely bad. It was not until late in life that she began to see that her grandmother's view of French history might be too narrow.

In the meantime, Lucy Saunders's suggestion that Elinor was, however distantly, related to French aristocracy and that her father Douglas Sutherland had also come from a titled family fed the girl's pride and fostered a snobbishness that she was never completely to lose.

As a result of all these stories of the French court Elinor accepted willingly her grandmother's rigid code of behaviour. She felt important living up to the high standards of her distinguished background. She identified with Marie Antoinette when she tried not to show fear or emotion. And she accepted willingly Lucy Saunders's belief in hierarchies and the great social responsibilities that went with great positions. All her life she was committed to the notion of *noblesse oblige* as defined by her grandmother. She commented on her relationship with her forceful grandmother saying, 'My dramatic instinct responded to her demand for elaborate manner, aloofness, strict discipline and righteous pride.'

Elinor's belief in the wonderful world her grandmother had described was reinforced when the annual Christmas parcel, the *tonneau bienvenu*, arrived from France. The Saunderses no longer really needed help from their relatives as they had once done in their early days of poverty and hardship. But the tradition was established, and if the contents of the *tonneau* were not strictly needed they were still very welcome because they gave a glimpse of a world far removed from that of provincial Guelph.

For Lucy and Elinor, whose whole lives as far as they could remember had been spent within the narrow confines of Summerhill, the opening of the *tonneau* was a magical occasion. Both of them were especially amazed by and attracted to the dresses and hats from Paris. They began at this early age to acquire a taste for Parisian clothes which in Lucy's case was to develop into a successful career.

Both girls were sent to a small local school along with their cousins. Lucy did not learn much because she was not interested, and she was often in trouble. Elinor was serious and well behaved but her mind was usually elsewhere. Already she was beginning to be absorbed in her own imaginary world. She did not welcome the intrusion upon this world of the clergyman whom her grandmother chose to instruct her in religion. For once she and Lucy were of one mind. They disliked the man and refused to believe anything he said.

The lasting effect he had on Elinor was to make her despise orthodox Christianity and to make her even more susceptible to alternatives she found in her reading. She could not accept the Christian God as described by the Canadian clergyman. But her belief in hierarchies made some potent ruling figure necessary to her. Only when she began to read classical literature did she find such figures.

At the end of her six years in Canada a good deal of Elinor's future character had been determined. What Edith Wharton said of herself is just as applicable to Elinor. 'A child of four stores up by anticipation so much of what the mature self is later to enjoy that the adventures of a little girl may incalculably enrich the inner life of an old woman.'[4]

In both cases the adventures being stored up were those of the imagination.

4 A SUITOR

Although at this time in their lives their mother spent comparatively little time with them, both Lucy and Elinor loved to be with her when she could rouse herself from her continuing grief and depression. For she also had stories to tell them. They learnt from her what a romantic and handsome figure their father had been, how he had been a poet and a musician as well as a brilliant engineer. Above all Elinor Sutherland stressed what a perfect love match her marriage had been.

Thomas and Lucy Saunders, however, were beginning to show signs of impatience at their daughter's protracted period of mourning. They had been happy to take her back into her old home on a temporary basis, but they felt that simple common sense suggested she should make a new life for herself and her children. They agreed that it was high time for Elinor to think of the future rather than the past, and they began to look around for someone who would make a suitable husband.

Suitors had come for Elinor Sutherland over the last few years for she was an attractive young woman. She had, however, turned them all away. She used her grief and the fact that she was in mourning as an excuse, but she never explained to anyone a further and important consideration which weighed heavily upon her mind. All the young men who had wooed her were confirmed Canadians. They saw their futures as being in Canada and they would have expected her to feel the same way and to bring up her daughters as Canadians. If Elinor had accepted any one of them she would have had to resign herself to the fact that she could never fulfil Douglas Sutherland's dying wish that his children should be brought up in England.

Her parents were unaware that Elinor dismissed all her suitors because of this ambition to return to Europe. Just as she had shown an unexpected stubbornness when she wanted to marry Douglas Sutherland, so now she showed a similar wilfulness in turning down other possible husbands. They were at a loss to understand her attitude.

Then David Kennedy, who had been a neighbour and acquaintance of the Saunders family for many years, and had even attended Elinor and Douglas's wedding, began unexpectedly to pay court to the young widow. He was still a handsome man and he gave every impression of being deeply in love. Elinor did not find him particularly attractive especially when she compared him with her dead husband. He was more than twice her age for a start. He had reached the age of sixty-three without ever marrying and he seemed set in his bachelor ways.

When he first proposed Elinor turned him down without even seriously considering his offer. She told him that she did not want to marry anyone; that she still mourned the man she had married in 1861 for love and that she would probably never love anyone else in her life.

However, despite his prosaic taciturnity, David Kennedy proved a more persistent suitor than all the young men who had gone before him. He was not deterred by Elinor's first refusal. When she continued to turn him down he enlisted the support of Thomas and Lucy Saunders.

Even the young Elinor knew that her grandparents believed in love matches. Aunt Henrietta had told her that it was because Elinor had been so in love with Douglas Sutherland and he with her that her parents had agreed to the match despite their worries and reservations. Now, however, they felt that some of their fears had been justified, for here was their daughter left alone without an income and with two children to raise. They were not inclined to indulge her a second time. From their point of view David Kennedy was a good match despite the difference in ages. Lucy and Thomas Saunders were persuaded that he did love their daughter, and, although he was so much older than her, he did have the advantage of being a property owner and was apparently well able to support both Elinor and her children.

They began to put pressure on Elinor, reminding her that she had to think not only of her own future but that of Elinor and Lucy. They suggested that it was her duty to put ideas of love behind her in her children's interests.

It was nearly impossible for Elinor to resist her forceful mother whom she was accustomed to obeying. It was also becoming apparent to her that her prolonged stay in her parents' home was becoming a burden to them. More and more frequently there were tensions between the strait-laced grandmother and Lucy which even her good-natured and tolerant father could not easily resolve. And she was aware that her younger daughter was daily more absorbed in a world of make believe than was perhaps healthy.

But what made Elinor look most kindly on David Kennedy was something which her parents had not considered at all. For what distinguished David Kennedy from all Elinor Sutherland's other suitors was the fact that he remained in close contact with his relatives in England and Scotland. Elinor began to hint that she might look more favourably on the idea of marriage if David Kennedy would take her and the children back to Europe.

At first David Kennedy laughed at this suggestion. But to his surprise Elinor continued to refuse to marry him. Gradually he realised that she was serious. He was by now so determined to marry her that he gave in and promised to do as she asked if she would marry him. And so on 14 November 1871 the ill-assorted couple were married. Elinor's feelings as a bride could not have been more different on the occasion of her second marriage. Lucy says in her autobiography, 'Mother looked very sad, I remember, on her wedding day.'

When Elinor and David Kennedy returned from their honeymoon the two girls, Lucy aged eight and Elinor aged seven, moved from Summerhill to the Kennedy farm and to what had been for so long a bachelor establishment.

David Kennedy was in no hurry to keep his promise to his young bride once he had secured her. He had hoped that it was just a passing fancy which her new position as his wife would cure. He had, after all, sunk most of his savings into his farm and he had no other source of income with which to support the family he had taken on. He had no wish to sell his farm and to commit himself wholly to leaving Canada. He did, however, have a sneaking fancy to surprise his relatives and show off his beautiful young bride. He began to consider the possibility of a protracted visit to Scotland and England.

He finally decided that he would try to find a suitable tenant for the farm. This solution would at once provide him with an income and secure his ultimate return to Canada. It took him a year to settle matters to his satisfaction, but at last he was prepared to leave and to keep his promise to his wife.

Elinor Kennedy believed that she had made the right decision. Whatever she had to put up with as David Kennedy's wife, she had at least kept faith with her first husband and was about to take her children back to England. She took pleasure in seeing that Elinor and Lucy were wild with excitement at the prospect of seeing for themselves all those wonderful places they had heard about from their mother and their grandmother. And Lucy, at least, was 'jubilant' at the prospect of leaving behind what she was later to describe as 'dirty little Guelph'.[1]

5 THE NEW LIFE

In the event everyone was disappointed with the immediate outcome of their departure from Canada.

Neither David Kennedy nor Elinor Sutherland had fully appreciated what changes marriage would bring into their lives.

All the time that the older man had been courting the young widow her children had for the most part been kept out of the way by their aunt. When David Kennedy did see them they were on their best behaviour and he made himself acceptable to them by giving them small gifts.

He was not a particularly imaginative man and he did not understand what it would mean to have two small children suddenly a part of his life. Perhaps he vaguely imagined that the two girls would continue to be out of sight most of the time. He had no clear idea that the woman who was about to become his wife was also a mother and that once she moved away from her parents' home that role would inevitably become more demanding and take more of her time and attention.

Under any circumstances it would have been difficult for a sixty-three-year-old bachelor whose health was not of the best to face bringing up two girls both under the age of ten. For David Kennedy the problems were so much greater because those two children were unusual.

Even before Lucy and Elinor moved to their new home Lucy had been at odds with her grandmother. If this stern and confident woman who had brought up nine children of her own and who was accustomed to having young grandchildren around her could not manage the boisterous Lucy, what chance had David Kennedy who was completely without experience of young children. Although Elinor was quieter and more disciplined, she too could throw a temper tantrum and even at seven was disconcertingly opinionated. She had a strong sense of herself as the descendant of aristocratic families and had adopted her grandmother's *ancien régime* outlook and conduct enthusiastically. Both girls could see for themselves that this new husband of their mother's did not measure up to the picture she had painted of her first husband, their real father.

The journey by sea from Canada to England put a strain on the new family from which it never recovered. Previously there had always been sufficient room for them to escape from each other. Now they were all cooped up in a small space. They were tossed about by heavy seas and David Kennedy became ill. Naturally he expected his wife to nurse him. The children were bored and restless and even a little afraid. Equally naturally they demanded the company and attention of their mother and wanted to be entertained by her just as before she had remarried. Elinor Kennedy found herself torn apart as she desperately tried to fulfil the incompatible roles of devoted mother and wife centred whole-heartedly on her husband.

When she could, she read to the girls. But they did not like her first choice of *Alice in Wonderland* at all. Elinor in particular had fixed ideas about kings and queens and how they should behave. The world depicted in *Alice in Wonderland* where values are topsy-turvy and where kings and queens are foolish and undignified offended her greatly. With *The Princess and the Goblin* by George MacDonald it was a different matter. Here was a world the children wanted to believe in, where princes and princesses are finally recognised despite their apparently lowly status. Elinor could readily identify with this story. She was sure that one day it would be discovered that she too was really a princess in disguise.

During that long voyage David Kennedy had plenty of time to question his own judgement. Why had he been so eager to marry? Did having a young, beautiful and submissive wife make up to him for having to put up with her two far from submissive children? And why had he allowed himself to be persuaded to make this foolish journey in the first place? He could see little good for himself coming from it. His resentment against the two girls grew whenever his wife left his side to attend to them.

Throughout their lives both Lucy and Elinor felt that they had been badly treated by their stepfather and they felt that their mother had wasted her youth looking after her tyrannical husband. Influenced by Elinor's description of David Kennedy, her grandson Anthony Glyn, who was not born until long after Kennedy's death, said of him,

'Kennedy's affection for his wife had been shortlived and his true character had already appeared – cruel, selfish, overbearing, mean.'[1] This was Elinor's judgement of her stepfather. Neither she nor Lucy were ever able to see that the position David Kennedy found himself in was not an easy one.

The whole family looked forward to the time when the appalling sea crossing would be over. But again they were disappointed. They landed at Londonderry in Northern Ireland. Their imaginations still full of the fairy stories they had been told, Lucy and Elinor fully expected to step straight off the boat into the sort of world their grandmother had described to them. The reality that confronted them was a severe shock. Londonderry was cold and wet and the roads were muddy. The hotel where they were to stay the night was quite unlike anything the girls had ever known. They were appalled at the dirt, their room where the wallpaper was peeling off the walls, and, horror of horrors, the bugs which they found everywhere.

Thoroughly disillusioned and dismayed by this first encounter with Europe Elinor and Lucy were relieved to leave the next day and travel on to Galloway in Scotland. Here they were to stay with Peter Kennedy, David Kennedy's elder brother, at his home at Balgnegan Castle. Elinor and Lucy brightened up, for this was more like the kind of place they had expected to see. For Balgnegan was a real castle with large, impressive rooms, odd staircases, grand bedrooms and turrets. There were even footmen in livery. Better still, the romantic appearance of the castle was justified: there were stories to hear about the castle as a centre where Jacobites met to plot to restore the monarchy. At first the two little Canadians were thrilled to be at Balgnegan, and for a short time they looked at their stepfather with a new respect. He was, after all, the brother of the owner of this delightful place which was so very different from Summerhill.

The newly married couple were well received by these relatives. They admired Elinor Kennedy but they also made it plain to David Kennedy that they could not understand why at his age he had given up his comfortable bachelor life and saddled himself with the responsibility of a young wife with two children. And why, they asked him, had he then made life even more difficult for himself by setting out on his travels with this young family? All David Kennedy's doubts which had filled his mind during the voyage were only reinforced by his family's attitude and questions. He began to feel that his resentment against Lucy and Elinor was quite justified. He had no compunction, therefore, about making sure that during the stay in Scotland he had the company of his wife without that of the children. Perhaps because she felt guilty about having spent so much time with her daughters during the voyage from Canada, and perhaps because of all that was implied by the attitude of her new relatives, suggesting as it did that she had somehow taken advantage of David Kennedy, Elinor acquiesced in the arrangements which the Kennedys made for the girls during their stay in Scotland.

Once again the children had an unpleasant shock. Up to this point in their lives Lucy and Elinor had always been very much in the midst of the family. Aunt Henrietta or their mother had cared for them and they were never shut away from the adults as a nuisance. Now, suddenly, in this strange and very unfamiliar place they were abandoned by their mother and put in the care of a strange nursemaid.

This young woman had no interest in them whatsoever. She knew that they were there only on a visit, that the family did not really welcome their presence and that no one would enquire too closely into how well she looked after them. So she took advantage of the situation. During the day she would lock her charges into the unheated billiard room while she continued her affair with a fellow servant.

There was no one to whom Elinor and Lucy could protest. At night it was even worse. They were put to bed in rooms far away from their mother and stepfather and left alone in the dark. The castle which had seemed so romantic and thrilling by daylight now appeared cold, gloomy and frightening. All the stories they had heard about the ghosts which haunted the castle now became terrifying. Lucy, who was usually the first to rebel when things did not please her, let everyone know how she felt by screaming and screaming until someone came to see what was the matter.

The Kennedys were scornful about the children's distress. They suggested that they were not well brought up, that normal children of their class would behave very differently. Elinor felt a mixture of shame and anger: she had failed to live up to her grandmother's standards but she hated being treated as if she did not matter. With obvious reluctance and disdain the Kennedys arranged that the girls should have a light at night.

Elinor never forgot this introduction to her new life. What she did not realise until many years later was that most children of the upper classes received similar, if not worse, treatment. Her childhood in Canada had protected her from the common lot of those she liked to think of as her peers. She blamed David Kennedy for her mother's apparent neglect at this time without realising that Elinor Kennedy was only behaving in a manner considered normal by the society of the time. George Curzon, who was to become so important a figure in Elinor's life, rarely saw his mother. He was consigned to the care of servants one of whom was extremely sadistic, perhaps even mad. But he felt that his childhood was not so strange or so different from that of his contemporaries.

Elinor Kennedy found herself in a difficult position. Left to herself she would have treated her children differently. But, after all, one of the reasons she had left Canada was so that her daughters could be brought up in the English fashion. She also knew that she was the object of much curiosity, a colonial girl, a strange choice for the wife of David Kennedy. She did not wish to make herself and her children more conspicuous and more obviously outsiders than they already were by insisting on special treatment.

The round of family visits continued in Yorkshire but nowhere else made the deep impression on Elinor that Balgnegan had done.

David Kennedy had originally planned to settle for a while in the north of England or in Scotland. But as he began to develop the asthma that was to plague him for the rest of his life he revised his plans. He consulted doctors who advised him against the dampness of the north. They suggested that a more suitable climate for him was that of Jersey and he determined to follow their advice. To Elinor Kennedy's dismay she realised that she was to return to the very place where all her troubles had begun. But there was no persuading David Kennedy this time. He was totally preoccupied with his health.

They were to sail from the south coast and so Kennedy decided that they would first spend a few days in London. Young Elinor was overjoyed. She had high hopes of this capital city which she had heard so much about both from her mother and her grandmother. This was where the Queen and all the aristocracy lived. It must be both different from and better than everything she had seen so far.

But her expectations and hopes were cruelly dashed when at last she arrived in London.

In Canada there had been the mud and dirt of the countryside, especially in early spring. But Elinor had never seen the dirt of a large and populous city with many horse-drawn carriages, where the houses were crowded together and where the poor were very evident on the street. This was the London she saw in 1872. All her dreams of the golden city were shattered. She was deeply shocked by this last and most astonishing gap between reality and her dreams. For a while she no longer looked about her with eager interest. Instead she retreated into herself and brooded over the shattering of her hopes.

6 THE UGLY DUCKLING

Elinor was eight years old when she returned to the place where she had been born. She had no memory of it and cherished no expectations of it.

For her mother, however, the return was painful. When she had arrived on the island eight years earlier her future had seemed a bright one. What she faced now was very different. She now knew without any doubt that she could never love David Kennedy. But that very fact meant that she felt an obligation to him far greater than if she had loved him. It was painfully apparent to her that her children did not like their stepfather any more than he liked them. She saw clearly that she would always be torn between her duty to her husband and her love for her children. The best that she could hope for was that the pleasant climate would improve her husband's health and therefore, perhaps, his temper.

Though both Elinors had changed much in the eight years they had been away, Jersey had changed hardly at all. There was still the rigid division between the indigenous population and the growing number of English speaking immigrants, mostly elderly, who had looked to Jersey as a refuge because of its pleasant climate and old-fashioned ways. Those who belonged to Jersey were even visibly different from the newcomers; they were mostly short and dark. They were enterprising and independent: the men farmed, made cider, collected seaweed for compost and fished, while the women had a flourishing industry knitting stockings. Their separateness as a group was emphasised by their language, a patois based on Norman French which was more or less unintelligible to English and French settlers alike.

The English community considered itself superior. Royalist by conviction, the group found its centre at Government House where the Queen's representative, the Lieutenant Governor, resided. A royal militia was stationed on the island. Although at one time it had a real function in defending the Channel Islands from the repeated threat of French invasion, at this time it served a more decorative and social role. A big event in the Jersey calendar was the Annual Parade with the trooping of the colour in honour of the monarch's official birthday. It had been many years since Queen Victoria's visit to Jersey in 1846, but the royalist enthusiasm inspired by her appearance was undiminished.

David and Elinor Kennedy had sufficient claim to good birth to be accepted into the elitist Government House circle. It was a social level that suited David Kennedy particularly well. His worth was acknowledged without his having to exert himself unduly or spend a great deal of money.

For David Kennedy the decision to live in Jersey was initially only a short term expedient. He did not know whether the climate or the life-style would suit him. Therefore, he did not buy a house to live in but rented one. Being the kind of man he was, he cannot have failed to notice that by renting rather than buying he escaped having to pay the poor rates and the parish rates. The house he chose to rent was a furnished one called Richelieu just outside St Helier on the road to St Clement.

During this otherwise rather miserable time both Elinor and Lucy took pleasure in one aspect of their new home. On the walls were portraits by Lawrence, Gainsborough and Lely, the collection of Mrs Coombe, the owner of the house. Lucy made practical use of the portraits. She saw them in terms of the clothes the sitters wore. Her interest in dressmaking which had been stimulated in Canada continued. At first she made clothes for her dolls using ideas from the paintings. Gradually she became more ambitious and made clothes for herself and then her sister and mother.

Elinor was absorbed in the pictures for quite other reasons. After all her disappointments she had begun to fear that the romantic world of lords and ladies did not really exist. But here in these portraits was evidence that at some time and in some place there had been such people. Her imagination was once again set on fire by the lucky chance of seeing the portraits daily.

But the house, the attractive surroundings and the pleasant climate were hardly sufficient to counterbalance the miseries of family life which the change of circumstances had done nothing to improve.

Elinor Kennedy continued to devote herself to her husband and his needs. She made herself see her daughters from his perspective and she was not pleased with them. To suit Kennedy they would have to have been quiet, obedient and respectful towards their elders and betters. In fact, although the two girls were very different in personality, they both lacked the qualities which would have endeared them to their stepfather and thus brought a measure of peace into the house. In a vain attempt to try to discipline the girls Elinor insisted on a rigid household routine based on the needs of her husband. The only result was that Elinor and Lucy became still further alienated from their stepfather.

A simple solution would have been to send the girls to school. But this would have been to go against the custom of their social group on the island. And so there was a long procession of governesses. Because David Kennedy was not prepared to pay for well-trained and educated teachers, the governesses were not a success. The only lessons Elinor profited from were her French lessons. Remembering her grandmother's accounts of France, she was eager to learn the language in the hope that one day she would visit the country. Her teacher was not one of the 'stupid' governesses but an elderly man, Monsieur Cappe. Elinor always remembered his 'soiled linen, ridiculous moustache and unspeakable scent of patchouli and stale tobacco'. But she also developed a lifelong love for the French language and for French literature which she first began to explore under Monsieur Cappe's guidance.

After that first year on Jersey David Kennedy's health was sufficiently improved that he felt able to leave for a while and to pay a visit to his Yorkshire relatives. His wife and stepdaughters went with him. During this visit there occurred an incident which put to the test the training in keeping calm which Elinor's grandmother had insisted upon.

Elinor Kennedy had been invited to watch the meet of the local hunt. She took Elinor along with her for a rare treat. The two of them were sitting quietly in the back of their carriage with a coachman at the front. Quite unexpectedly one of their horses took fright at the barking of the hounds and bolted. The coachman was terrified. Without thinking of his passengers he dropped the reins and jumped from the coach. Mother and daughter sat alone in the open carriage as the horses rushed uncontrolled down the country lane. Elinor Kennedy tried to reach the reins but could not. Even if she had succeeded she did not have the strength or the experience to control the frightened horses. As the carriage careered on it seemed inevitable to both the passengers and the onlookers that it would overturn and that mother and daughter would be thrown out onto the road. But they were lucky. One quickwitted and courageous huntsman saw what had to be done. He galloped ahead so that he could intercept the horses. He managed to grasp the reins and slow down the headlong flight of the carriage. He had saved their lives.

Badly shaken though she was by this adventure, Elinor felt proud of herself. She had not screamed or become hysterical or shown the real terror that she felt. Outwardly she had appeared calm. But, the incident had left its mark on her. From that time forward she was always wary of horses and, though she would often have to ride for social reasons, she took no pleasure in it.

The unhappy routine of life in Jersey was once again broken in 1875 by another visit to relatives in England. This time David Kennedy stayed behind. Once again Elinor and her mother, and this time Lucy also, came close to losing their lives.

They were returning home to Jersey after their visit. The weather was stormy and the seas violent. The ship they were travelling in was driven by the gales onto the greatly feared and dangerous Casquet Rocks. Distress rockets were sent up immediately but there was no response. Before their eyes the passengers could see their wrecked ship being battered by the heavy seas and breaking up. There was no sign that their distress signal had been seen and it was clear to everyone that unless help did arrive very quickly they would all be drowned. The perilous situation made a deep and lasting impression on Elinor as her description written in her autobiography many years later vividly evidences:

> I can still picture in my mind the gloomy scene; the dark and stormy sky, the cries of the seagulls as they circled above, and the thunder of the waves pounding mercilessly upon the slanting deck. My mother held us silently by the hand, too well-drilled by Grandmamma to show the slightest fear, although several of the other passengers were screaming. She whispered to us that we must not forget Grandmamma's teachings and that this was an occasion for us to show that we understood them.
>
> My sister, who was always naturally brave, was not a bit afraid, and I believe she even thought it all a great adventure; but I was filled at first with a kind of superstitious terror. In my pagan imagination, storms

and disasters signified the anger of the gods and I did not believe we should be saved.

Just as the ship was about to break in half and it seemed that nothing could save the wretched passengers from drowning, a tug from Guernsey managed to reach them and to rescue them.

Elinor and her daughters had had a narrow escape from death. They arrived in Jersey deeply shocked. There was bad news waiting for them. At the moment when they had been facing death by drowning Colonel Saunders had died. By a strange coincidence, like the huntsman who had come to the rescue of his daughter and grandchild, Colonel Saunders had, at the age of eighty, attempted to control a runaway horse. But it had cost him his life. Elinor's fear of horses was reinforced.

Then a few months later came more bad news. Not long after her husband's death Lucy Saunders who had been deeply attached to him had died also. The family's strongest ties to Canada were broken.

The Lieutenant Governor of Jersey at this time was Sir William Norcott. He had a daughter, Ada, of about the same age as Lucy and Elinor. The three girls were good friends and spent a good deal of time together. Their favourite occupation was devising performances for a puppet theatre. Lucy, naturally, dressed the puppets, Elinor drew their features and she and Ada wrote the scripts. At Government House they gave their performances.

The three girls were such good companions that Elinor Kennedy had no qualms about leaving her daughters to stay at Government House when she and her husband visited England in 1876. Elinor and Lucy were delighted to be free of the oppressive company of David Kennedy.

Life at Government House was far more lively than at Richelieu. There were lots of formal social occasions and the children were allowed to see the ladies of the island in all their finery. They were especially delighted and thrilled when they learnt that Lillie Langtry was to attend one of these functions.

Lillie Langtry fascinated the girls not least because she too had lived on Jersey. In fact, like Elinor, she had been born there in

1853 at the Old Rectory in St Saviour. She had been christened Emilie Charlotte Le Breton. She was the only daughter in the Dean of Jersey's legitimate family of seven children. The Dean was a man better known for his romantic liaisons and his large number of illegitimate children than for his decorum or religious convictions. It was well known on the island that at sixteen Emilie had fallen in love with a neighbour, a handsome young man. The Dean had intervened to end the affair. With some embarrassment he had told Emilie that her suitor was his son and therefore her half-brother. There was no way she could be allowed to marry him.

But Emilie had escaped from Jersey and her uncongenial family situation. This too interested Elinor and Lucy greatly. In 1874 when she was twenty-one Emilie had married Edward Langtry. Perhaps her hopes for riches had not been fulfilled at that time and perhaps life with Edward Langtry had proved initially to be rather dull. But she had gone on to have a success of her own. As Lillie Langtry she had first been taken up by the painter John Everett Millais, himself a native of Jersey, and then by fashionable society. At the time of her visit to Government House she was enjoying great fame as a Professional Beauty, the genteel and elegant precursor of the pin-up girl. She had not yet met the Prince of Wales and so her reputation was as yet unblemished.

Under normal circumstances the three girls would have been able to get only a glimpse of the famous and fascinating Mrs Langtry. But their enthusiasm and excitement made them inventive. In the ladies' cloakroom was a large dressing-table with a frilled pelmet. Ada, Lucy and Elinor experimented and discovered that with some care they could all three hide under the dressing-table and through three little peepholes would be able to see the Beauty close to. At the most important moment, just as Mrs Langtry was standing before the mirror tidying her hair, the girls' excitement gave them away. Ada's irritated and embarrassed mother scolded them and made them come out from their hiding place. But Mrs Langtry was not annoyed. On the contrary she rightly interpreted their behaviour as flattering to herself and she treated her young admirers with great kindness, taking some time and trouble to talk to them.

The incident made a great impression on both Lucy and Elinor. Both observed Lillie Langtry very closely and in their respective memoirs each was able to give a detailed account of what she had been wearing. Elinor describes her as follows: 'She wore a white corded silk dress, with a tight bodice and a puffed-up bustle at the back. The low neck was square cut, with a stitched pleating round the edge, and her elbow sleeves had lace frills.'

No doubt Elinor's accuracy of description was helped by her habit of sketching people who interested her.

This meeting with Lillie Langtry was more important to Lucy and Elinor than either of them could possibly have realised at the time. Almost unconsciously they registered that here was an example worth following. Emilie Charlotte Le Breton had transformed herself from just a pretty girl without money or connections living on an offshore island to an acknowledged beauty, a woman famous in her own right and one well able to support herself. Her first step had been marriage to someone who did not live in Jersey. Luck had played a part in the second stage of her transformation. But it had been a sense of individual style that had secured her position. Lillie Langtry had not initially impressed by her extensive wardrobe or conventional good looks. She had worn the same simple black dress and done her hair without elaboration or undue concern for current fashion. She had set the fashion and when she did become well known and consequently had the credit to enable her to buy more dresses, for a long time she distinguished herself by wearing only black or white. On the occasion Elinor records she was, typically, wearing white. It must have been obvious even to the three young girls that Mr Langtry had played the most minor of roles in his wife's success and that she had become the dominant partner.

Elinor had another and particular interest in Lillie Langtry. Here was a woman whom everyone acknowledged to be beautiful. As a child declared by everyone to have unfortunate looks, Elinor longed to know the secret of being beautiful. By now she had come to believe that her looks were not socially acceptable. When she took part in plays she noticed sadly that she was never the one suggested to play the beautiful heroine. On the contrary she was given comic roles which involved padding and disguise. Her most conspicuous feature and the one most despised was her red hair. She had so often heard other women commiserate with her mother on the misfortune of having a daughter with red hair. In despair Elinor Kennedy had even tried combing her unfortunate daughter's hair with a lead comb as she had been told that this would darken the colour and make it less flamboyant and offensive. Elinor reports with some bitterness that 'the disgrace of having red hair in those days was very real, and there was no division of opinion about its demerits.'

Lillie Langtry had pale soft hair which Elinor could never hope to have. But this woman had created a new notion of what it meant to be beautiful. For the first time Elinor perceived that beauty was not an absolute; that ideas about it changed from generation to generation. In the meantime her sense of her own unhelpful appearance drove her still further into her world of fantasy. There at least she could imagine herself to be a heroine. She began to look to her imagination and to romance for what life had failed so far to provide. But the nature of her dreams had changed since she had first come to Jersey.

> It was impossible for me to live without a dream kingdom, but my new paradise was a much more realistic and worldly place than the old. It was no longer peopled with fairy princes and princesses possessing every quality and virtue, but with the rather peculiar heroes and heroines of my remarkable collection of books.

When the Kennedys returned to Jersey Lucy and Elinor had to leave Government House and return to Richelieu. The time they had spent apart made stepfather and daughters even less tolerant of each other than before. David Kennedy had been unwise to leave the island for his health was now worse than ever. He was impossibly irritable and self-centred. The only pleasure he still enjoyed was playing backgammon, and this he did hour after hour with his wife as a reluctant partner. She too became irritable and because she had to keep herself so much under control when she was with her husband it was her daughters who took the brunt of her bad temper.

Elinor's way of dealing with the situation was to turn her back on it and retreat into fantasies. Lucy, however, grew increasingly rebellious. Governesses left hastily, unable to cope with the two difficult girls. The tension between Lucy and David Kennedy grew to such a point that her harassed mother finally gave in to Lucy's pleas to be allowed to leave Jersey and make a protracted visit to relatives in Scotland and England. She was then sixteen. Unhappily, in this same year Sir William Norcott's tour of duty in Jersey came to an end so that Elinor was suddenly deprived of the companionship of both her sister and her friend Ada.

David Kennedy resigned himself to the fact that he was not well enough to live anywhere but Jersey and so bought a house at 55 Colomberie in St Helier. The move to the new house deprived Elinor of the pictures and books which had become almost as important to her as human companionship.

But there were compensations. Recognising her daughter's loneliness, Elinor Kennedy allowed her to have a collie dog for companionship. Elinor called her dog Roy and loved him passionately. The importance he held for her found a strange and unexpected outlet. Years later, writing that very adult book *Three Weeks*, Elinor introduced just such a dog as the beloved companion of the hero Paul. The rapturous feeling Paul has for his dog has its comic side as his gift of an elaborate jewelled collar suggests. But the importance of the dog in the young man's life undoubtedly echoes Elinor's feeling for her pet.

With the move to the new house came another unexpected freedom. Elinor had hated the governesses who were supposed to teach her but whom she had despised as ignorant. The argument that she used to persuade her mother that governesses were unnecessary was the one she later gave to her heroine Halcyone in the novel of that name. 'I shan't be ignorant – don't be afraid. I would not remain ignorant even if no other governesses came near me.'

In the absence of good teachers Elinor had already learnt by the age of fourteen that her best hope of gaining any kind of education was to read. She had haunted the library at Richelieu. No one had been very interested in what she had chosen to read. The only limitation on her selection was imposed by the lack of library steps: she had to be content with what lay within her reach. Her favourite book had been Charles Kingsley's *The Heroes* which had fed her imagination with Greek mythology. She had not been deterred by the governess who told her that this was unsuitable reading for a young girl. On the contrary the book had given her a thirst for more knowledge of the Greeks. It was a bitterness to her then and throughout her life that there was no one to teach her the language. She also read books of English history which confirmed the royalist sentiments which were the natural accompaniment to her romantic ideals and which her grandmother had so early encouraged. She developed a strong dislike for Cromwell not only because he was a Puritan but also because she considered him ugly. She read the Romantic poets avidly and formed a life-long taste for the *Maxims* of the French writer La Rochefoucauld.

Her sadness at leaving the library which had been such a source of joy to her during her first six years in Jersey faded when David Kennedy sent for his books and his library at last arrived at the new house. The books had been transported from Canada but they had remained with his relations in Scotland until such time as he felt more settled in Jersey. David Kennedy had by then little interest in the collection, but to Elinor the books represented a whole new world to explore. She never forgot the intensity of her delight when she was confronted by David Kennedy's boxes of books. In her novels heroine after heroine is made to express such a delight. For example, in *The Reflections of Ambrosine*, in the midst of all the sordid problems of her unhappy marriage, Ambrosine can cry out with joy 'My books have come, quantities of books!'

The programme of reading on which Elinor now embarked was a highly unlikely one for an ill-educated fourteen-year-old girl. The books she now read included the *Memoirs of the Duc de St Simon*, *Decline and Fall of the Roman Empire*, Sterne's *Sentimental Journey*, Voltaire's *Zadig*, Lord Chesterfield's *Letters to his Son* and Flaubert's *Salâmbo*. The effect of this strange selection was not entirely happy. In *Romantic Adventure*, Elinor suggests: 'Neither modern knowledge nor modern instruction were ever within my reach, and there was no influence in my life to counteract the depressing effect of reading so many cynical books at such an early age.'

Katherine Bush, the heroine of *The Adventures of Katherine Bush*, who has much the same kind of educational experience as Elinor, gaining knowledge where she can from whatever books come her way, is shown to be 'so advanced in certain branches of literature, and absolutely ignorant of the names even of others – showing that it had been merely chance and no helping hand which had guided her'.

What were the long term effects on Elinor of what seems to have been a lonely and often unhappy childhood? They were, perhaps, less detrimental than might be supposed. She did gain some benefits from her solitude, including a lifelong addiction to reading and the acquiring of knowledge. Her self-education may have led her into some strange byways but she was not, as were so many women of her generation, denied access to areas of knowledge considered proper only to males. She did not find herself in the position of someone like Cynthia Asquith who was allowed to learn Greek only on the condition that she kept her lessons a secret, her mother fearing that the more she was educated the less marriageable she would become.

Elinor's loneliness gave her a certain self-sufficiency, a sense of being set apart and of being superior. Secretly she nursed a feeling similar to that of Katherine Bush:

> Could it be that some gentle drop of gentle blood flowed in her veins, transmitted from this source and concentrated in her, having escaped the others, or was it simply from the years of her reading that her mind had developed? But it could not be altogether that, because she remembered instincts and tastes in uneducated early childhood completely aloof from the family's.

Rather than moping on her solitary state she looked at the matter much as does Evangeline in *The Vicissitudes of Evangeline*: 'I have no young friends. When it is getting dark, and I am up here alone, I often wonder what it would be like if I had – but I believe I am the kind of cat that would not have got on with them too nicely – so perhaps it is just as well.'

Most importantly, it was at this time that Elinor developed her acute powers of observation. She made sketch books full of drawings of people she saw around her pinpointing the significant detail that made a person or a costume individual. It was a skill that she developed first in her writing as a fashion journalist and then as a novelist. At the same time she began to write something more than the fairy tales and fantasies she had written so far. Her stories at this time are closer to reality and the everyday world and already show a turn of wit. Her decision to keep a diary was the beginning of that accumulation of the details of her own life on which she was later to draw so fruitfully.

7 LA BELLE TIGRESSE

For two years Elinor lived in a dream of books and writing. She would spend hours in the small downstairs room reading David Kennedy's books which were never properly unpacked. She pursued her interest in French literature, especially that of the eighteenth century, which was the period her grandmother had told her most about. She learnt about the Italian Renaissance and about Roman history. In reading Thackeray she encountered Becky Sharp and saw in her something to emulate: a quickness of wit, a sharpness of judgement and a burning desire to better herself. Much later she was to create her own Becky Sharp in the person of Katherine Bush.

When the resources of Kennedy's book collection failed her she would walk into St Helier to the library and consult reference works there. She had a passion to educate herself and was quite oblivious to contemporary conventional notions of the education suitable for a girl of her age and class.

It was her visits to the library which brought her to the attention of an elderly retired neighbour. He offered to help her by suggesting a coherent course of reading. Her awareness that this man's interest in her was becoming something more than a simple philanthropic desire to further her education at first shocked her. But she realised also that perhaps this meant that she was not as unattractive as she had been led to believe.

As usual money was short in the Kennedy household. David Kennedy's natural inclination towards thriftiness now verged on the miserly. His concern about money was not entirely without cause. His investments were not prospering, money from the farm in Canada was not reliable, and his continued ill health was a constant drain on his financial resources. Mrs Kennedy had never had more than a little money of her own and this went less and less far. There was no question of money being available for new clothes. In order to keep up even a reasonable standard of appearance at those few social events they attended, Elinor and her mother had to spend hours making clothes for themselves.

Slowly, however, Elinor's life began to improve. At a Government House function she met an eighteen-year-old boy from Eton. It is unclear from her diary entries whether he was called Duncan or Herbert. He was attracted to her and did not hide his admiration for both her looks and her intelligence. Elinor was drawn more and more into the small circle of young people on the island. She went to a dance where the Etonian's interest in her piqued other young men so that, to her surprise and delight, she found there was now competition for her company.

Looking at photos of Elinor at this time it is hard to imagine how she could ever have doubted how attractive she was. Perhaps her face shows more character and alertness than that of conventional beauties of the time, and perhaps the prejudice against red hair blinded her contemporaries to her good looks. She was undoubtedly a beautiful young woman. And now the tide was beginning to turn in her favour.

Her young admirer was only holidaying in Jersey and the time came when he had to return to the mainland. Elinor was sad to see him go but she had learnt something from the brief relationship. She now knew that she was not ugly, that she could attract men and that there were other people of her age who shared her intellectual interests and to whom she could talk.

Her new sense of herself was further enhanced when a young Frenchman called on the Kennedys with letters of introduction from David Kennedy's relatives. He met Elinor only on the most formal of terms but he took the first opportunity to follow up this meeting.

Also staying on Jersey was a Mademoiselle Duret. She liked Elinor and was sorry for the young girl who led such a lonely life with so few occasions of interest and pleasure. Was she prompted by Elinor's new admirer to issue the invitation to Paris for a visit? The invitation was gladly accepted by Elinor Kennedy on her daughter's behalf. At last, in the spring of 1880, Elinor was to see the city about which she had read so much and dreamt so often.

Unlike London, Paris was what Elinor had hoped for. She fell in love with the broad boulevards, the imposing buildings, the streetside cafés. She thrilled to the bustle on the streets, the beautifully dressed women and the elegant men. And at night there was the wonderful sense of light everywhere. How different she found it from Jersey.

At first, however, it seemed as if even in this glamorous city she would have to spend her time quietly. There were no young people in Mademoiselle's family and acquaintance. Elinor had hoped that she might perhaps meet her own French relatives, the Fouquet Lemaîtres but they were out of town for the period of her visit.

Anxious to give Elinor something which would make her first visit to Paris memorable, Mademoiselle Duret decided to take her to that most French of institutions, the Comédie-Française.

What the proper and correct Frenchwoman had not bargained for was that Sarah Bernhardt was that night playing the leading role. Elinor had already heard about this actress who had just returned from London with the company. In the roles of Phèdre and the Duchesse de Septmonts in *L'Etrangère* she had taken the city by storm. She was totally unlike any English actress of the time. Ellen Terry described those qualities which had so impressed the audiences:

> She was hollow-eyed, thin, almost consumptive. Her body was not the prison of its soul, but its shadow . . . No one plays a love scene better, but it is a picture of love that she gives, a strange exotic picture rather than a suggestion of the ordinary human passion as felt by ordinary people.[1]

She was in fact not at all typical of the kind of actress normally to be seen at the Comédie-Française. She had already left the company once and even in London had threatened to resign. When Elinor saw Bernhardt in Paris it was in her last role with the company before she did actually resign and set off on a tour which was to take her to the States and the kind of triumphant welcome which Elinor was herself to enjoy some years later.

As an old woman Elinor recalled that the play she had seen that memorable night had been *Theodora* in which Sarah played the title role. But she was mistaken. In the spring of 1880 *Theodora* was not yet written and would not be produced in Paris until December 1884. There are obvious reasons why she should have made this error as *Theodora* was later to have an extremely important influence on her.

What Elinor did remember accurately was the overwhelming

effect that Sarah Bernhardt personally had on her. As a young romantic she was particularly vulnerable to Bernhardt's style of acting. But she was not alone in feeling overcome after seeing this actress. The young Sigmund Freud was bewitched by Bernhardt and during his time in Paris went to see her on every possible occasion. Many years later D.H. Lawrence saw her perform and he too found himself almost in distress at the power of the emotional response she had evoked in him.

Instinctively Elinor recognised in Sarah Bernhardt that same forceful individuality, the ability to do things which were not possible to ordinary women which she had seen to a lesser degree in Lillie Langtry. Here was another role model for her to emulate.

In Sarah Bernhardt's performance that night at the Comédie, Elinor saw acknowledged for the first time in her life a woman's capacity for taking the sexual lead. The highly charged atmosphere of the performance stayed with her and found a powerful outlet in her own work when she came to write *Three Weeks*.

She was still absorbed in the new and entirely unexpected feelings aroused in her by her evening at the theatre when the young Frenchman whose acquaintance she had made in Jersey came to call.

His behaviour towards Elinor's hostess and towards Elinor herself was impeccably formal. He came, he said, on the prompting of his mother who wished to repay the kind attentions shown to her son by the Kennedys by entertaining their daughter.

Mademoiselle Duret was doubtful whether it was proper for her to allow Elinor to know this young man. However, she agreed to take Elinor to pay a formal visit to his mother. In this way the path was paved for the young man's suggestion that he should accompany the two ladies on their sightseeing in Paris. Mademoiselle Duret, with some misgivings, agreed. She could not believe that anything could go wrong as long as she was chaperoning her charge. What she had not taken into consideration was that while she spoke very little English Elinor's admirer was fluent in the language. So it was that right under the chaperone's nose he was able to woo Elinor in a manner which would have been considered entirely unsuitable had there been anyone but Elinor to understand his words. Still under the spell of the sexual excitement created in her by Sarah Bernhardt Elinor made no attempt to stem the flow of her suitor's passion.

And so it was in Paris that this young Frenchman provided Elinor with that image of herself which she ever after thought of as defining the quintessence of her nature. It was during a visit to the Jardin des Plantes that Elinor saw her first tiger. The association between the proud, tawny, feline creature and Elinor with her red hair, green eyes and startling black eyebrows was immediately obvious to the Frenchman.

'Belle Tigresse,' he exclaimed.

But Elinor was not completely swept off her feet. However intoxicating she found the young man's declarations of love and admiration, she was not ready for the next step he proposed. His suggestion that she should elope with him did not please her. Young as she was, she already knew enough about the French and the French way of life from her reading and from her family to avoid making the mistake of taking this to be a proposal of marriage.

Regretfully she parted from her admirer but not before she had received from him the gift of an elegantly bound copy of La Rochefoucauld.

She returned to Jersey with a great deal to think about and a new sense of herself and of her possibilities. She had not finally been offended by the suggestion that she should elope with her admirer, for she exchanged letters with him and continued to do so well into her old age.

Contrary to her expectations Elinor did not find Jersey as dull as she had expected. Lucy had returned home and, at eighteen, a beautiful, animated young woman, she was much in demand, especially at occasions which involved the young officers from the militia.

When Lucy was invited out she often took along her rather quieter sister. Elinor saw that Lucy was falling in love with one of the young officers. Lucy had often been in love before but this time Elinor saw that Lucy was more serious. She had high hopes that Lucy would become engaged.

In the meantime rumours about Lillie Langtry had filtered back to the island. First of all her affair with the Prince of Wales had become public knowledge. Then the somewhat scandalised islanders learnt that as the Prince of Wales had lost interest in his mistress, Prince Louis of Battenburg had fallen in love with her. The loss of the Prince of Wales's patronage had been a serious matter for the

Langtrys. To maintain a suitable lifestyle as the mistress of the Prince Lillie Langtry had been largely living on credit. Once it was known that the Prince had turned his attention elsewhere the creditors had closed in and Lillie Langtry had suffered the humiliation of seeing her home in Norfolk Street auctioned off to pay her debts.

Worse was to come. Mrs Langtry found that she was pregnant. The father could only be Prince Louis. There was no possibility of his marrying his mistress. All he could do was to make a financial settlement. In 1880 Mrs Langtry was back in Jersey.

Elinor and Lucy were very much aware that the woman they had admired so much was no longer received at Government House or in any of the houses of that circle who had made so much of her on her previous visit. Her social ostracism was made complete when the Dean's irregular life became increasingly difficult to ignore, and he was forced to leave Jersey in disgrace.

It was to Paris that Mrs Langtry fled to give birth to her daughter Jeanne-Marie in March 1881. Even the *New York Times* took note of Mrs Langtry's change of fortune asking the question 'Is Beauty deposed or has beauty abdicated?'

Suddenly events at home distracted Elinor from her interest in Mrs Langtry.

Just as everyone was beginning to assume that Lucy's future was assured, she quarrelled violently with her would-be fiancé and left the island without seeing him again. Shortly afterwards she wrote to her worried and disappointed family that while staying at Kings Walden in Hertfordshire she had met James Wallace, a forty-year-old bachelor. He had proposed marriage and she had accepted.

Elinor Kennedy reeled from the shock. To her the proposed marriage was not only unexpected but also highly unsuitable. She had herself encountered James Wallace, who was her contemporary, on her visits to her English relatives. She knew him to be a man inclined to heavy drinking and gambling, and he had a reputation as a womaniser. He was a very different proposition from the young officer Lucy had run away from. But nothing she could say or do would change Lucy's mind once she had announced her intentions.

Lucy admitted later that she had rather hoped that the news of her sudden engagement and impending marriage would send her young officer in hot pursuit to carry her off himself. Only such a romantic and dramatic intervention would have overcome her pride and enabled her to withdraw from what she knew from the outset was a far from desirable match.

There was no last-minute intervention to prevent the marriage and Lucy Sutherland and James Wallace became man and wife in a quiet ceremony in London on 18 September 1884.

Elinor was disappointed and disillusioned by the unglamorous and, to her, unromantic wedding. However, as it turned out, she was to benefit from this marriage more than anyone else involved.

8 BREAKING OUT

James Wallace had no home of his own to which he could take his young bride after the wedding. He was content to accept the offer of a small house for rent in the grounds of larger estate owned by friends of his father.

Lord and Lady Fitzhardinge were the wealthy, good-natured and sociable owners of Cranford Park near Hounslow.

Despite public knowledge that Lord Fitzhardinge had been conceived before his parents' marriage, and despite his consequent inability to inherit his father's title and estates, there were large numbers of the male aristocracy who were prepared to overlook his questionable situation for the sake of the abundant hospitality he provided. He also made welcome officers from the cavalry barracks at Windsor and the friends he had made through his interest in horse racing.

Lucy, as the wife of the tenant on the estate, was well received by the Fitzhardinges and drawn into their circle. At first James Wallace was proud of his attractive young wife and made sure that she had the money to dress well. There were no other young women quite like her in the Fitzhardinge set and they made something of a pet of her. Lady Fitzhardinge found her amusing, and when she discovered that she had a younger unmarried sister in Jersey she encouraged her to invite Elinor to stay and to take part in all the many social activities of Cranford Park. Lucy and her mother both saw in the situation a golden opportunity to introduce Elinor to some eligible and wealthy young men.

And so, for the next few years, Elinor moved backward and forward between Jersey and Lucy's house in the grounds of Cranford Park.

Neither household offered a very inviting view of marriage. In Jersey Elinor Kennedy continued to be the unhappy slave of a domineering and irascible husband. Her lack of financial independence made her totally vulnerable.

At Cranford Park Lucy quickly discovered that she neither loved nor respected her husband. The couple quarrelled incessantly. Their financial fortunes fluctuated wildly depending on the success or failure of James Wallace's gambling forays. Although Lucy had left Jersey in the hopes of achieving independence from her stepfather, she found that, as a married woman, she was as constrained as she had ever been. Still without money of her own she had simply exchanged dependence on her stepfather for dependence on her husband. The discovery that she was pregnant only two months after her marriage emphasised to her just how trapped she was.

Elinor's notions of romantic love were in no way confirmed by the examples of her mother and her sister. She determined, if at all possible, to avoid making the mistakes which had apparently ruined both their lives. For the time being at least she no longer looked to *The Idylls of the King* for an example of how to manage her future but to Thackeray's *Vanity Fair*. 'Like Becky Sharp, I determined that I would never stay where I was, or be content with an uneventful life.'

Becky Sharp's initial success is based on her ability as an outsider to see clearly the nature of society and the weaknesses of its members. She also uses that knowledge to manipulate people and events for her own advantage.

Although never as completely cynical as Becky Sharp, Elinor did have some of her ruthless clearsightedness which she used to make something of her own very difficult position. By the time she was eighteen she could see without illusions the very limited possibilities open to her. She had educated herself sufficiently to know just how deficient her education was. By class, education and temperament she was unsuited to take up the traditional occupation of impoverished young women, that of governess. No other form of paid employment was conceivable.

So what could she do? She could stay with her mother and stepfather, increasingly conscious of herself as a financial burden on a man she did not like. Or she could transfer her financial dependence to some other man by marrying him.

She was not, however, prepared to take this step as rashly as her sister had done. Lucy's example had taught her that 'marriage is an act which can mean almost life or death to a woman'.

If she was not in a position to marry for a grand passion then at least she could be guided by the notion that she attributes to the heroine of *The Vicissitudes of Evangeline*: 'It is wiser to marry the life you like, because after a while the man doesn't matter.'

It was important to Elinor to establish herself in her own right at Cranford Park not simply as the young sister of Lucy. She was successful. Lord and Lady Fitzhardinge were charmed by her immediately. They were taken by her unusual appearance and ready wit. Initially she was less charmed by them, for they made a very odd couple. Lord Fitzhardinge was a very small man whose eccentric choice of tall hats with hedgehog quills sticking out of the crown only emphasised his strange appearance. His lack of height was further underlined by the contrast with his wife – a very large lady indeed.

As Lucy's pregnancy developed, she tended to shut herself away in embarrassment at her changed shape. Elinor, therefore, became the uncontested darling of the Fitzhardinge circle and before long she was not only staying in the big house rather than in Lucy's cottage, but was also being taken about by Lady Fitzhardinge to parties in London and to race meetings at Kempton and Sandown where she began to meet fashionable society.

To her secret delight Elinor found that even in this group her physical attractions were no longer in doubt: men flocked around her. She remained, however, very conscious that her good looks were unusual and perhaps deceptive. Did she look more reckless and adventurous than she felt, she wondered. Would her new acquaintances, like those in Jersey, assume that anyone with red hair and green eyes must have at least a touch of wickedness?

Clothes became a worry. The wardrobe that had been adequate for her limited social life in Jersey would not do for someone trying to make an impression on the Fitzhardinge circle. Together with Lucy and her mother she spent long hours making and altering dresses. The details of how Katherine Bush in the novel of that name makes the best of the limited means at her disposal to contrive elegant costumes reflects Elinor's own preoccupation at this time.

In Jersey she had entertained herself regularly by making sharp little drawings pinpointing the personal idiosyncrasies of the people around her. Now she discovered that her caricatures had the power to amuse others. The Fitzhardinges were delighted with her efforts and showed them gleefully to their friends. Soon Elinor found herself being asked to other houses because of her talent. In a society often bored, her sketches had the invaluable quality of novelty.

Mrs Kennedy's desire for Elinor to meet as many people as possible in order to better her chances of finding a husband prompted her to solicit invitations for Elinor to visit most of her relatives and acquaintances in England. As a result Elinor found herself moving between two very different worlds. On the one hand there was the life of continual partying and pleasure-seeking which she enjoyed at the Fitzhardinges; on the other there was the staid family life of her relatives. In *The Vicissitudes of Evangeline* she depicts such a family visit. The household is run according to strict rules. The Christian virtues are ostentatiously upheld. The daughters of the house engage in such useful pastimes as poker-work and embroidery, and in general 'they never seem to enjoy anything – the whole of life is solid duty'.

In these households the clothes that Elinor and her sister and mother had taken such pleasure in making and which had been so admired in London and Hounslow were looked at askance. In *The Vicissitudes of Evangeline* there is an amusing incident in which Evangeline's nightdress is the object of scandal because 'no nice-minded woman wants things to look becoming in bed'. It is an incident based on Elinor's own experience as described in letters to her mother. In provincial England Elinor found that she was indeed looked upon as something of a red-haired adventuress.

But the biggest disillusionment for Elinor in these early forays into society was to discover the discrepancy between her expectations, largely derived from her reading and the descriptions of her mother and grandmother, and the reality she encountered. She found herself among people who ate too much, drank too much and did too little. Even manners left much to be desired when measured against her own standards. The notions of honour and morality which she had been taught to respect appeared to have no meaning at all in a society which operated unselfconsciously on double standards. In her novel *The Edwardians* Victoria Sackville-West, describing the situation from the perspective of the upper servants, gives a succinct account of the kind of confusion Elinor experienced initially:

> The upper servants . . . suffered most from this confusion of their feelings, for they brought to the consideration of the matter two entire but conflicting systems of opinion, the one learnt in youth in a home decently regardful of moral virtues, the other acquired through years of experience in an atmosphere where self-indulgence was the natural law.

Despite the kindness of some of her hostesses, in particular Lady Fitzhardinge, Elinor never felt other than an outsider in the new and fashionable circles in which she now moved. She felt herself to be not quite English, and what claims she had to be of good family were sufficiently distant to be without weight amongst her new acquaintance. And, of course, she had no money.

Because she was not part of society and was not, therefore, bound by its rules, spoken and unspoken, she could observe it with a fresh, unclouded eye. She began to record her impressions of people and places and wrote numerous letters to her mother in which she did not attempt to hide her scorn and disgust at much of what she saw. Although this time of visiting was neither comfortable nor happy, it was fruitful in providing Elinor with material on which she would later draw when she began to write in earnest. In the meantime Elinor was not allowed to forget that the principal object of all this socialising and all this attention to her wardrobe was for her to find a husband.

At first the family had high hopes, and their sacrifices seemed to have been well directed as proposal followed proposal in 1886 and 1887. But Elinor, who was still only twenty-two, was not yet sufficiently anxious to be married to put aside her distaste and marry any one of her suitors. She first turned down a middle-aged peer. She did not like his fondness for alcohol. Like her heroine Ambrosine, in *The Reflections of Ambrosine*, she 'had not realized up to this that gentlemen got drunk . . . [She] thought it was only common men in the street.' She was also put off by this man's moustache and his habit of sputtering when he spoke.

Her next suitor was even more unlikely. How did the penniless young redhead come to attract a proposal from the elderly Duke of Newcastle, a man who had previously been too interested in the details of ecclesiastical apparel to pay attention to any woman?

No one, however, was very pleased when she turned him down on the grounds that even being a Duchess would not compensate her for the life of absolute boredom she anticipated as his wife. She had a luckier escape than many another young woman, Consuelo Vanderbilt for instance, the young American heiress who was locked up until her wedding day for daring to resist the arrangements for her marriage to the Duke of Marlborough. Her subsequent life with her unloving husband demonstrated the truth of all that Elinor feared.

James Wallace took a particular interest in Elinor's next suitor, a millionaire. Elinor never seriously considered this man whom she found both physically and mentally unattractive. She escaped his attentions for a while by accepting an invitation to Hillersdon in Devon, the home of W.J. Grant. Billy Grant as he was known to his friends was in his forties at this time. He was a bachelor and would remain so all his life. He had a great zest for life and loved to throw parties. He even organised his own wake and held it before he died so that he would not miss the fun. Elinor was the kind of lively woman he liked, and the friendship that developed between them at this house party lasted until his death. At Hillersdon she had her usual success with the male guests and thus incurred the displeasure of the women. When she bewailed her situation to her sympathetic host he simply laughed and asked what she expected with red hair, white skin, a slim figure and her ability to dance beautifully and converse entertainingly.

Undeterred by her clearly expressed antipathy, James Wallace tried to coerce Elinor into marrying the millionaire. He must have hoped that some of the man's wealth would eventually come his way as Elinor's brother-in-law. Without consultation he accepted an invitation for Elinor, Lucy and himself to go for a cruise on the rich suitor's yacht. He tried to use the kind of arguments to persuade Elinor which she later used in *The Reflections of Ambrosine* when the heroine is being urged into a marriage which is most distasteful to her.

' "Remember, chère enfant," he said, "marriage is a state required by society; it is not a pleasure, but it can, with creature comforts, become supportable, and it opens the door to freedom et tous les autres agréments de la vie pour une femme." '

Still Elinor refused to marry. James Wallace, whose temperament was far from placid, flew into a tantrum when he learnt what Elinor had done. Elinor responded in kind. The result was that, despite Lucy's protestations, Wallace refused to have Elinor in his house any longer. She was sent back to Jersey in disgrace.

Much later in her life Elinor was better able to understand the exasperation felt by all those who were trying to help her make a good marriage.

'On looking back I realise that from the worldly point of view it must have seemed very foolish to throw away such apparently good opportunities of marrying well, but I was too incurably romantic to accept anyone who did not attract me at all.'

The winter of that year did nothing to dispel indignation on both sides. Elinor Kennedy was becoming seriously anxious about how to proceed in the difficult business of marrying off her wilful daughter. She was reluctant to send her back to England until the quarrel with the Wallaces had been healed. She decided that she would write to her French relatives, the Fouquet Lemaîtres. To Elinor's delight their response was an invitation for her to pay them an extended visit.

9 ♥ IN SEARCH OF A HUSBAND

It was a joy to Elinor to be back in France once more. At twenty-three she found herself there on very different terms from her earlier visit as a much younger girl under the chaperonage of Mademoiselle Duret. As if to emphasise the difference, she saw once again the young man whom she referred to in her diary as 'G' who had pursued her so ardently on her first visit.

She no longer found him handsome and exciting but stout and rather foolish. She now wondered how much of his former attraction had been the result of the highly emotional state she had been in after seeing Sarah Bernhardt.

The relationship between Elinor and the Fouquet Lemaîtres was a distant one. Nevertheless her cousins Margot and Auguste received her into their family as if she were a near relation. For the first time Elinor had the experience of being a part of the kind of family to which she felt she belonged by right. She was delighted to be taken to Bolbec in Normandy to the family's château, La Valasse, and then to their town house on the Champs Elysées. This broad street lined with elm trees had originally been the design of Le Nôtre. Now it was a busy but elegant thoroughfare on which only the younger members of the best families lived. Their older relatives continued to live in the long-established Faubourg St Honoré.

The family was well placed in Parisian society, an aristocracy which prided itself on its exclusiveness and which was still largely closed to foreigners. Amongst their friends were the Comte and Comtesse de Ségur who invited Elinor to accompany them on a trip down the Seine in their yacht.

There was a double pleasure for Elinor in this invitation. She was, of course, only too pleased to be noticed by members of such an old family. But she also had a special interest in them because she was familiar with the book about Napoleon written by one of the Comte's ancestors. The book's royalist stance reflected her own attitude. A portrait of the Comte de Ségur appears in *The Visits of Elizabeth* where he is named the Comte de Tournelle:

> The Comte de Tournelle is charming, he is like the people in the last century Memoirs, he ought to have powdered hair, and his manners have a distinction and a wit quite unlike anything in England. One can see he is descended from people who had their heads cut off for being aristocrats.

On this visit Elinor saw much more of French life and there was a great deal that puzzled her. She was extensively read in the history of eighteenth-century France but she knew very little about contemporary French society. Strongly royalist herself, she could not understand why her French aristocratic relatives took such matters lightly. Even the Comte de Ségur in spite of his promising appearance was not as royalist as she was. In their turn her new French friends were vastly amused by this young woman's partisanship of kings and queens and nobles long since dead.

What these people did not take lightly were certain conventions, which were rigidly observed. Although her French family was very kind to her, Elinor, nevertheless, could not fail to feel an outsider. As a young unmarried French girl she would have been treated very differently. Because she was English, and because she was clearly without a '*dot*', or dowry, and therefore no threat to the prospects of her unmarried cousins, she was given an unusual amount of freedom. She recorded her experiences at this time in letters to her mother which she drew on freely when she came to write *The Visits of Elizabeth*. As she reports in that novel she was aware that even the visit she was then making to her cousins would not have been possible for her French counterparts for 'it is not considered proper for young French girls to go without their mothers'.

She quickly realised that in England she enjoyed a degree of freedom which she would not have had in France. To be unmarried in France meant that 'even up to forty . . . you mayn't go to the nice theatres, or talk to people alone, or even speak much more than "Yes" and "No".'

Because the Fouquet Lemaîtres did not feel responsible for finding a husband for Elinor, they did not feel the need to protect her reputation as they would have if she had been their daughter.

She was allowed to meet young men and talk to them and play tennis with them. She became a great favourite and her looks were much admired. Young men flirted with her but it was understood by everyone that her lack of *dot* made her unmarriageable. She points out in *The Visits* that the looks which made her popular were a positive disadvantage in seeking a husband: 'You haven't much chance if you are pretty and lively; as she says, the men only like you to be that when you are married to someone else.'

The Fouquet Lemaîtres were astounded to learn that Elinor had received proposals of marriage and had turned them down. They may have teased her about the Duke of Newcastle and his proposal saying, 'Les yeux bleus vont aux cieux, mais les yeux verts vont a l'enfer', but there is no doubt that they felt that such a marriage would have been highly suitable, and that Elinor's family were positively remiss in not insisting on it. In response to Elinor's protest about the lack of romance in arranged marriages, they explained that things were organised differently among their class in France. Everyone knew that marriage and romance were not the same thing at all. Marriage was for maintaining the family and securing proper financial arrangements. Romance was to be found outside marriage and in a civilised society such as that of France everything could be arranged discreetly and to everyone's satisfaction.

Elinor resisted this idea at the time. But when she came to write her autobiography her attitude had modified and she writes almost approvingly of the French system.

'Nearly every married woman in the "chic" society of Paris had a lover, but the greatest care was taken to avoid advertising the fact . . . When they wanted to meet, the lady went to have "five o'clock" at the man's garçonnière.'

Whereas in England lovers were expected to offer gifts and even sometimes to buy clothes and pay bills, in France there were no presents and so, no scandal: 'Things must be done in such a way that the husband could retain his public honour, and no family difficulties must arise.'

It was whilst she was staying with her cousins in 1888 that Elinor first saw that place she had visited so often in her imagination. Her grandmother had spoken glowingly of the splendours of Versailles. In her reading of the many volumes of St Simon Elinor had become familiar with the details of the palace and the rituals of life there. She knew the lay-out of the state rooms and their functions. She knew who had peopled the rooms and how they had behaved. What concerned her was that the reality would fail to live up to her expectations, as had happened so often already in her life. On this occasion she was far from being disappointed. Versailles thrilled her in 1888 and continued to do so whenever she revisited it, even when years later in 1919 she came to live just beyond the palace walls. It was an enthusiasm which she tried to communicate to others many times, not always successfully.

This first visit to her French relatives was a great success and the invitation was repeated in subsequent years. Elinor got to know the English and American ambassadorial staff and developed a close friendship with an English diplomat, Alexander Condie Stephen. She met Mrs Paran Stevens who treated her kindly. This lady was well known for arranging marriages between wealthy young American girls and European titled aristocracy. She had succeeded in making a good marriage for her daughter Minnie. But, though she took Elinor yachting with the eccentric American newspaper proprietor Gordon Bennett, she could do nothing for her in the way of helping her to find a suitable husband. Any girl she took on had to have money.

It was at a ball given at the American Embassy which Elinor attended dressed in a becoming white tulle dress given her by her cousin and with her hair elegantly dressed by Marcel, the French hairdresser who became famous for making regular continuous waves in women's hair, that she encountered the beautiful American heiress, Mary Leiter. Elinor could not have foreseen how years later their futures would become connected.

Although she had a great success at this and other glittering occasions and although she attracted great admiration as she rode her cousins' horses wearing her figure-revealing English riding habit and tall hat, Elinor realised that the years were going by and that, despite the pleasure of her visits to France, they were not fulfilling their original purpose of helping her to find a husband. All that she was ever likely to take back to England with her were the wonderful lacy Doucet dresses which her cousins no longer wanted and the vivid impressions recorded in her letters and journals.

In August 1885 Lucy's daughter Esmé had been born. Gradually the tension between Lucy and David Kennedy had eased so that Lucy and her family were now able to visit Jersey occasionally.

But as Lucy became more reconciled to her stepfather, she became increasingly estranged from her husband. As David Kennedy began to mellow slightly, James Wallace became more drunken and violent. Elinor and her mother were aware of the misery of Lucy's life but there was little they could do to help her.

In 1888 Lucy and her husband and daughter moved from Cranford Park to London and rented a house there. In the same year David Kennedy, who was eighty-one, took the startling decision to leave Jersey and live in London also. He wanted to have access to London doctors for he was convinced they were better than those in Jersey. The inevitable distress and upheaval the old man went through in making a move at his time of life made him as bad-tempered and irritable as he had ever been. Elinor and her mother had a wretched time as they packed up the house at 55 Colomberie and prepared to take up residence in the house that Lucy had found for them at 54 Drayton Gardens.

But neither of them was sad to leave Jersey. Their life there had been straitened and dull and often unhappy. Perhaps Elinor thought again about Lillie Langtry who had left the island seven years earlier and had then gone on to have a successful stage career in the States and who had even become an American citizen. She must have hoped that her fortunes too would change once she was away from her place of birth.

Initially, however, it seemed that they had only exchanged one kind of unhappiness for another. Despite being closer to the doctors he favoured, David Kennedy's health deteriorated. Lucy's marriage had reached breaking point and finally James Wallace left his wife and child to run off with a dancer.

Then in 1889 David Kennedy died. Although she had never pretended to care for him, Elinor felt some pity for her stepfather at the last. There is a remarkable similarity between the death of Mrs Carruthers, the guardian of Evangeline in *The Vicissitudes of Evangeline*, and the death of David Kennedy. In both cases death is the result of bronchitis and heart failure brought on by anger. Evangeline voices Elinor's response when she says 'I am sad, of course, because death is a terrible thing, and to die like that, saying spiteful things to everyone, must be horrid.'

Despite any unhappiness and difficulty brought about by the

simultaneous loss of the two men in their lives, 1889 proved to be an important turning point for the three women.

First of all they decided that for reasons of economy they should not run two households. Neither Lucy's house nor the house in Drayton Gardens was quite suitable for the new arrangement they proposed. So both houses were given up, and Elinor Kennedy rented a new home for the whole family at 25 Davies Street. Since David Kennedy had left what money he had to his wife she was not too badly off. But immediately the finances of the small household were put under a great strain. Lucy decided that she had to be completely free of James Wallace. On no account did she want him to try to come back into her life. The only sure way of achieving this was to divorce him. Surprisingly enough Elinor Kennedy supported her in that decision, knowing full well that the legal fees would cost her dearly, and divorce would cost Lucy her reputation and her entrée into certain circles. Herself only recently freed from a marriage which had consumed the greater part of her youth, Elinor Kennedy was sympathetic to Lucy's desire for freedom.

However, once the divorce was paid for there was barely enough money to maintain a household of four. Elinor and Lucy knew that they had to do something to relieve their mother's financial burden. Elinor could not disguise from herself the fact that the time had come when she could no longer afford the luxury of being so fastidious about whom she would or would not marry. Like the heroine of *The Vicissitudes of Evangeline* she realised with regret that

> Nice feelings are for people who have money to live as they please. If I had ten thousand a year, or even five, I would snap my fingers at all men, and say, 'No, I shall make my life as I choose, and shall cultivate knowledge and books, and indulge in beautiful ideas of honour and exalted sentiments, and perhaps one day succumb to a noble passion.'

A 'noble passion' seemed as far off as ever, and Elinor began to feel selfish in remaining unmarried when money was so short. Once again she began the round of visits to country houses. At twenty-six she felt she was already regarded as 'a worldly heartless society coquette'. She includes an ironic description of herself as she was at this time in the person of Miss La Touche in *The Visits of Elizabeth*: 'Jane Roose says Miss La Touche will never get married; she is too smart, and all the married women's men talk to her, and the best tone is to look rather dowdy.'

However, Elinor's new campaign to find a husband did not include 'looking dowdy'. Quite the contrary, for Lucy's idea for making money involved Elinor in looking smarter than ever.

Lucy quite simply decided that she could earn her living by exploiting her very real talent for making clothes. At first she worked from home and had to rely on her clothes being seen in society to obtain clients. Her first paying customer was a young socialite, the Hon. Mrs Arthur Brand, a woman with more engagements than money for clothes. The tea gown Lucy made for her inexpensively was a great success and brought other orders quickly. But it was Elinor, visiting everywhere wearing Lucy's designs, who gave the new business its greatest publicity. Since weekend occasions in country houses required women to have at least four changes of clothes daily – morning dress, tweeds or luncheon dress, tea gown and evening dress – Elinor had ample opportunity to show off Lucy's creations. In turn she benefited from Lucy's skill because she enjoyed always being beautifully dressed.

Lucy's success came quickly and she was soon in business as Lucile Ltd. Elinor had less to show for her efforts.

But Elinor's situation was about to improve as the result of a coming-of-age ball in Devon, to which she had been invited by Billy Grant.

Her stunning appearance at this ball had the men flocking round her as usual. Towards the end of the evening when a great deal of alcohol had been consumed, four of her admirers got into a quarrel. For some reason they decided to resolve their dispute by swimming fully clothed in the icy cold water of a nearby lake.

The incident gave rise to a great deal of talk. Clayton Glyn who had recently returned to England after travelling in the Far East was one of those who heard the story and for the first time learnt about the beautiful and sophisticated red-haired Elinor Sutherland who drove men to such mad acts. He resolved to see this intriguing beauty for himself and he arranged with his friends the Chisenhale-Marshes that he should be invited to a house party at their estate, Gaynes Park in Epping Forest. Elinor Sutherland was to be invited too.

10 ♡ MARRIAGE

Henry Clayton Glyn (who was always known as Clayton) was ten years older than Elinor and in his late thirties when they finally met at Gaynes Park towards the end of 1890. They had not met previously as, for the most part, they moved in different circles, and because for the last ten years Clayton Glyn had been away from England travelling in the Far East and Asia.

Hints had been dropped to Elinor about Glyn's interest in her so she was predisposed to look kindly on him. He was not, however, quite the dashing figure of romance she would have liked him to be. On the contrary he was rather stolid looking, though tall with broad shoulders. But his 'merry blue eyes and perfect teeth and . . . his faintly arrogant point of view about everything' were attractive to her and she was charmed by his head of thick, wavy, prematurely silver hair.

For his part he found Elinor just as fascinating as he had been led to expect. He can hardly have failed to be aware that she had no money, for this was common knowledge. But her elegant appearance and confident manner may well have clouded his judgement.

To all outward appearances Clayton Glyn was a man of some substance. Elinor found out that he owned an estate on which there was a large Georgian House, Durrington Hall, and a smaller three-hundred-year-old farmhouse, Sheering Hall, and a small house called Lamberts. She might have wondered briefly why Glyn was not living at Durrington Hall itself. It was let to tenants. But as she found out more about her new admirer, she discovered very good reasons for this. For, although this elegant Georgian House was where Clayton Glyn had been born, it had also been there that his father had died in 1887 and where, just one year later, his mother had been killed in an accident. To Elinor it seemed quite understandable that a confirmed bachelor who liked to travel and whose house had unhappy associations should choose to let it rather than live in it.

She learned from conversation with Glyn himself that on his return from his travels he had taken up farming and established a herd of pedigree Jersey cows and that he was taking a close interest in the stocking of his woods with young pheasants ready for the autumn shoot. It was quite easy for Elinor to convince herself that it had been practical and emotional reasons rather than financial ones that had influenced Clayton Glyn in his decision not to occupy the family home, Durrington Hall.

In their next meetings she observed that he lived well, taking a close interest in his food and drink, that he mixed with the wealthy and the aristocratic with no apparent strain on his resources. She was impressed when he told her his plans for developing the Homerston Estate on his land.

If Clayton Glyn had appeared at an earlier point in Elinor's life she would probably have refused to consider him as a possible husband. She would have seen clearly how little they had in common and how distressing she would find his 'detestation of fuss or other sentiment' and his tendency to hide 'his real feelings behind a mask of cheerful humour'. Most of all she would have resented his matter of fact attitude towards her and his total inability to make romantic love to her.

At twenty-seven, however, she was alert to the positive aspects of a marriage to a man with a position in society, an establishment, and the means of keeping it up. Because she still took to heart the words of Saint-Simon who, in his *Memoirs*, claims to have said firmly at eighteen 'Yet not for millions would I have made a misalliance; neither fashion nor financial stress would ever have made me to stoop so low', she had to persuade herself now that marriage to Clayton Glyn would be no very bad thing and no real betrayal of her principles.

One obstacle remained to the marriage: Clayton Glyn's failure to propose. For more than a year he hesitated; he appeared to assume that they would marry but he never actually made a formal proposal. He knew what Elinor did not know, that his financial situation was by no means secure. Even while at Oxford studying law he had begun to accumulate debt. His building work on the Homerston Estate was being kept afloat by mortgages on the houses on his property. It was questionable whether he could afford to marry a woman who was not rich herself.

In February 1892 Elinor and her mother went to Monte Carlo. Did this suggest to Glyn that after all Elinor had some money or did her absence finally persuade him that he cared for her? Whatever the reason he set off in pursuit and in Monte Carlo he proposed.

He offered Elinor and her mother a generous marriage settlement and he presented his fiancée with a large diamond engagement ring from Cartier. This gesture exhausted his limited ability to show romantic feelings for he returned to England immediately afterwards to check that all was well with his young pheasants!

The wedding had been set for April, so Elinor and Mrs Kennedy also left Monte Carlo and travelled to Paris. They had two objectives: to visit the Fouquet Lemaîtres and announce their good news (which they knew would come as a great surprise) and to give Elinor the opportunity to buy her trousseau. The French cousins were indeed confounded and impressed by the splendid engagement ring. They were, however, a little confused by the absence of the prospective groom – things were not done like that at all in France – but they were happy that their attractive cousin was not after all to be left an old maid. Elinor even managed to persuade her handsome cousin Auguste to act in lieu of a father and to give her away when the marriage took place.

On 27 April 1892 Elinor became Mrs Glyn in St George's Church, Hanover Square. It was a setting she was to use frequently in her novels.

Despite the lack of romance leading up to the occasion, Elinor, in the words of her sister Lucy, 'looked like the living incarnation of a fairy-tale princess' as she left the church on the arm of her tall husband. Lucy had rightly seen in the occasion an opportunity to demonstrate what she could do. She was responsible for the dresses of the bridesmaids and of the bride. Both sisters wrote a detailed account of exactly what Elinor wore for this especially important occasion in both their lives. Her dress was of very thick white satin. The bodice was cleverly cut on the bias so that there were no seams visible and the fastenings were hidden under the arm. The elbow-length sleeves were of old Honiton lace and the skirt had a satin ruche. From the shoulders was a train of satin brocade lined with satin also finished with a satin ruche. Orange blossom aigrettes matched the spray at her waist and echoed her bouquet of orange blossom, gardenia and stephanotis. Her fishnet veil was held in place not with the traditional orange blossom but with a diamond tiara given to her by Clayton as a wedding gift.

Elinor's appearance charmed everyone, and as Lucy had hoped she soon had other customers wanting her to make wedding dresses. She was particularly pleased to have an order from Maud Cassel, the daughter of Ernest Cassel, the financier and close friend of the Prince of Wales. Since the Prince had been invited to Maud's wedding Lucy knew that her dress also was likely to send rich customers her way.

Judging from the evidence of Elinor's novels, her first experience of sexual relations on her honeymoon did not greatly please her. Frequently in her fiction she depicts a young woman's disgust at the lust and brutality of a husband on the wedding night. In *The Reflections of Ambrosine*, for example, the heroine reflects: 'No one can possibly imagine the unpleasantness of a honeymoon until they have tried it. It is no wonder one is told nothing at all about it.' An even more emphatic response is that of Theodora in *Beyond The Rocks* when her husband suggests a second honeymoon: 'A second honeymoon! The first was a horrible, fearsome memory which was over long ago, but the thought of a second . . . Oh, it was unbearable – terrible – impossible! better, much better, to die and have done with it all.'

Not all of Elinor's fictional marriages are depicted in this negative way, but the novels in which the couples do find sexual joy are those in which a union is achieved only after great difficulty and misunderstanding. They are relationships vastly different from that between Elinor and Clayton.

In her autobiography Elinor's account of her own honeymoon concentrates on a single dramatic episode. Clayton Glyn, so Elinor claims, was so desirous of seeing her swim naked with her long red hair streaming out behind her like a mermaid that he hired the Brighton swimming pool for two days just for her. If Clayton Glyn did indeed do this it was the last romantic gesture he was to make to his wife for some years.

The honeymoon over, Mr and Mrs Glyn returned to Essex. The tenants on the estate expressed their pleasure in Clayton's marriage and there were the usual embarrassing hints about hopes of a son and heir.

Elinor liked Sheering Hall and its gardens and she tried to be a good wife. She had not, however, fully realised exactly what would be required of her as the wife of a country gentleman. Before long she felt the severe limitations of her new life. For once he had his wife safely home Clayton took her presence very much for granted and, worse still, he expected her to participate in his daily routines. He and his friends and neighbours were more interested in outdoor sports than in any kind of intellectual or cultivated activities, and Elinor was expected to accompany him when he went out shooting or fishing. The clothes she had chosen so carefully in Paris were in no way suitable for the kind of life she suddenly found herself leading. Even when visits were exchanged with neighbours Elinor found that her stylish clothes evoked not admiration but hostility. She, for her part, found the other women poorly dressed and that among them 'it was considered a sin to look "foreign" and to have polished nails and Paris clothes!' In vain she rebelled against 'dull lives of routine' and absorption in 'parochial interests'.

In August the routines which weighed so heavily on Elinor were broken when husband and wife began a series of visits. The first of these to St Fillans in Perthshire was not especially to Elinor's taste for they were there for the shooting and there was more trailing around after the guns, wearing tweeds and heavy shoes. But at Shipley Hall in Derbyshire the company was more lively and included Mrs George Keppel, the woman who was later to become another mistress of the Prince of Wales. Part of Elinor's enjoyment in this visit came from her opportunity to shine and to show off her dramatic skills when the ladies entertained the gentlemen by performing in *tableaux vivants*. Mary Queen of Scots was a role sufficiently romantic even for Elinor.

Back in Essex Elinor got her first introduction to a very different kind of society from that she had previously been accustomed to. It was the society so well described by Winston Churchill in his autobiography *My Early Life*.

> In those days English society still existed in its old form. It was a brilliant and powerful body, with standards of conduct and methods of enforcing them now altogether forgotten. In a very large degree everyone knew everyone else and who they were. The hundred great families who had governed England for so many generations and had seen her rise to the pinnacle of her glory, were interrelated to an enormous extent by marriage. Everywhere one met friends and kinsfolk. The leading figures of Society were in many cases the

> leading Statesmen in Parliament, and also the leading sportsmen on the Turf. Lord Salisbury was accustomed scrupulously to avoid calling a cabinet when there was racing at Newmarket, and the House of Commons made a practice of adjourning for the Derby. In those days the glittering parties at Lansdowne House, Devonshire House or Stafford House comprised all the elements which made a gay and splendid social circle in close relation to the business of Parliament, the hierarchies of the army and Navy, and the policy of the State.[1]

Elinor had previously had no entrée into this closed and inward-looking circle. She first became fully aware of it at the Essex Hunt Ball. Her arrival at this occasion, just like her arrival at that earlier Hunt Ball in Exeter which had had such far-reaching results for her, created a stir as she had intended it should. Frances, Countess of Warwick, who was then Lady Brooke, recorded the occasion: 'I can remember the sensation created by the arrival, in the unattractive ballroom, of a perfectly lovely girl, with the most wonderfully red hair I had ever seen, dressed simply in quiet satin, with no jewellery and no make-up.'[2]

Was Elinor aware of the parallels between her appearance on this occasion and that of Lillie Langtry when she had first attracted notice? Did she hope for the same results?

To her discomfort Elinor was at first ignored, the reason being that 'One woman suggested that the young woman was far too attractive to be respectable . . . the County regarded such allure as indecorous, and she was given the cold shoulder for a while.'[3]

How fortunate for Elinor that Lady Brooke was present at the Ball with a party of guests who were staying at her home, Easton Lodge in Essex. Daisy, as she was generally known, had a mind of her own and was of sufficiently high rank to be able to flout the norms of her society when she chose to do so.

Lady Brooke who had been born Frances Evelyn Maynard was just three years older than Elinor, but in terms of worldly experience she was much more her senior.

Her worldliness had developed only after her marriage. For, despite her family's wealth and rank, Frances Maynard's childhood had not been so very different from that of Elinor. She and her siblings had been sheltered from the goings-on in the adult world, dressed in hand-me-down clothes and kept in ignorance of all sexual matters. She had, however, been fortunate in the fact that her stepfather, the Earl of Rosslyn, had taken a great interest in her education. Like Elinor she was a great admirer of Lillie Langtry and when she had her own establishment made a point of inviting the famous beauty to stay.

She had been only fifteen when Francis Greville, Lord Brooke had fallen in love with her. From that point her life had the elements of romance so sadly missed by Elinor in her life. Lord Brooke had been forbidden to approach Daisy until she was eighteen. In the meantime the family began negotiations to marry off their beautiful daughter who was an heiress in her own right to Queen Victoria's youngest son, Prince Leopold. Matters were coming to a satisfactory conclusion when the prospective bride and groom got together and each confessed to loving another. The negotiations proceeded no further.

Lord Brooke proposed to Daisy the moment she was eighteen and she accepted. Her parents, after their initial dismay and disappointment, accepted the situation. There was a splendid ball at Grosvenor House to announce the engagement followed by a spectacular wedding in Westminster Abbey in 1881 with a grateful Prince Leopold acting as best man.

At nineteen Lady Brooke was the mistress of a house in Carlton Gardens and of Easton Lodge.

Like Elinor, however, Daisy had found that romance and marriage were not at all compatible. The young couple had soon found that their interests diverged. Daisy was mad about horses and hunting and bored by the shooting parties which so absorbed her husband. Even worse from Daisy's point of view was the fact that, once he had married her, Lord Brooke lost interest in her sexually. He took it for granted that she would have her admirers and he would have his mistresses. It was only now that she realised what the true mores of her class were and she began to follow the example of her husband.

By the time of the meeting between Elinor and Lady Brooke, the latter had already been involved in a series of much publicised love affairs and there was even some doubt as to who was the father of her children. In 1888 she had become the mistress of the Prince of Wales following in the wake of Lillie Langtry.

This worldly, wealthy woman was greatly attracted by Elinor's beauty. She made a point of singling her out for attention and found her to be 'very simple, artless, generous and kindly'.[4] She ensured that Elinor became the belle of that ball and by inviting her to Easton Lodge as a house guest gave her the social cachet which gradually established her in the County set.

With the memory of this first meeting very much in her mind Elinor wrote a similar incident into *The Reflections of Ambrosine*. In the novel it is Lady Tilchester, who is confessedly modelled on Lady Brooke, who rescues the embarrassed Ambrosine. Lady Tilchester is described as follows: 'She has gracious beautiful manners, and although she could not know anything about me or my history, there seemed to be sympathy in her big brown eyes.'

Without Lady Brooke's patronage Elinor would have long, if not always, remained an outsider. But she was more than simply grateful for Daisy's social help; she was greatly attracted to the person she described as 'the loveliest woman in England, of high rank, ample riches, and great intelligence'.

Lady Brooke was, of course, well versed in the niceties of all social conventions. Elinor, who had never had to run any kind of establishment before, welcomed her friend's advice in such matters as who should or should not be invited to dinner at Sheering Hall.

It was not only the kindness of Lady Brooke that was to change Elinor's life at this point. The discovery that Elinor was pregnant made Clayton more attentive and solicitous. He was most concerned that Elinor should be safely delivered of a son to be his heir. No longer did he insist that his wife accompany him whenever he went out shooting or riding. In the interests of a healthy pregnancy he was content that Elinor should do what she had long wished to do. At last she was free to wear 'beautiful indoor clothes' and to sit by the fire reading for hours.

In 1893 Elinor gave birth to her first child. It was a daughter. If Clayton Glyn was disappointed that his child was a girl he did not make too much fuss. After all, he reasoned, there would be plenty more opportunities to produce a son. He made no objection when Elinor chose to name the baby after her French cousin Margot Fouquet Lemaître whom she asked to be godmother.

Somewhat to her dismay Elinor discovered that she was not very interested in babies. But then she was by no means unusual for the time. Her attitude towards having a baby was quite unsentimental. She felt then, and later wrote in *The Philosophy of Love*, that 'females must bear children, and go through months of suffering, during which time they are physically unfit to fight hardships, and have to be protected in some measure'. It was the process that all women shared but their responses afterwards were not all the same. Some women, she declared, were animal mothers and able to dedicate themselves to the purely physical wellbeing of their children. Others, however, were spiritual mothers, and such women could only relate closely to their children once they had passed the baby stage and needed care and guidance beyond the merely physical. It was in the latter category that she unabashedly placed herself and thus, with a clear conscience, was able to delegate the responsibility for looking after her baby daughter to a nanny while she resumed her social life.

Once she had regained her figure, Elinor began to spend a great deal of money on clothes, most of which she ordered from Lucy. Her sister, whose business continued to thrive, was thrilled that she now had Lillie Langtry as one of her customers. When Elinor was not parading in her new clothes she whiled away the hours by adding to the detailed and illustrated catalogue of her wardrobe which she had begun some years earlier.

Many of the social exchanges she was involved in were sterile and uninteresting. How could it have been otherwise? The men had little to do but hunt and race and make love; the women's time was occupied by changing from one outfit to another, gossiping, and making love. A major preoccupation of both sexes was the consumption of heavy meals. It was customary at weekend parties to begin the day with a hearty breakfast. This would be followed by an elaborate lunch. Then there would be tea and finally a dinner which could run to nine or ten courses. As Babykins says in defence of her set in *The Reflections of Ambrosine*, 'We have always eaten and drunk rich food and wine in our class, and have not had enough to do, so we can't help being as we are, can we?' The generally condemning picture of Edwardian social life found in Elinor's early fiction is supported by J.B. Priestley's comment in *The Edwardians*. He writes: 'this Edwardian high society can justly be regarded as shallow, self-indulgent, stupid, not worth to the community a thousandth part of the money it spent trying to amuse itself.'

What was missing was a sense of responsibility and purpose; the notion stressed by Elinor's grandmother of *noblesse oblige*. Katherine Bush, in Elinor's novel, an outsider like Elinor herself, comments on the aristocracy she has come to know: 'You have become effete like the nobles before the revolution in France, who could only die like gentlemen, but not live like men.'

Again J.B. Priestley's observations support Elinor's picture: 'Taken as a whole it was not a society that accepted social or cultural responsibilities, unlike earlier aristocratic societies that had set admirable standards and produced notable patrons of the arts.'

There was, however, one house which Elinor loved to visit and where she found the company more congenial. Easton Lodge was only ten miles from Sheering. Fortunately Clayton shared her enthusiasm for visiting there as in Lord Brooke he had found a kindred spirit, and so husband and wife would frequently set off in their brougham pulled by their horses Pair and Impair and accompanied by vast amounts of luggage.

Lady Brooke, who became Lady Warwick in the course of 1893 on the death of her father-in-law, had qualities which Elinor missed in most of the women she associated with. For, although her friend Daisy could be as frivolous as the rest of them, she also had a more serious and responsible side which was later to develop to an extent which Elinor found alarming. Already she had begun to take an interest in the welfare of her tenants and had created employment for many of the women on her estate by founding the Easton school of needlework.

Daisy Warwick was the first woman with whom Elinor had been able to form a close friendship. Elinor's portrait of her in *The Reflections of Ambrosine* verges on hero-worship.

> She is the most fascinating personality I have yet met. There is something like the sun's rays about her; you feel warmed and comforted when she is near. She looks so great and noble, and above all common things. One cannot help wondering why she married Lord Tilchester who is quite ordinary.
>
> When she talks everyone listens. Her voice is like golden bells, and she never says stupid things that mean nothing.

She was so bedazzled by Daisy that she was even prepared to accept her justification for her love affairs. Lady Tilchester says: 'In my bringing up, the idea of taking a lover after marriage seemed a more or less natural thing, and not altogether a deadly sin, provided that the affair was conducted *sans fanfaronnade*, without scandal.'

Elinor herself, however, was never comfortable with the combination of rigid etiquette and loose morals. Unlike most of the men and women she was associating with, she had not grown up to take such behaviour for granted. Her romantic ideals were offended by the way in which the women she knew changed their lovers as often as their clothes. Her common sense told her that the difference between outward form and reality was simple hypocrisy. It was this perception, recorded repeatedly in her diary and in her letters to her mother, that she was later to use to such good effect in *The Visits of Elizabeth*.

11 ♥ DISILLUSIONMENT

The routine of daily life was echoed in the larger structuring of the year. In the first years of their marriage Elinor and Clayton would spend May and June in London for the season. Then they would go to Cowes for Cowes Week. After the first year Clayton would go alone for grouse shooting in August while Elinor would visit her relatives either in Paris or in Dieppe. The end of the year would be spent in a series of weekends at various country houses. January would find them escaping the English winter by going to the Mediterranean, usually Hyères, a resort described by one regular visitor, the art historian Bernard Berenson, as 'sheer paradise' with the 'fragrance of the pines and the cypresses' and 'the artistic beauty of the rocks above the opalescent sea'.[1] After refreshing themselves there they would travel in France or Italy before returning in time for the London season and the beginning of another cycle.

The baby was, of course, for the most part in the charge of a nanny, though when Elinor went to visit the Fouquet Lemaîtres she might take her small daughter with her.

The birth of Margot brought into the open the growing lack of sympathy between husband and wife. Clayton was not fond of babies, especially baby girls, so that all the nursery activities had to be kept out of his sight and hearing. He was not as attracted sexually to Elinor the mother as he had been before she became pregnant, even though Elinor diminished her maternal role as far as possible. Perhaps he would have turned to her again when they were in Hyères in January without Margot. But Elinor contracted typhoid fever from which she was slow to recover. The sickroom was no more appealing to the outdoor-loving Clayton than was the nursery.

From his point of view, therefore, the visit of one of Elinor's bridesmaids was most timely. Elinor was also grateful for the arrival of her pretty friend who, like Clayton, loved all country activities.

With relief she saw her husband and her friend setting off to wash dogs, rub horses and to tramp through the estate in the rain. She was grateful for the improvement in Clayton's disposition and happy to see how content her friend appeared to be. She could not at first imagine that under her nose in their own home Clayton was being unfaithful to her.

Any suspicions she might have had were confirmed later in the year. Clayton and Elinor had been invited to one of the large parties given by Daisy and her husband at Warwick Castle. In the usual pairing off for a stroll in the grounds Elinor was partnered by Lord Warwick himself. Although she had recovered from her illness, she was even paler and slimmer than usual and looking particularly beautiful and alluring. It was in the rose garden that the normally phlegmatic Lord Warwick became suddenly romantic. He declared himself to be passionately in love with Elinor whom he found more beautiful than any of the roses in the garden. He then took his astonished guest in his arms and kissed her. He was surely unprepared for Elinor's response. Other women to whom he had made similar declarations had known the rules of the game he was inviting them to play. But not Elinor. She pulled away from him horrified and offended and at the appearance of other house guests took her opportunity to escape.

Elinor relates in her autobiography how she debated with herself whether or not to tell Clayton about the incident. Did she really fear that he would make a scene about Warwick's improper advances to his wife and insist upon leaving? Or did she secretly hope that such tangible evidence of her attractiveness to other men would arouse his jealousy and possessive instincts and make him see her again as a desirable woman? She did not expect what in fact did happen when she made her announcement about 'the awful thing that had occurred'. For Clayton turned to her with a smile and said 'No. Did he? Dear old Brookie.'

Elinor could no longer deceive herself. Whatever romance there had been in her marriage was quite, quite gone.

That August Elinor was happy to turn her back on her husband and her disillusionment and join Margot Fouquet Lemaître in the more congenial atmosphere of Dieppe where art was more likely to be the subject of conversation than grouse and shooting.

Her pride and self-confidence were to a degree restored by the painter Jacques Emile Blanche's obvious enthusiasm for her looks which shines through his portrait of her and in his whimsical perception of her character shown in his painting of *Le Chat Nellie*. She was reminded once more of those passionate whispers of 'Belle Tigresse' in the Jardin des Plantes.

Early in 1895 Elinor learned with some interest that the Mary Leiter she had met in Paris had become engaged to George Curzon. They had in fact been secretly engaged since 1893. The wedding which followed swiftly on the announcement was a grand affair celebrated at St John's Church in Washington DC. There was a good deal of speculation in the British Press as to whether Mary Leiter was in fact Jewish and about just how wealthy she was. Curzon was very much in the news anyway, as in the same year as he married he was made Under-Secretary of State for Foreign Affairs.

Elinor herself gained some fame that year. In October a party gathered at Dysart, the home of Lord Rosslyn, the half-brother of Daisy Warwick. It was his idea that instead of the usual entertainment in which everyone took part in *tableaux vivants*, the company should take itself more seriously and put on a full scale production of a play, charge admission and give the proceeds to charity.

The idea appealed to Rosslyn's guests, especially to Mrs Willie James and Elinor. For three weeks Rosslyn rehearsed his actors and actresses vigorously. It was for all of them a novelty to work hard for an objective and with a deadline. Rosslyn's aim was to be ready after the three weeks to stage the play they were working on, an adaptation of a play by Sardou entitled *Diplomacy*.

Rosslyn had booked the Memorial Hall in Dysart for the first performance which would be in the nature of a dress rehearsal for his amateur company. Then they would take on the more difficult task of performing at the Empire Palace Theatre in Edinburgh.

The production was ready in time; a distinguished audience was attracted which included the Prince of Wales, and the reviews were all Rosslyn could have hoped for.

Elinor thoroughly enjoyed herself and read the reviews greedily. She particularly enjoyed one review which gave all the details of her costumes: she had herself provided the journalist with the information. But the following piece from *The Gentlewoman* was unsolicited praise: 'This was positively Mrs Glyn's first appearance in public, and if in her *debut* she could command so much favourable criticism, what may we not hope to see and hear of her in years to come.'

Neither Elinor nor *The Gentlewoman* could have foreseen exactly how that rhetorical question would come to be answered some years later.

Elinor's pleasure in the performances was only slightly marred when she fell badly in what should have been a controlled fall. She hit her head on a small table and suffered concussion. The audience applauded heartily when she insisted on playing her part to the end of the play. Lord Rosslyn nursed a secret suspicion that Elinor had engineered the situation to attract even more attention and sympathy than usual.

Clayton also was not impressed by her injury and did not let it interrupt their usual routine of moving from London to Cowes and then to Dieppe.

However, in the late autumn of this year they travelled to Italy, in particular to Rome and Venice. The two cities had a tremendous appeal for Elinor. In Rome she enjoyed the sense of history made visible as she marvelled at the ruins of places which had before existed for her only in books. She took to Gibbon once more to remind herself of all that had happened in the city which had once been the centre of a vast empire. Clayton was more interested in the society of Rome than in its history. He became bored with Elinor's enthusiastic delight. He knew that in Venice she would find even more to rouse her spirit of romance. He refused to be drawn in and to play the part of a romantic lover as Elinor so dearly wished. He agreed to humour her by taking her through Venice by moonlight in a gondola. But to ensure that she did not misunderstand his intentions he insisted that Elinor's maid, Williams, should have a treat and be invited along to make a threesome.

There was no mistaking his rejection. Elinor was bitterly disappointed and upset. Had she imagined and hoped that the ambience of Venice would penetrate even Clayton's stolidity and draw from him the declarations of love which were conspicuously lacking in their relationship?

When she realised that Clayton was completely unaffected by Venice she consoled herself by imagining what it would have been like to be in that city with a sympathetic and passionate lover. Her account of this episode in her autobiography *Romantic Adventure* is clear-sighted.

> At last, filled with depression, I flew to my journal and wrote, from sheer imagination, the passionate descriptions of love in Venice which ten years afterwards I re-lived in *Three Weeks*. Perhaps if I had really had a lover there I would not have written all that my wild imagination pictured in my disappointed soul!

To Elinor it seemed that already her marriage was one in name only and that Clayton had lost whatever feeling he had once had for her. Something of her state of mind at this time found expression later in the sad little comedy of the attempts of Amaryllis, the heroine of *The Price of Things*, to seduce her cold husband who hides away behind *The Times* and refuses to respond.

But Elinor had been mistaken. To her surprise and delight she found that her despair was premature; that there was still life in her marriage after all, as the next few months would prove.

Ever since she had been married Elinor had wanted to consolidate her position in society by being presented at Court. The occasion had been delayed for some seasons partly because of her recurrent ill health. At last, however, everything was arranged for her presentation at a Drawing Room in May of 1896.

It was, of course, Lucy, who could herself never be presented at Court as a consequence of her divorce, who designed the dress Elinor was to wear.

Elinor's excitement was increased when Clayton, quite unexpectedly, decided that for this season and for the foreseeable future they should lease a small flat in Sloane Street.

A few nights before the May Drawing Room a grand masked ball was held at Covent Garden. In high spirits Elinor plotted with Violet, Lady Rosslyn, with whom she had been very friendly since the previous year's theatricals, to attend the ball dressed as bats. They decided to increase the mystery by speaking French the whole evening. Their disguise was successful and the two young women were gleeful. Late at night they had supper with two gallants in the Turf Club Box. Elinor's handsome admirer begged to be allowed to know her identity so that he might meet her again. But Elinor remained firmly incognita.

On the great day of the presentation Elinor made her appearance in Court dress. She was delighted with herself. At last she was beginning to realise something of her dreams about her aristocratic lineage. The portrait of her in Court dress is revealing of her feelings at this time. She sits proudly confident, with her head held high, her back very straight, and her right arm posed in a curiously regal gesture. The details of her elaborate dress were, of course, duly recorded in her diary.

> White satin peau de soie, the skirt edged with silver gauze ribbon (very bright silver) this edged with narrow lace. The bows on the bodice and the train were of the same ribbon. The centre of each bow was a rosette of lace with a diamond button. The sleeves were of best old Buckingham lace (three yards in each). The train of white brocade lined with satin and ruched inside with silver ribbon and lace, and trimmed with festoons of wide old Buckingham lace fastened with bows of silver pink.

The diamond tiara which she had worn at her wedding secured the feathers of her headdress.

Fully aware of her own beauty and aided by her experience on the stage, Elinor carried out her part in the ritual flawlessly managing her six curtsies without becoming entangled in her long train. But her pleasure and excitement did not prevent her from making her usual sharp observations of the scene. She drank in the details of the royal rooms and of the Princess of Wales herself who was presiding instead of Queen Victoria. She took stock of all the other women present and found that most of them did not measure up to her own high standards either in their dress or in their complexions.

On her way into the Drawing Room she had caught sight of her ardent admirer of a few nights earlier now also in Court dress in his official capacity as one of the Queen's equerries. He had clearly not recognised her now that she was dressed as a lady of the court speaking English and not as a bat speaking French. She disturbed the young man's calm poise by whispering mischievously to him as she left the Drawing Room, '*chauve souris*'.

Was it Elinor's high spirits consequent upon her success that season that made Clayton see her again as he had before they were married and feel attracted to her once more? Or was it, perhaps, his feeling that it was time for another child, hopefully a son this time?

His renewed interest in her was what Elinor had passionately hoped for but not expected: 'Clayton seemed to fall in love with me all over again, and the past was forgotten.'

Despite the earlier period of coolness between Elinor and Clayton, Mrs Kennedy had become increasingly attached to her son-in-law. She had appreciated, more than her daughter, Clayton's willingness to let his wife spend great sums of money on clothes from Lucile. Not only had this helped the business directly but the clothes Elinor had worn in company had successfully advertised Lucy's work and indirectly helped the business by bringing more customers. As an investor in the business Mrs Kennedy was well pleased.

At the end of 1895 Lucy was sufficiently prosperous to be able to set up a shop and workrooms in Mayfair at 24 Old Burlington Street. Circumstances had changed since Mrs Kennedy had established herself and her family in the Davies Street house. Lucy now had money of her own and did not need to live with her mother for reasons of economy, and Esmé was now old enough not to need the watchful eye of her grandmother on her while Lucy worked. Mrs Kennedy was beginning to think that it was time to make a move. So, when Clayton proposed to his mother-in-law that she should leave London and occupy Lamberts, a house on his estate, she was happy to accept his offer. The spacious old house was modernised for her arrival. From now on Mrs Kennedy became an increasingly indispensable member of the Glyn household. When Elinor and Clayton set off for Europe as usual in the winter, they now travelled with a larger party than formerly as Mrs Kennedy and Margot joined them.

In Rome there was much socialising, and then followed a quieter time spent at a villa in San Remo where their host was Sir William Walrond, the Conservative Chief Whip.

By the end of 1897 Elinor's reputation as a beautiful and elegantly dressed woman was firmly established. So that when Lord Rosslyn decided to publish a magazine *Scottish Life* it was to Elinor he turned to write articles for him on fashion and beauty. Elinor went one better and offered to illustrate her articles with her own sketches. Her articles began with the first issue of *Scottish Life* in May 1898 with the title of 'Les Coulisses de l'élégance by Mrs Glyn'. They were written as letters from Suzon to Grizelda. It was a form with which Elinor felt quite comfortable as for years she had written regularly to her mother giving her the same kind of details of dress illustrated with sketches.

It was, however, her first venture into journalism and it established a particular style of writing which she was to develop in the course of her writing career.

The commission for these pieces could not have come at a better time. Elinor was once again pregnant. If she could not herself wear the beautiful clothes which were so important to her at least she could get some satisfaction from writing about them.

But the pregnancy was difficult and Rosslyn ran out of money for his venture into publishing so that before the baby was born Elinor gave up this foray into journalism. Subsequent events put this, her first appearance in print, into the shade. Anthony Glyn says of his grandmother '. . . she seems to have forgotten in her later life that they were in fact her first published work.'[2]

On 15 December 1898 Elinor's second child was born. The birth was very painful. Still weak from the experience Elinor was told that she had given birth to a beautiful daughter, but she should not risk having another child.

Clayton's hopes for a son were utterly destroyed. His disappointment was such that he could hardly bear to be in the house with the new baby, and shortly after her birth he left England. His destination could hardly have been more ironically chosen. It was to Monte Carlo where he had proposed marriage to Elinor that he now made his way.

12 A NEW LEASE OF LIFE

Christmas was a bleak occasion at Sheering Hall that year. Along with post-partum depression Elinor had to face the implications of Clayton's abrupt departure. She had enjoyed their brief period of apparent reconciliation when she had felt her husband truly loved her. Clearly that was over. Even when she began to go about in society again she remained depressed and was increasingly aware of the emptiness of the life she was leading. And there seemed to be no prospect of any change. Years of more of the same thing stretched ahead of her.

In this state of physical and mental depression Elinor was unable to resist illness. A cold that she might have thrown off easily in another situation developed into rheumatic fever. She became seriously ill. Mrs Kennedy nursed her devotedly but she feared, perhaps correctly, that Elinor might die simply because she appeared to have lost the desire to live.

Then suddenly Elinor's strong will reasserted itself. She stopped flirting with the idea that to die young would be 'rather touching and romantic', and made up her mind not only to live but to make something of her life.

Her illness had made her physically immobile. She was happiest sitting in a deck chair in the sun with her mother by her for companionship. The baby, Juliet, was looked after by a nurse and Margot was in the care of her efficient and loving governess Mary Dixon.

As Elinor and her mother sat in the sun and talked over old times an idea began to develop in Elinor's head. Her series of letters in *Scottish Life* had come to her quite easily and she had started from scratch with them. Why shouldn't she make something of all those letters she had sent to her mother and the detailed diaries in which she had recorded all her visits to country houses when she was in search of a husband?

Mrs Kennedy, eager to promote anything that made her daughter more lively, collected together the letters and diaries and Elinor began to read them. She had forgotten how entertaining and perceptive they were. They even made her laugh. She saw that she could use many of the incidents she had recorded and the descriptions of her fellow guests, but she needed to give the letters a shape that would prevent them from being purely autobiographical. What she needed, in fact, was a heroine other than her own young self. Since the letters were to have such a strong relation to reality anyway, she thought she might as well base her heroine on a real person. There was a splendid candidate to hand: the half-sister of her good friend Daisy, Lady Angela St Clair-Erskine. This young woman had good looks, a title and plenty of money. More importantly, when she had first come out she had been regarded as something of an *enfant terrible* because of her naive outspokenness and her ability to ruffle the feathers of more sophisticated women. Elinor had described in her diary one particular occasion on which Lady Angela had caused great consternation at a house party. Having previously led a very sheltered life, she was not familiar with the kind of thing that went on at weekend gatherings after everyone was supposed to have gone to bed. She was, therefore, very disturbed to hear movements in the corridor outside her bedroom door. She got up to investigate and saw in the dim light a tall grey figure stealthily making its way into the room of a fellow guest just a few doors beyond her own. Convinced she had seen a ghost she reported to the assembled company the next day that she was absolutely sure the house was haunted and she gave a detailed account of what she had seen the previous night even mentioning through whose door the 'ghost' had disappeared. It was some time later that she had understood why the party had fallen silent, why some guests were hard put to hide their amusement and why others were embarrassed, even angry, and why they claimed that she had either dreamt or made up the whole thing.

In this incident Elinor found the perfect point of view from which to write her sequence of letters.

Delighted to see her daughter recovering some of her old animation, Elinor Kennedy hurried into the village and bought the blue school exercise books in which *The Visits of Elizabeth* was written. For days Elinor scribbled away thoroughly enjoying herself, and then gave her efforts to her mother and Clayton to read.

There is some dispute about what happened next. After her

experience with *Scottish Life* Elinor almost certainly had in mind at least the possibility of publishing Elizabeth's letters. The Countess of Warwick claims in her memoirs that Elinor showed her what she had written. Daisy was agreeably surprised and introduced her friend to Mr Drummond then acting editor of *The World*.

Anthony Glyn in his biography of his grandmother says that Clayton took the notebooks with him to London and 'over lunch at the Cavendish Club' showed Elinor's work to Samuel Jeyes, the assistant editor of *The Standard*. Clayton's intention, his grandson suggests, was not so much to get Elinor's work published, since 'To have a wife who had written a book was at that time and in that society a matter more for shame than for anything else', but to return home with a 'friendly comment from an established literary man' as a 'nice surprise for the convalescent'.[1]

It is questionable how much of a disgrace it was for a society lady to publish a book. Millicent, Duchess of Sutherland, for example, had published in 1889 her first book, *How I Spent My Twentieth Year*, with no apparent harm to her reputation, for now she was in the process of publishing a novel entitled *One Hour And The Next*. It is possible that already Clayton was sufficiently anxious about his growing financial problems that he was more than ready to encourage Elinor in pursuing a course which might at least produce enough money to offset her large expenditure on clothes.

However it was that the letters came into Samuel Jeyes hands, there is no disputing the fact that he liked them very much. He tried them out on a number of friends and found that they were just as entertained as he was.

A few days later Elinor received a telegram from Samuel Jeyes. The very wording of this suggests that he had been consulted in the first place about their suitability for publication, for the telegram said quite simply 'Elizabeth will do. May I come and see you?'

It was not in *The Standard* that the letters were published but in *The World*. Serialisation began on Wednesday, 9 August, 1899 and immediately caused a stir. As the Countess of Warwick commented, 'They created a sensation, for frank intimacies of their kind were unknown.'[2]

Elinor's health began to improve rapidly, suggesting that much of her physical weakness, as also that of many of her female contemporaries, was the result of the kind of life she was leading – too much rich food and too little sense of purpose.

Her delight in her success was compounded initially by the fact that no one knew the identity of the author of the *Visits*, for she had been persuaded by an editor with a good feel for publicity that to publish them anonymously would add to their spice. In the social group in which Elinor moved, everyone was aware that only one of their number could possibly have known their stories and their conventions. There was much speculation about the unnamed author. The temptation to reveal herself became too much. Elinor confided in a friend who laughed her to scorn, saying, 'But, Nellie darling, it can't possibly be you. A really clever person must have written those letters.'

After her long period of illness and convalescence Elinor was now ready to go about in society once more. This time she had a new sense of herself as someone who had caused a stir by something more than her good looks.

She maintained her close friendship with Daisy Warwick but she was concerned about the changes that were taking place in the older woman's life. In 1895 when Elinor had been out of England Daisy had given a particularly elaborate costume ball. All the guests were required to appear in the court dress of Louis XVI. Daisy herself had dressed as Marie Antoinette. It was the kind of occasion which would have delighted Elinor. But it had not delighted a certain journalist, Robert Blatchford of *The Clarion*, who had written an extremely hostile piece about the irresponsibility of wealthy aristocrats. Daisy had never before viewed herself in that light. She was hurt but she was unable to ignore the criticisms levelled against her. She visited Blatchford and began to be influenced by his socialist views. She took an increasingly close interest in the running of her estates and in 1899 created Warwick Estates Ltd to ensure greater efficiency in their management. She was now known as the Red Duchess. The more socialist she became the more difficult it was for her to maintain relationships with her society friends. She had appreciated the criticisms of her set that Elinor had made in *The Visits of Elizabeth* but knew that at heart Elinor remained a Conservative and that she did not want to upset the social order, merely to have everyone play their allotted roles responsibly. At this time Elinor felt that she was showing sufficient social responsibility by participating in the kind of charitable performances then fashionable among ladies of good family.

In February 1900, for example, Lady Arthur Paget invited her to be in a *tableau vivant* at a matinée performance at Her Majesty's Theatre.

Elinor had known Minnie Paget, as she was familiarly called, for some time. She was the daughter of Mrs Paran Stevens who had been so kind to Elinor in Paris. Minnie Paget and Elinor had more in common than just their green eyes and their determination to get on. Born in New York in 1853 and thus eleven years older than Elinor, Mary Stevens was the daughter of Paran Stevens and his second wife Marietta. Paran Stevens had been a wealthy widower in his forties when he had met Marietta. She was the daughter of a prosperous grocer and a friend of his daughter. At nineteen she was grey-eyed, spirited and voluptuous. Paran Stevens had fallen in love with her and married her despite the difference in their ages. They had two children, Mary and a son who was for a while engaged to Edith Wharton. One of Paran Stevens's business ventures had been a partnership in the Fifth Avenue Hotel in New York. It was here that the Prince of Wales frequently stayed and Marietta Stevens took care to make his acquaintance. When her husband died in 1872 Marietta had determined to take her already glamorous daughter to England and to use her social connections to make a good marriage for her. She knew only too well that she would do better in New York society once she had made her mark in Europe.

The Prince of Wales was instrumental in launching Minnie's career, as once society saw that she was invited to Sandringham and to Marlborough House other invitations were quickly forthcoming.

But Minnie was not independently wealthy like so many of the young American girls seeking to make their way at that time. The money her mother had would eventually go to her brother. Like Elinor she found herself doing the rounds of country houses being greatly admired but not receiving proposals of marriage. At twenty-five she had decided to set her sights a little lower than a Duke and had then captured Arthur Paget, the grandson of the Marquis of Anglesey.

Her social position had been made absolutely secure when the Prince of Wales stood godfather to her first son. And she put this position in England to good use both in helping her mother to run a kind of transatlantic marriage bureau and in organising events to raise money for charity.

In 1900 Mrs Arthur Paget was busy raising money for the orphans and widows of soldiers killed in the Boer War. She had a personal interest in this cause as her husband was the General commanding the Scots Guards in South Africa.

She chose the ladies for her *tableau vivant* not only for their beauty but also for their red hair. The subject chosen for them to represent was an imaginary Titian painting entitled *The Five Senses*. Performing along with Elinor were the Baroness D'Erlanger (her full name was Marie Rose Antoinette Catherine de Robert d'Aqueria de Rochegude), Mabel St Oswald, Lady Mary Sackville and Winifred Curzon wife of George Nathaniel Curzon's brother Francis. Mrs Curzon was then enjoying the reflected glory of her brother-in-law, now Lord Curzon, who had the previous year achieved the distinction of being the youngest man to be appointed Viceroy of India. His arrival in India with his beautiful Vicereine on a tour of duty, largely financed by his father-in-law Levi Leiter, had been much publicised, as had his parting dinner with that group of his friends who were known as the Souls.

The performance of *The Five Senses* was a great success. Elinor, looking back, marvelled that the very red hair which had been such a bane in her young life, was now a much praised asset to her beauty. She cut out all the accounts of the performance taking especial delight in the following from *The Ladies Field*: 'In the centre stood "Hearing", represented by Mrs Clayton Glyn, looking superbly handsome in a dress of bright purple velvet trimmed with sable and revealing a skirt of cloth of silver studded with pearls and emeralds.'

Elinor was happy that her dress was so praised as she had paid for it herself.

In the meantime her literary venture was also prospering. After the serialisation of *The Visits of Elizabeth* had finished in *The World* the editor, Samuel Jeyes, had the idea of showing it to a friend of his who was just setting up his own publishing house and was looking about for suitable books. Gerald Duckworth enjoyed the letters, saw their larger potential and responded to Jeyes immediately, asking for an introduction to the author as soon as possible.

So it was that in August 1900 Gerald Duckworth met Elinor Glyn for the first time. Neither of them knew on that pleasant summer day that their partnership would continue for the next thirty-three years.

Although Duckworth was impressed by the letters, he saw that they were not sufficient by themselves to make a book. He broached this concern when he met Elinor to see how she would react. He was afraid that she might have written all she had to say in those serialised letters. But Elinor was not at all put out by the request for more material. Quite the contrary. When she had visited her relatives in France for the first time she had kept a journal which already had a certain amount of artifice in its structure, for it was written as a series of letters home. So, rather than simply adding more letters from country houses along the lines of those she had already published, Elinor decided to reshape her material and to use the English country house letters as a framework for a sequence of letters recounting Elizabeth's adventures in France.

For a first novel *The Visits of Elizabeth* is a remarkable achievement. It has a deceptive ease and artlessness. Just how carefully contrived this effect is can be seen if the novel is compared with the real autobiography of Lady Angela St Clair-Erskine, the ostensible heroine of the novel, whose photograph as Elizabeth was used as a frontispiece for the published novel.

Memories and Base Details, as Lady Angela entitled her book, has none of that sharpness of detail and characterisation which we find in *The Visits of Elizabeth*. Incidents such as the haunted house story used to such effect by Elinor are barely mentioned. The account of her husband's proposal is recorded as follows: 'When J. asked me that evening to marry him, I said: "Yes! if I may have your chestnut horse." '

What we do have in detail are descriptions of hunts, of races, of horses and lists of people who were good at hunting. What she says of Margot Asquith's *Autobiographies* is in fact true of the first half of her own venture into the genre:

> Like a good cook giving you a badly ordered dinner, she has chosen the dullest stories and selected the most unattractive episodes of her life; she has concealed the most interesting details and has given place and prominence to domestic anecdotes which would have been most happily ignored.

It is from this unpromising material that Elinor Glyn created a novel which is, as Anthony Glyn says, 'a polished rounded whole, a witty, sparkling, shrewdly observed, sometimes malicious description of society'.[3]

Not surprisingly, since Elinor's own experience is the basis of the story, it is a novel about marriage. In her sequence of visits Elizabeth, a naive and well-brought-up young girl, observes with a fresh and innocent eye the complicated relationship between men and women. In France she witnesses at close hand the negotiations to secure an unwilling young man as a husband for her unattractive cousin, Victorine. And all the time she is gently pursued by Lord Valmond to whom, inevitably, she becomes engaged at the end of the novel. The skill lies in the deft handling of the point of view. We only ever have Elizabeth's account of events and people, and yet we are allowed to understand much more than she ever does. The haunted house incident mentioned earlier is a very good example of this. The gap between what Elizabeth sees and what she understands is the source of much comedy.

Although each letter is written from a country house and each describes basically similar occasions, there is none of the tedious repetition which occurs in Lady Angela's autobiography, for each letter has a specific focus. There is the smart set of Nazeby with perhaps a hint of the Souls in Miss La Touche's use of the word 'deevy', (a word Margot Asquith used often); there is the political set at Carriston Towers; the social climbing parvenus at Folyambe Place and the socially haphazard situation such as Elinor had experienced at Cranford, here thinly disguised as Retby.

All of this is examined afresh when seen in contrast with French society as Elizabeth visits her relatives in France. The French section differs from the English in that there is a smaller cast of characters, but even here each letter focuses on an incident which illustrates a specific aspect of French behaviour and attitudes.

Elizabeth herself is not simply the medium through which society is observed and satirised. Her letters give us a strong sense of her character, though again she herself is not fully aware of what she reveals. Her uncertainty undercutting her expressions of determination is most visible when she writes to her mother of Lord Valmond: 'I don't want to see him any more. It is too fatiguing quarrelling all the time, and one could not forgive him and be friends I suppose after such behaviour as his at Nazeby – could one, Mama?'

The book concludes with two postscripts which underline the

enfant terrible aspect of the letter-writer of which she is unaware. 'P.S. I shall get married before the Drawing-Room in February, because then I can wear a tiara. P.S. again. Of course an English marquis is higher than a French one, so I shall walk in front of Victorine anywhere, shan't I?'

When she had finished reshaping her material into a novel Elinor had to decide what name to use as the author of her book. Gerald Duckworth advised her against remaining totally anonymous. She consulted Daisy Warwick because she knew that Millicent, Duchess of Sutherland, had used a pseudonym for her books. The two women agreed that the name Elinor Glyn might well be taken for a pseudonym anyway, as all Elinor's friends were accustomed to calling her Nellie, and so this is the name that appeared on the cover and title page when in 1901 the flat-backed book with its apple-green cover with white label and gold lettering was launched. Elinor Glyn had published her first book, and for the first time in her life found herself earning substantial sums of money.

13 FINANCIAL TROUBLES

Much to everyone's surprise *The Visits of Elizabeth* was an immediate success. The critics were approving of its originality, wit and high spirits. Elinor collected all her reviews and pasted them into a large scrapbook with a binding of embossed leather. She was thrilled to see piles of her distinctively bound books in the shops and to learn from her publisher that a reprint was already under way to meet the unexpected demand for it. What pleased her most of all was that she was earning money. By now she had realised that the family's financial situation was far from healthy and that the extra income was not just helpful but necessary.

Elinor first became aware of something wrong when she received a letter from the family solicitor advising her to postpone payment of her marriage settlement. It was now that she discovered that, robbed of all possibility of a male heir, Clayton was no longer planning for the family's future. The money they were at that time living on was borrowed against the Homerston Estate which was steadily diminishing in value as collateral as it became more and more heavily mortgaged. Elinor found financial details hard to grasp. But even to her it was clear that, apart from the unexpected earnings from her novel, they would have very little in the way of income that year, or any other year for that matter.

They were not alone in finding themselves in this precarious financial situation. The kind of social life led by their contemporaries as the Victorian age drew to a close was draining the resources of even the most wealthy and highly placed of their circle. Before long even Daisy Warwick's income would prove unequal to her spending and Warwick Estates would be declared bankrupt. Her half-sister, Lady Angela Forbes, would soon find herself not only without her beloved horses but also without a home. Lady Randolph Churchill's finances were in desperate straits as were those of the Duke of Marlborough and George Curzon.

The men solved their problems by marrying rich heiresses. This practice was so widely accepted that American papers published lists of Peers who were on the lookout for rich American ladies.

There were a number of ways in which the women attempted to sustain their extravagant life-style. There were those, like Minnie Paget, who made money by arranging the introduction of English Peers to ambitious American mothers. Consuelo Vanderbilt knew clearly that her meeting with 'Sunny' Marlborough in Mrs Paget's house at 35 Belgrave Square was no chance encounter but an opportunity provided in return for a cash payment. What she remembered most vividly of that occasion was not her future husband but 'a pair of hard green eyes'[1] which belonged to her hostess.

Another profitable business for titled or well-placed ladies was to take under their wing wealthy foreigners, Jews or the newly rich. They would act as hostesses for their clients' dinners, thus ensuring a good guest list. They would help to organise the purchase of prestigious houses and their decoration in fashionable taste. On these occasions they would expect an additional benefit in the form of commission from tradespeople.

The husbands of the ladies 'running' those aiming at social acceptance also preyed on these ready victims. They would lead them into playing for high stakes at cards, or help them set up a stable of carefully chosen and expensive horses, or make introductions to exclusive hunts.

A more risky way of continuing to afford a wardrobe of beautiful clothes when cash was in short supply was to take a wealthy lover and send the dressmaker's, furrier's and jeweller's bills to him. Lucy saw a good deal of such behaviour at Maison Lucile and discussed it with her sister.

Although no one appeared to understand it at the time, a whole way of life, even the structure of society as they had known it, was coming to an end. The extravagant spending of the late Victorians and Edwardians simply speeded up a process which the 1914–18 war was to bring to completion. As Harold Nicolson comments in 'The Edwardian Weekend', 'It was an age of fevered luxury; at the same time it was an age of peculiar human ineptitude.'[2]

Elinor's friend Lord Rosslyn was a spectacular example of the kind of disintegration that was taking place in society. First of all in 1896 he had found it necessary to sell Dysart, the house where Elinor had stayed during the rehearsals and performance of

Diplomacy. Then his wife and children had left and were living apart from him under the care of his father-in-law. Worse still, in 1897 he had been compelled to register as a bankrupt and had been left with nothing. This once wealthy man had spent everything on high living, expensive mistresses and compulsive gambling. In his feverish spending he had even hired special trains to take him to the races. In the year in which Elinor began to understand the extent of her financial difficulties, the Earl of Rosslyn under the name of James Erskine was making his living as an actor, thinking himself lucky to be hired by Lillie Langtry to play opposite her in her company.

But none of these ways of supplementing a diminishing income was available to Elinor. She was not sufficiently well connected to 'run' socially ambitious couples, even if she had cared to do so which she did not. In *The Visits of Elizabeth* she makes it very clear that she found such activity repellent, even dishonest. Her moral code inherited from her grandmother and her mother, and her own sense of romance inhibited her from becoming involved in what was really little better than high-class prostitution.

The unexpectedly good sales of *The Visits of Elizabeth* temporarily pushed many money worries aside. There were as yet no serious retrenchments. The nanny and the governess were retained as was Elinor's personal maid and other domestic staff. Elinor continued to dress well and expensively whilst Clayton saw no reason to stint himself in the matter of champagne brandy and the choicest of food. Indeed his concern for the latter is described by Mary Davson in an article in *The Listener* of 14 November 1974 as amounting to an obsession such that 'rather than sit up with, or go to bed with, his wife, he would sit up all night with a pear in order to eat it at the acme of its ripeness'.

No attempt was made to economise by curtailing the regular winter trips abroad. On the contrary, in 1900 Elinor and Clayton began to plan their most ambitious tour to date. Because it was then fashionable to visit Egypt they decided that was where they would go. This time they would travel alone.

Elinor's attempt to instil some romance into her moribund marriage by making this journey with Clayton was probably prompted by the changes that had taken place in her sister's life.

Lucy's business was now thriving. Among her customers she now had the Princess of Wales and several members of the group of friends known as the Souls, including Margot Asquith, the Duchess of Rutland and Lady Desborough. In 1895 she had taken on as a business partner Sir Cosmo Duff Gordon, who even at that time was in love with her. He was only prevented from marrying her by his mother's refusal to accept a divorced woman as his wife. Lucy had other admirers, however, and when she went for a break from work with her mother to Monte Carlo she was pursued by one of them who proposed and was accepted. At this moment Cosmo's mother died and the way was at last clear for him to marry Lucy. He set off immediately for Venice where the newly engaged couple were staying. In a scene which would have delighted Elinor he routed his rival and there and then in Venice in May 1900 he married Lucy and carried her off on a honeymoon to Abazzia.

In January 1901, underlining the fact that a certain way of life was indeed coming to an end, Queen Victoria died. Elinor spent a few days in London staying with Lucy to see the funeral procession before departing with Clayton for Egypt. She left England with a feeling that a new era was about to begin, one which she was reluctant to acknowledge too quickly.

Egypt's popularity as a place in which to spend the winter had begun some years before. It was to Cairo, for example, that Margot Asquith, then still Margot Tennant, had journeyed with her parents in 1891, and it was in that romantic setting that Alfred Milner had proposed to her. He was there at that time as Financial Secretary to Sir Evelyn Baring, the man largely responsible for the establishment of a lively British Colony in Egypt.

Major Baring had gone to Egypt originally as the British representative on a commission to investigate Egypt's debt to French and English bankers who held shares in the Suez Canal. He had remained in Egypt as British Consul General and, although he was nominally only adviser to the Khedive, he did in fact run the country, backed up by the presence of British troops. Under his good management Egypt had begun to prosper. The budget now balanced thanks to improvements in agriculture and irrigation. It was altogether an attractive place for British visitors. The presence of the troops gave a reassuring sense of security without taking away the air of exoticism stimulating to jaded British palates.

There were three hotels in Cairo that catered for European visitors and it was in one of these, the Savoy, that Elinor and

Clayton settled for a few weeks. They found themselves part of a society that held itself aloof from most Egyptians with the exception of governing royalty such as the Khedive. Men and women alike continued to dress in much the same way as they would have done at home except that the parasol became an absolutely necessary part of a lady's wardrobe whilst some of the men took to wearing the fez to protect their heads from the heat.

Flirtations and affairs were less common than at home largely because most of the available men were occupied with business, government or the army, and lacked the kind of endless leisure that their counterparts at home enjoyed.

Elinor was enchanted by the vividness of the colours in this unfamiliar country and by the contrasts between the irrigated areas and the desert, between the austerity of the pyramids and the lushness of the gardens. In her diary she wrote enthusiastically about 'the beauty and colour of everything, the sapphire-blue sky, the brilliant green rice fields, the picturesque buildings, the domes and minarets, the camels, the desert, the sense of endless space and endless time'.

She was no less enthusiastic about the people she met in Cairo. In her autobiography she wrote at length about the British Consul, Evelyn Baring, by then Lord Cromer. He was just the kind of man to attract Elinor. His rule in Egypt, based on strong imperialist ideals, was what she herself believed in at that time. His methods and beliefs had much in common with those of George Curzon, still in India as Viceroy. Like him he was autocratic and hard working almost to the point of obsession, and they shared a deep interest in the history and archaeology of the areas they ruled. Cromer's quiet forcefulness and his interest in antiquities was a contrast to Clayton's aimlessness and lack of interest in the history of anything.

Although not an obviously romantic figure – his subordinates nicknamed him Overbaring – Elinor found in the story of his marriage much that appealed to her. She learnt that he had fallen in love at first sight in 1858 with Ethel Errington, the daughter of the Catholic Sir Rowland Errington, while he was serving as a subaltern in the Royal Artillery. It was the very year in which Elinor's parents had fallen in love. But Evelyn Baring was too poor to marry the woman he loved. He was, however, determined to do so as soon as possible and so he set about improving his position. For a long time the couple saw very little of each other but their love endured and in 1876 they were at last able to marry.

Then Ethel had become ill with Bright's disease. She should have stayed in London but instead went to Egypt to be with her husband during the Sudanese campaign. She had died in 1898, a month after the battle of Omdurman. Her devotion to her husband was remarkably similar to that of Mary Curzon to hers.

Eventually Baring had married again. The Lady Cromer Elinor met, Katherine Thynne, the sister of the Marquess of Bath, had been his wife for only a short time. She was the same age as Elinor and a lively and intelligent woman. The obvious devotion the couple showed each other made them for Elinor an ideal of married love. It was a relationship such as she had longed for and failed to achieve. The disproportionate amount of time she spends discussing the merits of this marriage in her autobiography suggests that she was herself half in love with Lord Cromer and somewhat envious of his wife. She concludes her discussion with 'What a fortunate woman to be the wife of such a man, and possess his love, as she obviously does.'

The high point of this Egyptian idyll was a moonlit ride to see the pyramids. The experience was so powerful that Elinor determined to visit Egypt again with her children so that they too could see the magic and the mystery of the pyramids in the glow of the moon.

Egypt had a strange effect on many of its Edwardian visitors. A.B. de Guerville in his book *New Egypt* commented that there was something in the air of Egypt which seemed to excite almost everyone and 'which almost maddens certain natures, especially of the weaker sex'.[3]

Elinor did not respond in the manner of many other English ladies who threw themselves into affairs with well-born young Egyptians, tourist guides and interpreters. Indeed one wealthy English woman rented a house near the pyramids for seven months so that she could dedicate herself to a passionate affair with her guide.

Although it was less obvious, Elinor too was affected by the weeks she spent in Egypt. The journey home taking in Naples, Rome and Florence and even making the acquaintance of a new admirer, Professor Thomas Lindsay, Principal of Glasgow College, who talked to her about medieval religion and manners, did little to calm Elinor. She returned to England with a restlessness and a longing. She thought a great deal about the relationship between Lord and Lady Cromer. She was, in fact, ready to fall in love.

Major Seymour Wynne Finch was not a new acquaintance by any means. He was one of the Prince of Wales's set, a Guards officer, a friend of Daisy Warwick and of Lady Angela Forbes who described him as one of the most handsome men in England. Elinor herself described his appearance in *The Reflections of Ambrosine* so accurately that his nickname in society became Sir Anthony Thornhirst, the name of the hero in her book.

> His brown hair crisps nicely and is rather grey above the ears; but he does not look very old – perhaps not more than thirty-five or so – and now that one can see both his eyes, one realises that they are rather attractive. A grayish-greeny blue, with black edges and such black eyelashes. They are as clear as clear, and I am sure he is a cat and can see in the dark. He laughed at some of the people, even the ones who think themselves great; and he made me feel that he and I were the same and on a plane by ourselves, which was delightful.

Not only was Seymour Wynne Finch handsome, he had style. While other men wore smoking jackets of plain red or blue velvet he wore one of paisley shawl with silk facings.

It was at Easton Lodge, that hot-house of love affairs and intrigues, that the two confessed their feelings to each other. When Elinor returned to Sheering, Seymour Finch visited her there; then there were meetings in London. Wynne Finch was as cosmopolitan as Elinor. He loved all things French and, although at that time it was not generally acceptable to take a lady out to dinner, he knew that Elinor with her French habits would delight as he did in dining at the Amphytron, one of the only two restaurants in London at that time. It was there that he introduced her to Sarah Bernhardt with whom he had enjoyed a passionate affair some years previously. She was in London along with Lillie Langtry at the invitation of the Prince of Wales.

Elinor might well have been jealous of this old flame. But she was not. It was a thrill to her to meet at last this actress who had so inspired her many years ago. She was not even upset to think that theirs was a relationship which had been fully consummated. For she knew that it was said that it was enough for Sarah Bernhardt to like a man to go to bed with him, and that she did not regard this as making a long term commitment to a lover. Elinor's own relationship with Seymour Wynne Finch she regarded as completely different. For although she loved him and loved the romance of their relationship, she was not ready to be sexually unfaithful to Clayton. Her upbringing still inhibited her as did the proximity of her mother who had never even considered anything other than fidelity to the difficult David Kennedy. Elinor's idea of this new affair was based on Tennyson's *Idylls* and notions of courtly love. But for a man as passionate and as in love as Seymour Wynne Finch the situation was intolerable. It was clear to him that they must either consummate their love or part.

With bitter regret Elinor decided they must part and her lover went away. Because the affair never became physical, it remained in Elinor's imagination as the most romantic of all her involvements.

But that did not stop her brooding about whether she had done the right thing, or whether she had thrown away her chance of love. She was very much aware that Sarah Bernhardt had not had the same scruples. Which of them had been right? Years later she was still asking herself this question when she met Sarah Bernhardt again in Paris. By this time the man they had both loved was dead. She wrote about the difference between herself and the woman she still admired. She saw Sarah Bernhardt as someone who had felt able to live out her love 'because she was a great actress and free', and herself as 'the immaculate and well-behaved wife of an English squire'. She wondered if she would have been happier if she had given in to her impulses or 'only more full of unrest'.

14 THE FIRST TIGER SKIN

The break with Seymour Wynne Finch came towards the end of 1901 and left Elinor unhappy and with a great gap in her life. Although they could not really afford the expense, Elinor urged Clayton to go to Egypt again, this time taking the whole family. Once again they would stay at the Savoy Hotel.

Because on their second visit they stayed longer, Elinor became much more actively involved in the life of the English set this time. Her particular friend was Lady Talbot who had been a close friend of Seymour Wynne Finch and who was ready to talk to Elinor about him and to sympathise with her unhappiness at the ending of the relationship.

The social life of the English in Egypt was not very different from that of their peer group at home. There were the familiar *tableaux vivants* for charity for example. Perhaps they were a little more spectacular than they might have been in England. Would Elinor have appeared in an English country house as Lorelei, 'clad only in tights, yards of green gauze and her hair', which she had combed out to its full magnificent length and which she had decorated with emeralds to match her eyes?

She was almost certainly remembering and relishing the impression she had made in this performance when she described Zara, the heroine of *The Reason Why*, who created a similar sensation dressed as Isolt from the *Idylls of the King*. Elinor's ability to appear overtly seductive in this performance was a foretaste of things to come in just a few years.

Such displays of female beauty as the *tableaux vivants* were open to disturbing interpretations by the non-English men present. After his wife's appearance as Lorelei, Clayton was surprised to be approached by an envoy of the Sultan of Turkey acting on behalf of his wealthy, princely master. He offered Clayton a considerable sum if he would sell Elinor to him. He expressed great admiration for her beauty and seemed confident that Clayton would be willing to sell her. Why else would he have allowed her to display herself in such a manner? He was sympathetic. After all, everyone knew that, although men were greatly attracted to ladies with red hair, they also tired of them quickly.

Clayton told Elinor the story and they laughed together at the Sultan's mistake. But Elinor thought ruefully to herself that there was after all an uncomfortable truth in the Sultan's words. For had she not seen for herself that Clayton had indeed quickly tired of her and that he was no longer moved or stirred by her beauty?

But the dressing up continued. A great ball was arranged by Lady Talbot. There was to be a variant on the *tableau vivant* as the centrepiece of the evening. Eight ladies were chosen, including Elinor, and each was to dress to represent a Romney portrait. Each was to be accompanied at her entrance by an officer from the 11th Hussars in full levée dress. What a strange and unlikely sight they must have been in that Cairo setting.

Even the children were drawn into the social life of the English colony. The High Commissioner gave a fancy dress party for them at the Residency. Margot and Juliet were dressed up like miniature adults with hooped skirts and powdered hair. They quickly forgot their pride in their fancy dress in their excitement when the gas-filled balloons appeared, and in their subsequent distress when these inevitably floated away out of reach and then stuck to the ceiling.

Millicent, Duchess of Sutherland, was also in Cairo for the season. She soon became as close a friend of Elinor as her brother and sisters were. It was she who persuaded Elinor to venture out of doors to watch the 11th Hussars playing polo. Elinor took the usual precautions to protect herself from the sun. She carried a parasol as well as wearing a large protective hat. But she did not take to the game. She remained as always largely without interest in such sports.

There were a number of celebrities in Cairo that winter. Usually to be seen together were Cecil Rhodes and Dr Leander Starr Jameson. Rhodes was an untidy, shambling man and his companion was no more prepossessing. Elinor described him in *Romantic Adventure* as looking from the back like an 'old rat with pink ears and a bald head'.

Despite their unattractive appearances the two men had been treated like heroes in London. Cecil Rhodes's appeal was his declared aim of bringing the benefits of peace, religion, enlightenment, trade and education to the uncivilised areas of the world. It was a declaration of the imperialism in which so many Victorians and Edwardians believed passionately. Even declared socialists such as Daisy Warwick found Rhodes's ideas inspiring and romantic.

Dr Jameson had been responsible for the Jameson raid. He had invaded the Transvaal with men from Rhodes's South Africa Company. His raid had failed and his force had surrendered. As a result both men had been summoned to London to face a Parliamentary Committee of Enquiry in 1897. Public sympathy was with them however, and they had not been treated as men in disgrace. On the contrary they had been wined and dined everywhere. The Prince of Wales himself had attended the hearings in Parliament, and to show where he stood in the matter he had openly entertained Rhodes at Marlborough House. In Cairo, where the English were for the most part staunch imperialists like their leader Lord Cromer, it had been the same story. Elinor was unusual in her mockery of Jameson's appearance and her lack of interest in his achievements.

There was, however, another member of the Marlborough House set – as those admitted to the intimacy of the Prince of Wales were known – in Cairo whose acquaintance Elinor was only too glad to make. She knew that Sir Ernest Cassel had indirectly helped Lucy's business by allowing his daughter to order her wedding dress from Lucile. But what really fascinated both Elinor and Clayton at this time of financial difficulty was Ernest Cassel's remarkable ability to make money. His financial abilities had gained him the Prince of Wales's friendship and he had consolidated this by being the ostensible host and escort of Alice Keppel, the King's mistress, whenever the two of them wanted to spend time together discreetly away from London. Because he had modelled his appearance on that of the Prince – he was 'portly, bearded, beringed, watch chained and cigar smoking' – he was a wonderful decoy.[1]

Despite his great wealth and power, Ernest Cassel was a quietly spoken and modest-mannered man. He had made his way in society despite being a German Jew when anti-Semitism was only just below the surface in British society. He made a very favourable impression on Elinor, one which surfaced when she was writing *Katherine Bush* in 1917. At a time when her former friend, Lady Angela Forbes, was writing virulently anti-Semitic comments in her memoirs, Elinor has her heroine involved in the following conversation:

> 'You found Jews agreeable to work with?'
> 'Very. You know where you are with them. They do not pretend, and they are very generous.'
> 'Indeed!'
> 'Yes. People have a preconceived notion of Jews, I find, quite faulty as a rule. They know what to pay for. They are far less fools than other races. I respect them.'

There was much to respect, in Elinor's view, in this man who had organised the loan which had made possible the building of the Aswan dam which in turn had made possible the irrigation on which Egypt's new agricultural prosperity was based; who had founded the National Bank of Egypt, and who was in Cairo that winter to supervise the take-over of the Agricultural Bank. He could not have been more different from the careless, spendthrift, idle men whom Elinor had become accustomed to meeting in English society nor from the Egyptian aristocrats such as Prince Mahomet Ali. The Prince entertained himself by giving elaborate parties in the desert with silken tents and exotic food, where conversation was likely to be rather more lively than would have been considered seemly at an English party.

The Khedive's Ball to which Elinor and Clayton were invited that year was similarly different in tone from its English equivalent. The presence of Grand Duke Boris with his entourage of handsome, if wild, young Russian noblemen may have contributed to the difference. It was at this ball that Elinor met Prince Griztko Wittgenstein. As soon as she set eyes on him in his colourful Cossack dress, staring with undisguised sexual interest at all those women he found attractive, she was provoked. She found him the most physically compelling man she had ever met. Not for him the courteous exchanges which might establish whether he and Elinor were mutually interested. He did not even wait to be introduced or to enquire whether Elinor wished to dance. He simply swept her away in a waltz holding her tightly in a close embrace. His answer to her protest at this familiarity was to kiss her passionately and then to walk away. Elinor declared her indignation at such treatment, but in reality she was fascinated and stirred in an unprecedented way. No man had ever behaved towards her in such a fashion before. She set out to discover more about him and found that his attitude towards her had been restrained in comparison with some of his exploits with other women. She was particularly shocked but intrigued by the story of his stripping naked a gypsy girl who had failed to please him before lowering her over the balcony of the room in which he was carousing right into the soup tureen of an amazed party of diners. She made detailed notes of his appearance and of the feelings he aroused in her. The journal which records her meeting with him was later to be responsible for an appropriately dramatic incident in her own life.

Elinor's pleasure in her new experiences was spoiled by another bout of illness. In her autobiography she attributes her collapse to a fall she had suffered when she had been bathing at the bath house earlier in the year. But in the light of subsequent events it seems more likely that Anthony Glyn's less romantic diagnosis of gall stones is more accurate. The pains were so intense that at times Elinor had to be given morphia. And, of course, she lost her appetite and began to lose weight. Prince Hussein of Egypt learnt of Elinor's illness and suggested that once she felt able to do so she should convalesce in his garden at his island palace Gezirih. In this 'fairytale garden' filled with 'giant violets, roses, lilies of the valley, bougainvillea and clematis' and with the refreshing sound of fountains and flowing water Elinor felt at peace. Perhaps for the first time she had leisure to think back over her romance with Seymour Wynne Finch. The sadness these memories evoked led her inevitably into thinking about her own marriage and its failure to be what she had hoped for. She remembered earlier proposals and wondered what would have become of her life if she had accepted any of them. Suddenly her thoughts began to cohere. 'I was filled with an impulse to write, and the idea of the story came to me from imagining what it would have been like to have married the millionaire whom my brother-in-law had so furiously cursed me for refusing, long ago in my first season.'

As she sat there in that exotic garden she began to write what would become *The Reflections of Ambrosine*, that novel with a setting and tone so far removed from the warmth and light of Egypt. And, as she wrote, once again, she began to feel better.

It was just as well that she did recover for before she had written very much it was time to leave Egypt.

Was it irritation that Elinor was absorbed in her new book that made Clayton so frankly out of sympathy with his wife as they began their circuitous journey back to England? Did he sense that Elinor was launched on a career which would gradually reverse the roles in their relationship?

Certainly the differences in their interests and their personalities became ever more clear during the next few weeks, which were spent in Italy.

When Elinor and Clayton arrived in Naples – their first stop – they found to their dismay that the hotel they had intended to stay in was full of passengers from a liner whose departure had been delayed. They had been travelling with an elderly American diplomat, a Mr Van Allen, who had taken the precaution of securing rooms for himself by sending his valet on ahead of him. This enterprising servant had secured the 'Royal' salon which had two brass beds along with various flimsy gilt sofas and armchairs. When the American saw the difficulties the Glyns faced, he offered to share his accommodation with them. They were only too pleased to accept his offer. There were, therefore, Mr Van Allen, Clayton, Elinor, Elinor's maid, Williams, and the valet to share the available space. Naturally the American gentleman had one of the beds. The second was put at the disposal of Elinor and her maid. Clayton settled for a sofa, but the valet, appalled at these irregularities, opted to sit up all night fully clothed in an armchair.

Williams was dismayed at having to share a bed with her mistress. Out of politeness she slept so close to the edge of the bed that inevitably she fell out. The thud of her fall caused uproar in the room. Waking up suddenly, Elinor realised that their American companion had so far spent the night gazing at her sleeping form. For the rest of the night he whispered to her his appreciation of her beauty.

Clayton was not impressed by his wife's power to keep their benefactor from his sleep. His response was just one more example of his hurtful indifference to her: 'Old fool – bothering about women when we were all so tired.'

After their adventure in Naples the Glyns travelled to Pompeii. Here Elinor had an experience which convinced her of the validity of the belief she had long held and which Clayton was inclined to laugh at. Elinor believed strongly in reincarnation and in a very particular kind of karmic law. In Pompeii she had an intense feeling of *déjà vu.*

When she visited Paestum, the ruined city near Salerno which had been founded by the Greeks in 600 BC, she had an even stronger experience. In the temple of Neptune she 'felt almost suffocated with the intensity of [my] weird, tigerish sensations', as though she had been suddenly transported to another age in which she had been another person.

If Clayton would not listen to her account of how she had felt at Paestum, there were others who would. In Rome where they attended the wedding of an Austrian Prince and Princess Frasso they met up once more with Lord Grey who was taking a break from his duties as Director of the British South Africa Company. A classical scholar himself, he not only listened to Elinor, but also undertook to educate her more about the ancient world. He told her of the marvels to be seen at Hadrian's Villa at Frascati, and the Villa d'Este. Clayton was quite unperturbed by the growing closeness between Elinor and her friend and admirer. When a party was organised to visit the Villa d'Este, Elinor chose to travel in the same car as Lord Grey because she wished to hear more about the marvels they were about to see. Clayton had no objection to this arrangement so he was amused when a young attaché from the French embassy who was also of the group fell into a jealous rage about Lord Grey. It fell to him, the husband, to reassure the younger man that there was nothing at all to be jealous about since Lord Grey was just 'one of Elinor's antiques'!

He was a little less complacent about Elinor's frequent visits to the Palazzo Barberini where she was sitting for the American sculptor Waldo Storey to whom she was evidently attracted. Clayton sensed the potential for scandal. But it was a relationship that did not survive their departure from Rome.

Because Elinor had not entirely recovered from the illness which had so devastated her in Egypt, she was advised by Waldo Storey to consult his friend, the Swedish doctor then most fashionable in Rome, Axel Munthe. This interesting man lived in the house where Keats had lived in the Piazza di Spagna. His first success in Rome had been the curing of an English banker's wife who had been given up as a hopeless case. Although his methods were based on common sense and the belief in mind over matter, he was judged to have effected a cure little short of a miracle. Word got about and wealthy patients flocked to have a consultation with him.

Axel Munthe had no illusions about what was wrong with most of the women who came to him for help. They were suffering from the common Edwardian complaint of idleness combined with 'over-eating, too many cakes or sweets during the day or too heavy dinners at night'.[2]

But he was also fully aware that the last thing anyone wished to hear from him was this honest diagnosis. While he had practised in France he had for some time sent many of his women patients away happy to believe that they had a problematical appendix. What he recommended as a cure was a more sensible diet and more exercise. When, however, word got out that in the United States appendicitis was being treated as a case for surgery, his clients were less happy to follow his cure. In Rome he had hit upon the term colitis as an acceptable alternative to a diagnosis of greed and excess. Margot Tennant had consulted him on her way back from Egypt to London. She had been as fascinated by him then as Elinor was to be in 1902.

Elinor attributed to him hypnotic powers, which indeed he did have. She found his eyes, hidden behind glasses with thick lenses, most disturbing. But she discovered that she had a lot in common with him. She shared his views about women. In his book, *The Story of San Michele*, written much later in 1929, he confesses that his treatment of his women patients, many of whom were hysterical, was based on the notions that 'Women, though they do not seem to know it themselves, like far better to obey than to be obeyed', and 'Love means to a woman far more than it means to a man, it means everything.' These are the very principles which form the basis of many of Elinor's novels.

Munthe was as interested in antiquities as Elinor herself. He talked to her about his views on Tacitus, and how he felt that the writer had damaged irretrievably the reputation of the Emperor Tiberius in whom he had a special interest. Tiberius had ended his days on Anacapri on the very spot where Munthe had bought an old stone house and the ruined chapel of San Michele. His descriptions of his finds of old Roman sculptures stirred Elinor's imagination and she was to remember his words when she wrote her novel *Halcyone*.

Elinor was well satisfied with her consultations with Dr Axel Munthe, especially as he concluded them by telling her that she belonged to that group of women he classified as Sirens. Perhaps she would have taken him a little less seriously if she had known that he had told Margot Tennant exactly the same thing.

But it was with this sense of herself as an irresistible woman that Elinor left Rome and travelled with Clayton to Lucerne. Here she tried to make her siren qualities work on her husband. She found her first sight of Switzerland, of the mountains and of Lucerne 'ideally romantic' for this purpose, but Clayton just laughed at her 'spring fancies'.

Feeling foolish and frustrated and vastly let down by Clayton who did not see in her what attracted other men to her, she reacted as she had done in similar circumstances in Venice. She put pen to paper to create those love scenes that to her dismay and lasting regret had not happened.

Full of the romantic fervour of a passionate love story that existed only in her imagination, Elinor went out to calm herself by walking in the streets of quiet, staid Lucerne. How could she ever have anticipated that the most unlikely object to be found in that Swiss town should immediately strike her eye.

There in a window displayed in all its magnificence was a tiger skin.

Elinor had to have it: she saw it as emblematic of how she perceived herself. Once again she remembered the whispered words, 'Belle Tigresse'. She thought of the portrait of herself as a cat and she felt again those strange 'tigerish sensations' that had come over her at Paestum.

But Clayton saw things differently. He did not regard Elinor's fancies as any justification for spending money on a tiger skin of all things. He laughed scornfully at the idea and flatly refused to give Elinor the money.

Elinor was enraged, but helpless to change Clayton's mind. She flounced out of their rooms determined to have one last long look at the coveted tiger skin. Before leaving the hotel she checked at the desk for letters. There was one from Duckworth. Inside was a substantial royalty cheque for sales of *The Visits of Elizabeth.* This sudden unexpected source of money seemed more than a coincidence to Elinor. She felt that she was meant to have the tiger skin.

Without stopping to consider any further she went straight to the shop where it was displayed. She bought it without even questioning the price and had it parcelled up and sent round to the Hotel National. Even now she believed that once Clayton saw the tiger skin with herself draped seductively upon it he would be won over. She set up the scene just as it appeared later in her novel *Three Weeks*. But Clayton was no fictional hero. He was not overwhelmed by the beauty of the scene. His first response was to laugh at Elinor's foolishness. His second response was to lose his temper with her for her wilful extravagance. Was it not enough, he raged, that she had already bought thirty-seven new dresses and countless new hats without this ridiculous indulgence which would necessitate their buying yet another trunk to hamper them on their journey home?

Thirty-four years later Elinor recalled the day she had made the fateful purchase and considered the effect it had had on her life.

> My sin of disobedience in ever buying the lovely creature deserved punishment no doubt, but the merciless fate which seems to have decreed that the name of Elinor Glyn shall for ever be coupled with the picture of a woman lying on a tiger-skin seems almost too like the imagination of Dante.

15 ♥ A CHANGING WORLD

Despite their cumbersome luggage the Glyns arrived back safely at Sheering Hall. In their absence their money troubles had not gone away. Rather they had been exacerbated by the expenses of their winter excursion. As Elinor learned from the family solicitor, Walters, just how little money would be left to live on for the year after debts had been paid, she was even more conscious of the extravagance of her purchases, especially that of the tiger skin.

Worry about money, and growing distress at Clayton's indifference made Elinor feel ill again. She desperately wanted to finish the novel she had begun in Egypt. She hoped that its publication might provide some financial relief. But at home, even with the children away at Lamberts with her mother, she did not find the atmosphere conducive to writing. Axel Munthe had suggested that Elinor might find taking the cure at Carlsbad helpful and so she decided to set off on her travels once more. Clayton did not wish to accompany her.

Carlsbad was all that she had hoped for. In its own way it was quite as much a social centre as Cairo or Hyères. For Elinor was not alone among society people needing to get away from the rigours of the Edwardian social round. She found the company at Carlsbad congenial, and she discovered that without Clayton's mocking observation she could make friends with people he would have had no time for or interest in.

On this first visit she met Sir Francis and Lady Jeune. The famous divorce judge was later to become Lord St Helier. What attracted Elinor to him was his devotion to the classics which he was prepared to discuss with her as they took the recommended slowly paced long walks through the pinewoods.

In the tranquillity of Carlsbad Elinor was once more able to write, and she quite quickly finished the novel she had begun in Egypt. She had planned to call the book *The Chronicles of Ambrosine*. At one point in the narrative the heroine declares 'This is not a school-girl love story I am writing, but the chronicle of my life.' Her statement makes clear the difference between this second novel and *The Visits of Elizabeth* which is, among other things, a school-girl love story. In Carlsbad Elinor decided on a new title which underlines still further the new tone and new perspective of this second novel.

Though *The Reflections of Ambrosine* is basically about the same world as *The Visits*, the difference in perspective is all important. Elizabeth is rich; she can afford to mock the arranged marriage of her cousin Victorine and she can afford to marry where she loves, no matter that the man she chooses happens to be a wealthy aristocrat. Ambrosine, in contrast, is poor and has to agree to an arranged marriage. It is from her point of view that the miserable realities of such an arrangement are examined. Whereas the whole business of lovers and intrigues is made funny as the result of the naive misunderstandings of Elizabeth, in this second novel the anguish and the sordid contrivances resulting from adultery are emphasised.

Although many of the situations in *The Visits of Elizabeth* are ones Elinor had herself observed, she is not Elizabeth. She was never able to afford such naivety. Ambrosine is a character closer to Elinor herself. In particular, the central experience of the novel, loving one man and being married to another, is Elinor's own. Like Ambrosine, she could not easily accept the casual view of infidelity expressed by Lady Tilchester (modelled on Daisy Warwick). Instead she had to endure the misery of dismissing a lover because her upbringing had made her regard adultery as a deadly sin. Ambrosine's cry of distress is surely expressive of Elinor's own feelings when she made a break with Seymour Wynne Finch. ' "Oh! what is this quality in me that makes me as I am – a flabby thing, with strength enough to push away all I desire in life, to keep untarnished my idea of honour, and yet too weak to tear the matter from my mind once I have done so." '

The differences between English and French society which are such an important part of *The Visits* are also examined in this novel. But whereas Elizabeth could stand aside from the customs of her French relatives, Ambrosine, like Elinor, has been brought up to respect many French notions of correct conduct. Although many of her grandmother's edicts stand her in good stead, she can also see the cynicism which lies behind the code. It is no accident that the most quoted book in this novel is *The Maxims* of La Rochefoucauld.

When Elinor had finished her novel she felt sufficient confidence in her new friends Sir Francis and Lady Jeune to show them her manuscript and invite their comments. The highly educated Sir Francis was dismayed to discover that this woman who had talked to him so earnestly and had appeared to understand his most erudite comments was incapable of spelling correctly or writing to strict rules of grammar. But he persisted in his reading and once he was able to ignore Elinor's school-girl errors he enjoyed the novel greatly. He spoke to her about it in a kindly and encouraging way whilst suggesting tactfully that she should try to improve her spelling. She was delighted with his response. She knew all about the faults in her writing, which she attributed to her scattered education. She was not too concerned; she knew that if Gerald Duckworth liked her work he would see to the necessary corrections.

Through the Jeunes Elinor met the novelist Sir Gerald Parker. He too was considerably older than Elinor and flattered by her interest in him. When he read her work his response was much the same as that of Sir Francis.

Encouraged by her social success and the completion of her novel Elinor returned to Sheering in good health and good spirits.

Her first thought was to take her new manuscript to London to Gerald Duckworth. The sooner the book could be published, she reasoned, the sooner she would have more money to meet her expenses.

Her new friends, the Jeunes, were happy to have her to stay with them when she arrived in London. Then she went to 3 Henrietta Street in Covent Garden where Duckworth had his offices.

Her experience in Carlsbad had suggested to her that her book might make a better impression if she read it aloud. That way the spelling errors would not be apparent. She read well, but in any event Gerald Duckworth was disposed to look on her work favourably. He was not only influenced by his personal admiration for her as a beautiful woman, he was also impressed by the unexpectedly good sales of *The Visits of Elizabeth.* It would be a good time to bring out a second novel while the first was still fresh in everyone's mind.

When Elinor could read no more and Duckworth began to feel his concentration weakening he suggested that they take a break and have lunch at the Savoy. What Elinor liked to eat on such occasions, according to Anthony Glyn, was fried onions, steak and boiled lettuce. After lunch it was back to the office and more reading of the novel until it was finished.

Gerald Duckworth was pleased with *The Reflections of Ambrosine*, even if it was not quite what he had expected.

Elinor returned to Sheering Hall with the promise of publication in December and an advance royalty cheque. She was in high spirits and very hopeful. When she met Ralph Blumenfeld, the editor of *The Daily Express* at a dinner party he was much struck by her. He had already seen her in the charity tableaux at Her Majesty's Theatre, but now he realised that she was not only a 'striking figure' but 'full of new ideas on literature, and so full of energy that nothing will deter her from finding expression for them'.[1] It is interesting to note that, although to most people Elinor continued to insist that she was not a professional writer and never would be, in the company of a fellow writer she was less modest and more willing to reveal that she did intend to write more.

In August the whole of society was swept along in the preparations for the coronation of Edward VII. Elinor was not herself directly involved in the ceremonies but her friend Millicent, Duchess of Sutherland and Consuelo, Duchess of Marlborough were two of the new Queen's canopy bearers. The word spread quickly that Edward had brazenly invited his mistress to attend the coronation, and that Mrs Arthur Paget and Sarah Bernhardt were to be seated together in good seats, much to the disgust of Queen Alexandra who spoke disparagingly of 'the ladies in the loose box'.[2]

When *The Reflections of Ambrosine* appeared in December in the same distinctive cover as *The Visits of Elizabeth*, the reviewers were quick to see that the second novel was no mere repetition of a successful formula. For, despite a protracted correspondence in *The Daily News* as to whether or not *The Visits of Elizabeth* was a scandalous novel, and despite one reviewer's observation that the book was not one for a 'jeune fille, or even for her English sister' and another's perception that this first novel had the serious purpose of revealing 'the mode of life of Society and on the whole the revelation is not particularly pleasant', *The Visits of Elizabeth* had been generally regarded as 'fresh' and 'piquant'. But there was no escaping the fact that *The Reflections of Ambrosine* presented 'Society' as neither amusing nor pleasant. It did not even sugar the pill with a conventional happy ending. Even those readers who did enjoy the novel and who regarded it as an advance on *The Visits* were perturbed by the fact that Lady Tilchester and Sir Anthony Thornhirst, the two people for whom the heroine expresses such love and admiration, were the parents of a child born as the result of adultery. The fact that Elinor was only being true to her intention of depicting Daisy Warwick accurately perhaps made matters worse rather than better.

1903 began with what was to Elinor shocking news. On 12 January the King and Queen of Serbia were assassinated. As a royalist, Elinor was appalled. She does not seem to have realised that the reign of the unpopular Alexander Obrenovich and his wife, Draga, had more to do with the political will of the Austrians than birth. The violence of their death, however, lingered in her thoughts.

A further blow was Clayton's decision that the only possible way to ease their financial situation was to take the measure he had used once before. The letting of Durrington Hall had helped him once. Now, he told Elinor, they must move from Sheering Hall into even smaller premises. He proposed that the whole family should share with Mrs Kennedy Lamberts, the house on the estate which she rented from him. It was a sensible and logical step to take. Margot and Juliet practically lived at Lamberts already. There was space enough for Clayton to have his own rooms. And anyway he was not at all averse to living at close quarters with his mother-in-law. He knew that she was very fond of him and usually took his side in any arguments with his wife. She would in fact be likely to look after his comforts in a way Elinor no longer did.

Elinor had little choice but to accept Clayton's plan. But she made one firm condition. If she was to continue her writing, and the income had proved very useful, then she must have a space all to herself in which she could do so.

Plans were drawn up to enlarge Lamberts to accommodate the whole family. Elinor was to have an extension built close to the original house and connected to it by a glass-roofed verandah. It did not escape the notice of either husband or wife that in this move they were making clear their intention to live as separately as possible while remaining under one roof.

While the extension was being built Elinor went once more to Carlsbad. Once more she travelled without her husband, though she planned to join Minnie Paget on her arrival.

Carlsbad had its usual soothing effect on her. She relaxed while Minnie related all the recent gossip to her. Lord Rosslyn, she reported to Elinor, had taken to the stage seriously and for money. He had joined forces with Lillie Langtry and was touring as a member of her company. Not much less shocking was the news that his half-sister, Daisy, was once more pregnant. Elinor felt some qualms about the portrait of Lady Tilchester then circulating in London. In return Elinor confided in Minnie her distress at the ending of her affair with Seymour Wynne Finch.

The company was then joined by Lord Milner, tired out after his time as Governor of Cape Colony and High Commissioner for South Africa, positions he had held since 1897, but pleased that at last the Boer War had ended.

The statesman and the two ladies had long discussions about Egypt. Milner knew their friend Lord Cromer, for he had served under him as Financial Secretary when Lord Cromer had still been Sir Evelyn Baring. What he did not discuss with his new friends was his romantic involvement with Margot Tennant, now Margot Asquith, and her refusal of his proposal of marriage made to her in Cairo in 1891.

Elinor found herself very much attracted to Lord Milner. She admired his dedication to work and to his country. He was shy and sensitive and not sure of himself with women. But she did not find herself in the position of Margot Tennant who had written: 'Alfred makes me feel a little too dependant on information to talk well . . . the fact is I do not know enough and all the imaginative insight in the world will not serve me instead of knowledge.'[3]

On the contrary Elinor found it easy to talk to Milner about their mutual love of the classics. In her company Milner relaxed and became positively boyish. As they walked and talked and even played surprisingly childish games in the pinewoods where Elinor had the previous year wandered happily with Sir Francis Jeune and Sir Gilbert Parker the atmosphere became charged with romance. It was, perhaps, all the more exciting because neither party had any intention of carrying the relationship further. Milner, just as much as Elinor, shied away from the thought of adultery.

In the evenings Milner read aloud to Elinor from Plato and Elinor flattered him saying he must be the reincarnation of Socrates. She wrote later that 'His stern face grew soft when his eyes rested on me. We talked for hours in the firelight and he forgot his duties and his dinner.'

Elinor began to write *The Damsel and the Sage*, a book which owes much to her absorption in La Rochefoucauld the previous year. She told Milner that he had been her inspiration, though in fact many of the epigrammatic sayings come out of her experiences with Clayton. She was, for example, surely commenting on the course of her own marriage and remembering the days of her honeymoon in Brighton when Clayton had hired the pool for her when she wrote: 'I who swam about freely and showed my glittering scales in the sun, am now caught and in a basket, with no prospect but suffocation and death in front of me.'

But perhaps Milner took as an oblique reference to their relationship the following words: 'Some things cause pride, some pleasure. There is only one thing which causes infinite bliss and oblivion of time, and this one thing, unless bound with chains, is called immoral.'

Elinor's respect for Milner and her gratification that he had chosen to spend so much of his time with her increased when a message arrived for him from Prime Minister Arthur Balfour asking him to become Colonial Secretary. Milner declined the honour and decided that he had to return to South Africa.

And so the time came when the Carlsbad party regretfully had to break up. Elinor gave Milner as a keepsake a tiny new moon of diamonds designed by Cartier. He in turn gave her a copy of the poems of Henley. He decided to accompany the two women as far as Nuremburg but there came the parting of their ways.

Back home in Essex Elinor had little time to pine over Milner even though a long and affectionate letter soon arrived for her. Uppermost in her mind was the matter of delivering her manuscript to Duckworth and the supervision of the move from Sheering to Lamberts.

Her new suite of rooms was not prepossessing from the outside. But she set about creating inside an environment which she felt expressed her personality. It was the first time she had designed rooms starting with bare walls and floors. At Sheering Hall she had simply made changes and additions to what was already there. She threw herself into interior decoration with enthusiasm. Reminded of Marie Antoinette's Petit Trianon by the relationship of her own modest rooms to those of the three larger houses on the estate she gave it that name. She chose French furniture for herself, a bed with a canopy and, remembering Hadrian's Villa d'Este, she had a Roman-style sunken bath fitted in her bathroom. To contrast with the austere and blatantly utilitarian board and rough cast of the outside of her new home she decorated the interior with a profusion of pink silk roses which she made herself with the help of all the other females in the household.

For days when the weather was too fine for her stay indoors she had a platform built in an apple tree in the garden. What she was trying to achieve above all was the possibility of isolating herself from the reality of family life the better to explore fully and without disturbance that romantic world inside her head.

When *The Damsel and the Sage* was published in October it was greeted far less kindly and enthusiastically than her two previous books. It is worth noting that the scrapbook into which Elinor had pasted all the reviews good, bad and indifferent of her first two novels has no reviews of *The Damsel and the Sage*. But the disappointment that Elinor felt at her book's critical reception was offset by the fact that it sold well, especially in the de-luxe edition at Christmas time.

The social round continued as usual. Elinor's fortieth birthday in October 1904 brought with it some soul searching. It was true that she was in the prime of her beauty, she did not lack admirers, and her writing was proving successful. But still missing from her life was that much sought-after element of romance.

Then in 1905 she met Lord Alistair Innes Ker, the second son of the Duke of Roxburghe and an officer in the Guards. He was tall, fair, strong, handsome and young. He could have been a hero from an Elinor Glyn novel. But best of all, he fell in love with Elinor.

From the start of their relationship Elinor was very conscious of being older, better read, even more worldly than her admirer. Until now she had always sought the company of men older than herself. Perhaps she consoled herself with the fact that two of the women she most admired had also become involved with much younger men when they reached their forties. Sarah Bernhardt had married a man eleven years younger than herself, and in 1899 the forty-six-year-old Lillie Langtry had returned to Jersey to marry the twenty-eight-year-old Hugo de Bathe. And there was the example of Jennie Churchill, Winston Churchill's glamorous mother.

Elinor's relationship with Alistair Innes Ker was very different from that with Seymour Wynne Finch. This time she was the leader, the educator. The young man visited Lamberts regularly. He played with the little girls, he went shooting with Clayton, he visited Elinor's rose-covered boudoir and he accompanied husband and wife to dinners and Saturdays to Mondays.

It was not his mind or his conversation or his knowledge of the classics that Elinor admired so much but his youth and the beauty of his appearance. He brought a new liveliness and playfulness into her life.

It was in the high spirits this new love had given her that she wrote *The Vicissitudes of Evangeline*. The book is dedicated to 'The Women With Red Hair'. The heroine, Evangeline, has a good deal in common with the young Elinor, including her admiration for Becky Sharp: 'I wonder if it is amusing to be an adventuress, because that is evidently what I shall become now. I read in a book all about it; it is being nice looking and having nothing to live on, and getting a pleasant time out of life – and I intend to do that!'

The difference in Evangeline's life, however, is that she escapes marriage with an older man and marries the young man of whom she says 'Lord Robert is such a beautiful shape, that pleased me too; the perfect lines of things always give me a nice emotion.'

Lord Robert is a recognisable portrait of Alistair Innes Ker. Like *The Visits of Elizabeth*, *Evangeline* is a light-hearted but sharply perceptive comedy of manners.

It was as if the relationship with Innes Ker had given Elinor a new creative energy. For no sooner had she finished *Evangeline* than she started on another novel, *Beyond The Rocks*. This time the tone was less light-hearted and Elinor began to touch on aspects of women's lives not generally dealt with in contemporary fiction. Like Ambrosine, Theodora, the heroine of *Beyond The Rocks* is forced into marriage with an older man in order to provide money for her feckless father. Something of what Elinor remembered about her mother's marriage is used in the novel. Theodora, once married, 'had fallen into her place, a place occupied by many wives before her with irritable, hypochondriacal husbands'.

What is especially striking in the novel is Theodora's expression of emphatic distaste for sexual relations with a man she does not love and her acknowledgement that she could enjoy physical passion if only it were with the man she does love. Hector Bracondale is once again a hero modelled on Innes Ker. But although he is shown to be handsome, courtly and a highly desirable match, he is not just a knight in shining armour. He is presented with a greater degree of realism than Elinor's previous heroes had been: he is very much a young Edwardian aristocrat, with all that that implies: 'He suddenly realised that his days were not more amusing than hers, although they were filled up with racing and varied employments – while the thoughts of his nights sickened him.'

The novel does have a happy ending of sorts. Theodora's rich and ailing husband, Josiah, dies, leaving Theodora to marry the man she loves. But the happiness of this ending is not absolute. Josiah, the inconvenient and unloved husband, is not a straightforward villain like Ambrosine's husband. He is generous by his lights and he cares for his young wife. His only real faults are a lack of fineness, his age, and the fact that he marries a young woman who does not love him. He is shown to be just as much a victim of the values of society as is Theodora herself.

Clayton must have had some misgivings when he read this, the latest of Elinor's novels. He was after all himself, like Josiah, finding he had less and less in common with his wife. He too was experiencing ill health, largely because he was drinking and eating too much. He must have wondered if the helpful death of Josiah was what Elinor secretly wished for him. He began to look a little less kindly on the model for Hector Bracondale.

Elinor's attachment to the young Innes Ker, however, had not stopped her interest in Alfred Milner, and their correspondence continued in affectionate terms. Everyone in their circle knew all about Lord Curzon's resignation of the Viceroyship of India after well-publicised arguments with Kitchener. Milner wrote to tell Elinor that in the unseemly haste to replace Curzon he had been offered the position but had decided to turn it down.

Elinor was pleased to be privy to this behind-the-scenes political manoeuvring. She looked with new interest at Curzon when she met him once more at a weekend party at Radcliffe. This tall, upright man with the pale, smooth face and inscrutable expression was accompanied by his wife Mary, whom Elinor had met several times previously. She had seen the photos of Mary in her peacock dress during her time as Vicereine and she had been as impressed as everyone else. She was, therefore, shocked at the difference in the appearance of the woman she had once praised for her glowing good looks. Mary Curzon had been so ill that she had almost died the previous year but then, despite all medical advice to the contrary, she had insisted on joining her beloved George in India for the last painful months of his Viceroyship. In so doing she had undermined her health irretrievably. She was now pale and thin and looked as ill as she felt. Curzon's love for her and his concern was apparent. But on the matter of the Viceroyship he was silent. His bitterness at the way he had been treated was well hidden.

Elinor was intrigued by Curzon and wrote to Milner giving her impressions of him. She felt that he was a man who concealed a great deal of himself. Milner confirmed her suspicion that there was probably a very different man hiding behind the cold public façade.

When in July Elinor learned of the death of Mary Curzon and of her husband's distress and temporary withdrawal from society she was not surprised by the news.

As she moved through the regular visits and routines of the year Elinor puzzled over the three men she was interested in. All three had similar backgrounds and education, but whilst Curzon and Milner were men occupied in serving their country, Innes Ker took life lightly and spent his time amusing himself. Was it simply a matter of the difference in age, she wondered. And when while on a visit to Lord Kintore at his home near Glamis Elinor experienced a moment when she saw the young man for what he really was and what he might be. As he lounged on the rug before the fire playing with his dog he seemed to her to be 'a typical product of Eton and Oxford, endowed with a splendid physique, personal charm and innate good qualities of the highest order, but intellectually and emotionally sound asleep.'

What would it take, she mused, to awaken such a young man. When the assembled company called on Elinor to entertain them in some way in the empty time before they changed for dinner she obliged them by telling them a story. Almost teasingly she made Innes Ker the subject of her tale and recounted how the passionate love of an older woman, a woman like Theodora as Sarah Bernhardt had played her, brought him to life.

The story she told that night must have been a mere sketch of the novel developing in her mind, for her companions applauded her. No one was shocked or displeased. The story stayed in Elinor's head and began to grow, fed by the constant presence of the young man who had inspired it.

In September the whole family set off for Paris to see Margot settled into a school there. Despite Clayton's growing misgivings

1. The Saunders Family. Henrietta, Elinor's youngest aunt, 'a deliciously romantic creature', is on the extreme left. Next to her is Juliet and then Elinor Saunders before her marriage, 'gay and full of life with a sense of humour and a ready wit'. Mrs Saunders on the extreme right is the young Elinor's grandmother, who 'demanded elaborate manners, aloofness, strict discipline and righteous pride'. The young man seated is Elinor's uncle, Thomas Saunders.

2. Douglas Sutherland, the father Elinor never saw. He was said to be 'tall and handsome and debonair, very sure of himself, and sure of life in general'.

3. Summerhill, Guelph, Ontario, Canada in 1949. The house had been drastically changed and divided since Elinor lived there in the late 1860s.

4. Elinor and Lucy and a cousin in 1871 just after the marriage of their mother to David Kennedy. At this time Elinor was a 'serious, good little girl' while Lucy, the tomboy, found her happiness threatened by the severity of her grandmother.

5. Elinor aged seventeen. She no longer felt an 'ugly duckling' since her young French admirer had said that she had 'something of Sarah Bernhardt about her eyes'.

6. Elinor is front left and Clayton is centre back in this photo taken during the annual visit to Cowes. Elinor had been attracted to Clayton by his 'merry blue eyes and perfect teeth, and by his quaintly arrogant point of view about everything'. In this first year of their marriage, 1892, Elinor was 'very happy on the whole'.

7. The authoress of *The Visits of Elizabeth* in 1900. Like her heroine she was 'candid, unconventional, versatile, and not sparing in her criticism of the people she met'.

8. *Above:* 'Le Chat Nellie', Jacques Emile Blanche's teasing portrait of Elinor echoed her own sense of herself.

9. *Right:* Lord Alistair Innes Kerr, the inspiration for Paul in *Three Weeks*. According to Elinor he was 'a typical product of Eton and Oxford' with 'innate good qualities of the highest order, but intellectually and emotionally sound asleep'.

10. Alfred Milner, later Lord Milner. When she first met him in 1903 Elinor described him as 'the reincarnation of Socrates'.

11. Major Seymour Wynne Finch. Elinor's love affair with him was 'sentimental and refined'.

12. Margot Glyn, Elinor's eldest daughter, who for many years accompanied her mother on her travels.

13. Juliet Glyn, Elinor's younger daughter who was sent to school in Eastbourne but left before she was eighteen to volunteer as a VAD.

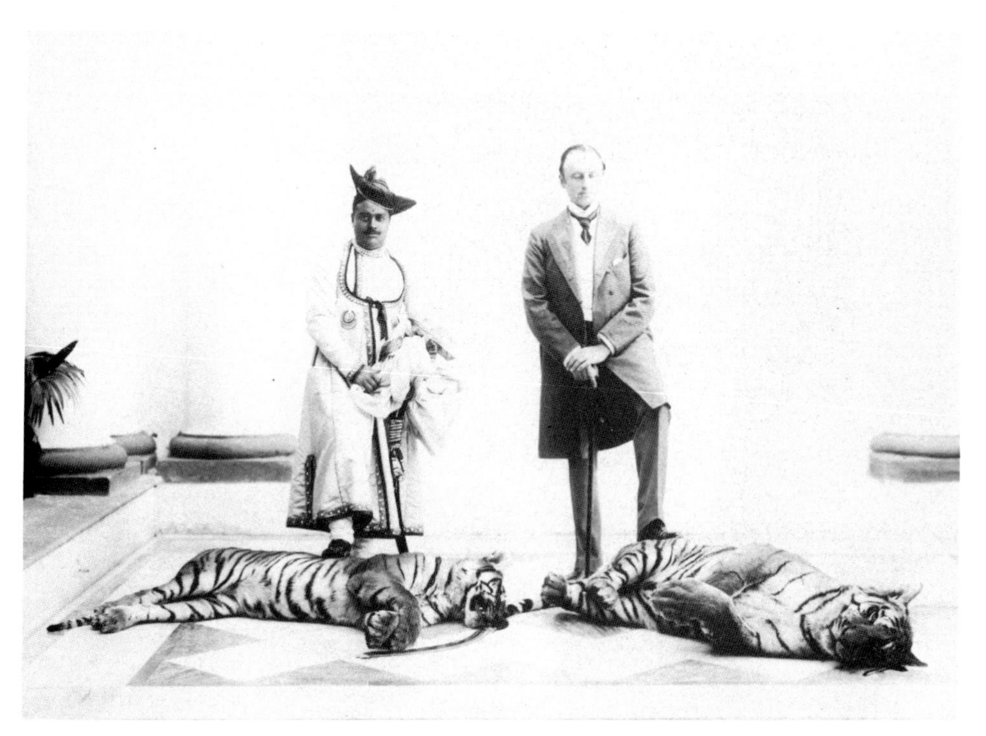

14. George Nathaniel Curzon, Viceroy of India, and Maharaja Scindia with tiger shot by each, 1899. Curzon gave Elinor a tiger skin shortly after their first meeting.

15. Staff group at Simla, 1901. Lord Curzon is seated, centre, with his wife, Mary, and daughters, Irene and Cynthia.

16. Curzon (*right*) and Lord Lamington (Governor of Bombay), 1904.

about Innes Ker, the young man was still sufficiently a part of the family to accompany them to France. Elinor was in her element, and she wanted to share with Innes Ker the pleasure she had experienced when she first saw Versailles. Perhaps she saw this as a first step in his necessary education. In her view the long façade which overlooks the tapis vert, the smooth expanse of grass, and the fountains was the best and the most dramatic. She tried to set the scene to make the maximum impact on the young man. She walked with him up the steep approach to the front of the chateau and then ordered him to close his eyes while she led him to the right and along the front terrace to the very centre. There she told him to open his eyes and she stood back to watch the effect on him of the full magnificence of Louis XIV's creation.

Was he really as unimpressed as he pretended to be, saying in a startled voice 'What a lot of lightning conductors', or was he just affectionately teasing Elinor for her enthusiasm? Whatever the reason behind his response, that response was noted and quite soon put to fictional use.

As soon as Elinor was back home at her Petit Trianon she took to her bed. She was not ill; she was seized by inspiration and a burning, urgent need to put together on paper all the frustrated emotions of the last few years which had suddenly been set free by the love of Alistair Innes Ker.

While she wrote she ate little and slept little, keeping herself alert with repeated cups of black coffee. At the end of six weeks she was exhausted but triumphant. Her novel *Three Weeks* was finished. The writing of this book which was to change her whole life always remained a vivid memory. When she wrote about it in *Romantic Adventure* the passions of the time swept over her once again.

> The book meant everything to me; it was the outpouring of my whole nature, romantic, proud and passionate, but for ever repressed in real life by the barriers of custom and tradition, and held fast behind the iron mask of self respect and self-control which had, perhaps fortunately, been locked round my throat by Grandmamma in Canada long years before. The writing of *Three Weeks* was the echo of the day when I saw Sarah Bernhardt in 'Theodora'; of the lonely nights in Venice and Lucerne; of the Egyptian desert and the eternal message of the sphinx; and of all the dreams of love and romance which had occupied my mind throughout my youth.

Clayton Glyn had watched the affair between his wife and Alistair Innes Ker with some amusement. He liked the young man and he knew that Elinor's rigid moral code prevented her from involving herself sexually. He saw Innes Ker as a kind of English *cavalière servente*. He had, however, been a little alarmed by the transparency of the story Elinor had told at Lord Kintore's. And then, when, after the Paris visit, Elinor had become totally immersed in her writing, he took fright. He must have had some notion of the power of her work. He was afraid that this new book glorifying the young man would make him look foolish. And so he did what he had never done before and told Elinor that she had gone too far, that she was a bad influence on the young man, that she was spoiling his marriage prospects whilst offering him nothing in return. No good could come of the relationship, he insisted, and so Elinor must ask Innes Ker to go and she must not try to be in his company alone again.

Dismayed but obedient, Elinor sent the young man on his way. Like so many other love-lorn young officers he began to make arrangements to go to India. Elinor was in great distress at his departure. Clayton was kind. He thought the worst was over and that he had averted a scandal. Little did he know that, on the contrary, it was about to sweep over them with full force.

16 SCANDAL

A combination of relief and exhilaration overcame Elinor when she finished her novel *Three Weeks*. She felt it was the best and most truthful book she had so far written. Yet when she read it through from start to finish she had some misgivings, which Clayton's attitude towards Innes Ker had done nothing to relieve. Had she been too honest in her depiction of the young Englishman Paul, initiated into a grand passion by an older woman to whom he was not married, whom indeed he scarcely knew and whose name remained a mystery to him until after she had left him? Was the Edwardian reading public ready to shed its hypocritical attitudes towards a woman's sexuality and acknowledge that it was not only men who experienced physical passion?

She took her manuscript to that worldly friend who had been involved in so many love affairs herself and who would be unlikely to be shocked by what Elinor had written. She asked Daisy Warwick for her opinion of this new novel.

Lady Warwick read *Three Weeks*. She confessed that she had enjoyed it, that she had found its poetic and erotic sensuousness powerful. But she strongly advised Elinor not to publish the book. She told her that in her opinion its publication would be the end of Elinor's hard-won position in society. No one would be prepared to accept the honesty of her vision and everyone would accuse her not only of having had a love affair with a younger man, but worse still of having boasted about it.

She pointed to various episodes in the novel which were recognisably autobiographical. Everyone in their circle knew that Elinor herself had a tiger skin; everyone knew how she loved Lucerne and Venice; they had all seen or heard about her 'rose bed' which was the obvious inspiration for the final moments of passion in a bower of roses in Venice. She reasoned that their friends would think that if so much was taken from Elinor's life, perhaps the rest was also. And it would not do to confess so frankly that you had seduced a young man.

Elinor's confidence was undermined: if this was Daisy's response what could she expect from her other less experienced, less honest and less tolerant readers? She confided her problem to Alfred Milner describing to him in general terms the narrative line of the novel. He was understandably guarded in his response, but on the whole felt that it would be unwise to publish the novel at that time. Though he added that he thought that in the future it might be possible to hope for a more kindly reception.

At this point the confused writer learnt from Walters that even after Sheering Hall had been let on the best terms he felt he could hope for, the family would still be in debt.

The only way that Elinor could improve her situation was to publish another book. She could not hope to produce a second one with the same speed with which she had written *Three Weeks*. Anyway, in her heart she felt that her novel should be published despite all the advice she had received to the contrary. She took it to London and showed it to Gerald Duckworth. He immediately saw its commercial possibilities, though even he could not have known or hoped that the sales would be as immediate and spectacular as they proved to be.

In June 1907 *Three Weeks* was published. Gerald Duckworth presented it as, 'A Novel for those who are neither old nor young. A study of a strange woman. An Episode in a young man's life.' Elinor's own life was changed for ever.

Despite the warnings of Lady Warwick and the hints of Alfred Milner, Elinor was not prepared for the outcry which greeted the novel's publication. On the whole she had so far been treated kindly by the reviewers, but in June she was assailed by a barrage of hostile criticism. Only *The Sunday Times* spoke of the 'record of a honeymoon unsanctioned by the church's blessing or the state's approbation' in positive terms, saying 'Mrs Glyn has never written before with anything like such poetic sentiment or such admirable descriptive power.' This reviewer concluded that the story was 'narrated with too much emotional intensity to deserve the reproach of lasciviousness', and that 'Readers who can tolerate in fiction a defiance of the conventions will find *Three Weeks* a very dainty romance.'

The accurate perceptions of this reviewer were singularly untypical.

Elinor was hurt by what she saw as the misunderstanding of her work in the press, but she was hurt even more by the responses of people she knew personally. Society closed its ranks against her. She found that she was invited to fewer and fewer houses as Daisy had correctly predicted. When an old friend, Professor Lindsay, came to spend the weekend at Lamberts he rebuked her for putting such a scandalous book into print. Elinor in her own defence challenged this Scottish Professor of the History of Religion to identify for her the parts of the book he considered immoral. Somewhat shamefacedly the old man confessed he had not read the novel, only the reviews. Elinor insisted upon giving him the book and sending him away to read it. In *Romantic Adventure* Elinor records his tearful response: ' "Lassie," he said, "I'm ashamed of my thoughts on it yesterday. Posterity will justify you." '

'I cried too, with sheer joy that this stern old man had understood.'

Alfred Milner, to whom Elinor had sent the book with a defiant letter justifying her decision to publish it, wrote back more positively than she had expected, saying that the book had many strong points and that he would not join those who were attacking her as immoral.

Encouraged by these two men and by supportive letters from Mary, Duchess of Abercorn, whom Elinor had met in Egypt, and from Minnie Paget, Elinor tackled the headmaster of Eton, Dr Edward Lyttelton, when he banned the book in his school. He too had to confess that he knew the book only at second hand. Elinor sent him a copy. He read it and retracted his accusation of immorality but maintained that, nevertheless, the book was not suitable reading for his boys.

Inevitably, the more the book was banned and condemned, the faster it sold. When that insatiable womaniser, Edward VII, that 'arch vulgarian' or 'Edward the Caresser' as Henry James called him, refused to have the book even mentioned in his presence, he boosted sales immeasurably. At Harrow Cecil Beaton read a copy which had been smuggled into the school. Nancy Cunard was typical of many young girls who managed to get hold of copies to read illicitly in bed. Nancy's governess found the banned book under her pupil's mattress and reported the matter to Lady Emerald. This woman, so notorious for her own love affairs, was appalled, and punished her daughter severely.

Another young society lady, Clare Frewen, read the book just before she got married. On her first night she set the scene just as in *Three Weeks* but using a bear skin instead of a tiger skin. When her new husband Wilfred found her posed seductively on the rug he simply said 'Come on, jump into bed. You're not supposed to be a mistress. You're supposed to be a wife.'

There were those who mocked the book but they did so in a way calculated to draw attention to its so-called immorality. No one knows exactly who started circulating the rhyme which was to be for ever associated with Elinor from this time on:

Would you like to sin
With Elinor Glyn
On a tiger skin?
Or would you prefer
To err with her
On some other fur?

So what exactly had Elinor written to cause such a furore? Was the uproar simply an example of the 'stupendous hypocrisy of the Edwardian age', as Elinor later claimed?

The narrative line is quite simple. A young Englishman, Paul, falls in love with a local girl, Isabella Waring. This large, jolly, country girl is not considered to be a suitable mate by his parents who send him off to Europe to cool down. But in Switzerland he meets a beautiful and mysterious lady who fascinates him and with whom he soon falls in love. The Lady sees his potential as a lover. At first she hesitates: ' "You are so young, so young – and I shall hurt you – probably. Won't you go now – while there is yet time? Away from Lucerne, back to Paris, even back to England?" '

Paul is too smitten already to be able to leave and so the Lady initiates him into the arts of love and sensuous experience. It is she who is the leader, the teacher, the setter of scenes. In Lucerne her room has a couch covered with a tiger skin and a profusion of pillows and drapes in purple velvet and silk. 'The whole picture was barbaric. It might have been some painter's dream of the Favourite in a harem. It was not what one would expect to find in a sedate Swiss hotel.'

Then the Lady orders her young lover to meet her in Bürgenstock. Here they are to experience passion in a different setting. In her sitting room is the tiger skin which Paul had chosen with such care and presented to her as a gift: 'A magnificent creature the beast must have been. The deepest, most perfectly marked, largest one that he had ever seen.'

(Paul clearly feels about his tiger skin what Elinor felt about hers.) But the tiger skin is the only thing this room has in common with the hotel room in Lucerne. For here there are 'some simple cushions of silk; sweet peas and spring flowers decorated the vases – there were no tuberoses, or anything hot-housed or forced.'

In this pastoral setting Alfred Milner must have recognised with some misgivings and uncertainty, some of the experiences he had shared with Elinor. The mention of the crescent moon would have brought to his mind the keepsake Elinor had given him after their time together walking in the pine woods of Carlsbad.

The third setting which is to be their 'souls' wedding' is Venice and a palazzo on the Grand Canal.

> All the simplicity of the Bürgenstock surroundings was gone. The flowers were in the greatest profusion, rare and heavy scented; the pillows of the couch were more splendid than ever; cloths of gold and silver and wonderful shades of orange and green velvet were among the purple ones he already knew.

In these three meetings of the lovers, 'With brilliance and relish, Mrs Glyn plays every variation in this sensual symphony for full orchestra', as Cecil Beaton explains in his preface to the 1974 re-issue of the novel.

Despite this the act of love is not described, only the preliminary stirring of passion and its aftermath. An image suffices for the rest. 'And outside the black storm made the darkness fall early. And inside the half burnt logs tumbled together causing a cloud of golden sparks, and then the flames leapt up again and crackled in the grate.'

So perhaps Elinor's contemporaries would have forgiven her the exotic sensuality of her novel which is, after all, not so very far removed from the scene setting in Keats's *Eve of St Agnes* and Flaubert's *Salâmbo* had they not been within the context of the Lady's comments on love and marriage.

The Lady makes no pretence that her relationship with Paul can ever lead to marriage. From the outset she sets a time limit on their love and insists upon secrecy. Indeed she positively scorns the way society seeks to regularise and make permanent a love such as theirs. Her words, honest assessment of reality though they are, were totally unacceptable to a social class steeped in hypocrisy.

> 'Here we are you and I – mated and wedded and perfectly happy – and yet by these foolish laws we are sinning, and you would be more nobly employed yawning with some bony English miss for your wife – and I by the side of a mad drunken husband. All because the law made us swear a vow to keep for ever stationary an emotion! Emotion which we can no more control than the trees can which way the wind will bow their branches!'

Elinor's first shocked readers were not appeased by the fact that the love of Paul and the Lady is always a doomed tragic love, as the mention of many other doomed lovers underlines. Cupid and Psyche, Marguerite and Faust, Lancelot and Elaine, Desdemona and Othello, Pericles and Aspasia, Anthony and Cleopatra, Justinian and Theodora, Belisarius and Antonina are all mentioned as parallels. From their example the Lady concludes that 'In all ages it is undoubtedly not the simple good women who have ruled the hearts of men.' And she adds that of these passionate women 'Not one of these was a man's ideal of what a wife and mother ought to be'. The Lady proposes another morality to replace the conventional one. 'But to live a life with one's love, if it engenders the most lofty aspirations, to me is highly moral and good.'

As Elinor repeatedly pointed out, the conclusion of her novel is highly moral. The hero and heroine are allowed only their three weeks together. Later the Lady gives birth to a son who in time becomes King and who is the hope of better things for his nation. But this does not happen until after the Lady herself has been brutally murdered by assassins hired by her husband. The clear implication is that her relationship with Paul had a larger purpose than simply the indulgence of her senses.

As for Paul, he suffers when he is left alone and he suffers more to know that he has fathered a son whom he can never claim. But he too takes from the relationship something which is turned to the good of the larger community. His love has given him 'an awakened soul' and once he has recovered from his extreme distress at the loss of his Lady, he turns away from the idle pursuits of his youth and determines to pursue a serious political career.

Few contemporary readers in England seem to have read and

understood this ending of the novel so preoccupied were they with the passion at its centre. Few critics commented on the careful structuring of the novel and its relationship to fairy tale and legend in its emphasis on rituals and patterning. Cecil Beaton is quite right in describing it as 'the work of an extraordinary fantaiste'.

Even the most discerning and sympathetic critics seem to have been blind to the important element of comedy in the novel. Paul's stature as a serious adult male at the end of the novel is the more impressive because of the comic figure he cuts at the beginning. He is not a heroic figure at this point but a young man who is 'sound asleep'. He declares his undying love for Isabella Waring before he departs on his travels but any sense of tragedy that this scene of parting lovers might contain is undercut by their meeting in the 'pouring rain under a dripping oak' and by Isabella's parting words: ' "Goodbye old chap," she said, "We have been real pals, and I'll not forget you!" ' and by the accompanying chorus, ' "Cuckoo!" screamed the bird in the tree.'

On his travels Paul is as gauche and ignorant as can be. 'He did not like Paris, he found Versailles, Fontainbleau and Compiègne "beastly rot".' He is incapable of writing a proper letter to his love. He has no appreciation of fine food or wine. At one meal he is 'progging at some olives with his fork, one occasionally reaching his mouth'. At another where he has tried to outdo the Lady and has grossly over-ordered, he finds himself, 'trying to get through two mutton chops à l'anglaise' and thinking 'what a frightful lot there was to eat'.

When Paul falls under the Lady's spell and buys the tiger skin for her, the romantic gesture is offset by his clumsy attempts to gift wrap his offering: 'It is not a very easy thing to fold up a huge tiger-skin into a brown paper parcel tied with string.'

Despite the sneers and reproaches the book went on selling well. It was quickly translated into other languages but still the furore in England did not die down. Yet Elinor faced the criticism, the hostility, the innuendoes and ostracism with courage. But she remained puzzled about accusations of immorality. She was aware herself that had she been truly immoral and had she engaged in wild passionate love affairs she would have had no real need, and no pent up frustration to draw on, to write the book. She wrote in *Romantic Adventure*:

> How odd it is that real immorality might have preserved my public character, without even losing my private one, for I am sure that Clayton would not have given me away. He was far too generous a character ever to play the part of a dog in the manger, and I think my faithfulness was almost an embarrassment to him.

It was almost certainly to get away from all the publicity and unpleasantness that Elinor decided to spend some of the proceeds of *Three Weeks* on more travel. She decided to take her family to Japan as part of a round-the-world tour. But first of all she had to collect Margot from her school in Paris. There for a while she felt sad remembering how the young Innes Ker had been with her when she had taken Margot to school in France. Things had changed so much in her life since then that she felt almost a different person.

She was further distressed to learn that even her daughter had been touched by the *Three Weeks* scandal. Margot had been found reading her mother's novel. The book was confiscated by scandalised teachers and Margot was punished for daring to read it.

Elinor found consolation in buying new dresses and hats and shoes to take on her trip. She met some of her old friends including the Grand Duchess Kiril of Russia. She was greatly cheered to be told how much the Duchess had enjoyed *Three Weeks*. She listened sympathetically as Elinor told her about the difficulties she was having over the book in England and how no one seemed to understand her essentially moral message. Elinor explained that she found that many of her readers never troubled to read the end of the book. The Grand Duchess thought that she could see a way to get round this problem. If Elinor were to dramatise her novel then her audience would be more or less compelled to see her work as a whole. It was an idea that interested Elinor and she might have begun work immediately had she not at that moment been struck by another and more potent suggestion.

17 ♥ ELINOR VISITS AMERICA

On this visit to Paris Elinor was staying with her friend from New York, Mrs Moore. Her hostess had been surprised at how upset Elinor was at the reception of *Three Weeks* in London. She knew that Elinor's novel had also created a sensation in America but it was her view that as many readers were favourably impressed by the book as had been scandalised. She was well aware that Elinor was worried about money. Why, she asked, was Elinor proposing to make a world tour which would only cost her money when by investing in a trip to America and by confronting the furore she could actually make money? A personal appearance in New York and perhaps elsewhere would boost sales of the novel immeasurably, she reasoned.

Elinor was struck by this new way of looking at her problems. She had good reason to trust the judgement of her American friend. She had, after all, despite her comparatively humble background created a position for herself as an international hostess through sheer ingenuity.

Like Mrs Paran Stevens, she had realised that the way to be accepted into American society was through friendship with the Prince of Wales. But Kate Moore knew no one who knew the Prince of Wales. So she set out to make his acquaintance in an unorthodox way while he was holidaying in Biarritz incognito. She made it her business to find out the Prince's regular routine, and then she simply had her chauffeur follow the royal car whenever the Prince went out for a drive. She gambled on the fact that all cars of the time were sufficiently unreliable that at some point the Prince's car was sure to break down. Her hopes were realised and the day came when she was able to pull her car alongside his disabled one and offer him a ride home. A friendship developed, and once Kate Moore was seen to be on good terms with the Prince, her position was secured.

Elinor listened carefully to her friend; she turned over in her mind the idea of a trip to New York, and when she left Paris with Margot it was with letters of introduction from Kate Moore to her influential friends in America.

Back in London she discussed the possibility of an American tour with Minnie Paget. As an American herself Minnie Paget saw the sound business sense of Kate Moore's idea. She encouraged Elinor to go to New York and she too offered letters of introduction. Elinor finally made up her mind when support came unexpectedly from her old friend from her early days in Paris, Sir Condie Stephen who was then in London and a groom-in-waiting to the King. His travels as a diplomat had given him many useful contacts and he too could provide the right introductions for Elinor in New York.

One problem remained. What was to happen about the trip she had planned to make along with Clayton and the girls? What had begun as an expedient way of escaping controversy had turned into something the whole family was looking forward to. Elinor felt she could hardly ask them to relinquish this treat while she set off for her own adventure in America. She did on this occasion what she was to do more and more frequently. She asked her mother and the children's governess, Dixie, to go in her place. Plans were made for her to meet up with the family party at a later point, although this in fact did not happen.

And so in October 1907 just days before her forty-third birthday Elinor set sail for New York on the *Lusitania*. Even more than on her visits to Carlsbad she felt the excitement of setting out alone. This time she was definitely travelling as Elinor Glyn, the authoress, rather than Mrs Clayton Glyn. She was reminded of the time before she was a married woman: 'I felt independent and gay, as in the long ago days when I had visited my French relatives'.

Also travelling on the *Lusitania* were Lady Ponsonby, a close friend of Sir Condie Stephen, and the Duchess of Manchester and her mother Mrs Yznaga.

Consuelo Yznaga, after whom the young Duchess of Marlborough, formerly Consuelo Vanderbilt, had been named, had been one of the first 'Dollar Princesses' to marry into the English aristocracy when she had left Saratoga Springs as the wife of Viscount Mandeville, the son of the Duke of Manchester. Her marriage to this dissolute young man had proved no happier than that of her namesake to the Duke of Marlborough. But she had used her position as one of the

Prince of Wales's set to push forward other young Americans looking for husbands in England. She was a close friend of Minnie Paget and had been responsible for her initial introduction into English society.

This lady who had been uninhibited enough to demonstrate the cancan to Edward when he was still the Prince of Wales was not the kind of person to be shocked by *Three Weeks*. On the contrary she was kindly disposed towards its author. And as she and her mother were well-versed in the ways of New York they spent the voyage preparing Elinor for what she would encounter when she arrived. They even helped Elinor to choose from her extensive Lucile wardrobe suitable clothes for her first appearance in the American city. For they warned her that she was likely to be mobbed by the press and immediately made into a very public figure. Elinor listened to their advice even though she felt sure that they were exaggerating what she could expect.

The one regret the travellers had was the fact that they were missing Minnie Paget's Versailles Ball which she was holding in the Albert Hall. As they discussed the guests and their costumes, Elinor heard for the first time about the beautiful and wealthy Grace Duggan, the young wife of the Argentinian Alfred Duggan who had recently settled in London and who had already been accepted into even the most exclusive circles. Elinor, who was still smarting from her own exclusion from these same circles, felt some jealousy towards the young woman she had not yet met.

The press were indeed out in force to greet Elinor when the ship docked in New York. Mrs Yznaga had done well to advise her what to expect. Dressed in a romantic and striking purple outfit designed by Lucy, Elinor looked the part the press wanted her to play. She revelled in the attention and the limelight and the demands of New York society to meet her.

Instead of going straight to the Plaza Hotel as had been her original intention, Elinor was whisked off along with Consuelo and her mother to stay with Mrs Frederick Vanderbilt in her palatial house at Hyde Park on the Hudson river. Mrs Vanderbilt was a character straight out of Edith Wharton's *The Age Of Innocence*, with her determination to cling to the ways of Old New York and her rigorous scrutiny of her guest list.

Elinor had met Mrs Vanderbilt in England. She hardly recognised her as the same woman, for Mrs Vanderbilt behaved with a degree of formality in her New York home which contrasted startlingly with her casual behaviour in English country houses.

Elinor was, however, suitably impressed by the luxury of the bedrooms in Mrs Vanderbilt's house with their *en suite* plumbing and by the ostentatious display of wealth in the furnishings of the rest of the house. But finally she found this American stately home far less attractive than a house such as Easton Lodge. It was not only the conspicuous lack of books and writing materials in the bedrooms she objected to; she also missed the sense of being in a house which had grown over the years, where furniture had been accumulated gradually and where the portraits were of the family. What struck her unfavourably about this house in Hyde Park was the unsuitability to their surroundings of all the newly acquired antiques. She confided her views to the Duchess of Manchester who was surprisingly in agreement with her. Over the years she too had become accustomed to English style and now found that of her compatriots shockingly vulgar.

There were other wealthy and influential New Yorkers whom Elinor met. Some, she discovered, were out of sympathy with Mrs Vanderbilt in her enforcement of old ways. One of these was Mamie Stuyvesant Fish. Elinor described her as 'a shrewd, very intelligent woman who knew the exact purpose and value of everything which she did or countenanced', a woman with a 'merciless wit'. At dinner she was heard to comment 'They say in Europe that all American women are virtuous. Well, do you wonder? Look at the men!'

So bored was Mrs Fish with the traditional lengthy, many-coursed and predictable meals of her group that she had arbitrarily declared that in her house no dinner party could sit at table for longer than fifty minutes. While she approved of this innovation, Elinor was shocked to learn that to relieve her boredom Mrs Fish had indulged in such antics as dressing up a monkey to act as her butler and inviting to an elaborate tea party not her friends but her friends' cats and dogs.

More to Elinor's taste than the hot-house atmosphere of New York society were the days she spent outside the city staying with friends in countryside which reminded her of her childhood days in Canada: 'Old memories of Summerhill came back to me when I saw the glorious colours of the maples.'

Then it was back to the city and the Plaza Hotel and a round of social engagements in her capacity as famous authoress. Elinor found New York exciting. It was as different from London in its own way as Paris had been from Jersey. She recorded her responses in *Romantic Adventure*. 'I was properly impressed with the tall buildings, only a comparatively small number in those days, and none so immensely high as now, but still imposing.'

But what struck her most forcefully was the sense of vitality, the feeling that everyone on the street had a purposeful and determined air. She was interested in everything from the food which she found good to the cocktails which she described in *Elizabeth Visits America* as being 'like ipecacuanha wine mixed with brandy and something bitter and a touch of orange, but you have not swallowed it five minutes when you feel you have not a care in the world and nothing matters'.

She was amazed to find it was generally accepted practice to dine in public rooms, not in small private rooms as in England.

The appearance of the women, even of those who were not wealthy, impressed her as showing far more care and attention to grooming and smartness than she was accustomed to seeing in England. She wrote of them admiringly: 'The American woman is unquestionably the most beautiful, the best dressed, best turned out and consequently the most attractive of all women.' She was quick to observe that women did not only dress up for the company of men but would take just as much care for a luncheon party attended exclusively by women. This, she realised, was one aspect of an entirely different relationship between the sexes. In America she found none of that 'traditional contempt for woman, as the weaker vessel, which the average Englishman had inherited as second nature'. On the contrary, it seemed to her that women dominated their husbands, seeing them primarily as sources of income. But she was not altogether pleased by this reversal of roles in American society. She felt that the relationship between men and women had been irretrievably damaged by American insistence on the importance of accumulating wealth.

> The appalling struggle for existence – success being measured entirely in terms of wealth – which characterises the life of men of all ages in the States is difficult to realise in Europe. It tends to bring to the top those types which are the most pliable, the least hampered by

> traditional standards of manners, morals and ideas. The classical education which produces the philosophical, contemplative type of mind, and the high level of personal integrity typified by the English Civil Service, is unknown in America, except in circles entirely devoted to literary and cultured aims to which I have already referred, and would be considered a distinct handicap there among everyday people. The idea is that attention must be devoted exclusively to the business of getting on, since only thus can a man fulfil what is believed to be his inevitable destiny, namely the advancement of his material well-being and that of his family.

Such values, she concluded, tended to make gold diggers of women and to drive young men to the point that 'the escape into temporary oblivion offered by drink becomes a positive necessity'.

That Elinor, an outsider, had judged American society of that time with some accuracy is confirmed by the portrait Edith Wharton paints of the same society in her novel *The Custom of the Country*. The American writer shows in fictional form exactly the same motivating forces described in the above passage by Elinor.

If Elinor had any lingering doubts about her status as a professional writer they disappeared when she was honoured by a visit from the great American author Mark Twain. He called upon her at the Plaza Hotel and was complimentary about *Three Weeks*. He encouraged her to visit him at his house in Washington Square. His attention flattered and excited Elinor. She regarded their meeting as being of sufficient importance for her to record it, and it was her intention to publish her account. She did, however, take the precaution of showing her piece to Mark Twain first. She was dismayed by his lack of enthusiasm and his suggestion that she had perhaps overstated his enthusiasm for *Three Weeks*. Somewhat deflated she agreed not to publish her account after all. There was then a slight coolness between the two authors, one so experienced and the other just at the beginning of her writing career, which was only dissipated when later during her stay Mark Twain made a speech commending Elinor's work at a dinner given in her honour.

Back in England Lucy was fascinated by her sister's picture of her brilliant life in New York. As always she reported what everyone was wearing and what was fashionable in the American city. Lucy determined to join Elinor. She wanted to sound out the possibility of opening another branch of Lucile in the States.

Elinor was not overjoyed to have Lucy's company in the Plaza Hotel. Although Lucy writes at length about this visit in her memoirs, Elinor fails even to mention that Lucy was with her during this period. She was, perhaps, a little jealous of Lucy's status as Lady Duff Gordon, the mother of the recently married Esmé, wife of Viscount Tiverton. The fact that Lucy was a successful business woman was not held against her in New York as it was in both England and France. And, although rank was not supposed to count in republican America, a title always went down well. Elinor was also afraid, with some justification, of what Lucy might do or say, knowing as she did that Lucy was fully in favour of the American notion of self-advertisement.

The two of them went about together a good deal with Elinor taking a pride in being already sufficiently accepted in the best circles in New York to be able to introduce Lucy into them. The sisters were even invited to meet President Theodore Roosevelt. Though it does seem that the meeting made a greater impression on them than it did on the President who failed to distinguish between Lucy and another Lady Duff Gordon, one of her husband's ancestors.

Elinor was not, however, altogether sorry when Lucy decided to return to England after Christmas. There was talk of Elinor making a tour right across the States to meet more of her fans. The idea attracted her and she suggested to Clayton that he should make his way back to England via the Pacific so that they could all meet up on the west coast of America.

But not all her time in New York was spent socialising and promoting her work. Elinor kept in mind the suggestion that the Grand Duchess had made to her in Paris. The reception of *Three Weeks* in the States had renewed her confidence and she decided to try her hand at dramatising it. She confided her plan to Sir Condie Stephen. He approved of her idea of clearing her name of the smirch of immorality and he promised to give what practical help he could. He offered to speak to the Lord Chamberlain, who would have to approve her play, and to try to get the King to give the work his blessing.

Throughout this time Elinor was in regular contact with journalists who were eager to report all that she did, said and wore. One of the men employed by the Hearst Press took Elinor to the newspaper offices where he worked to see how newspapers were produced. She did not at this time meet the owner himself, William Randolph Hearst, though she heard a great deal about him. She learnt that he was only slightly older than herself, that he came from a rich family which he had made richer through his newspaper enterprises. She was told how he had defied his mother by marrying at thirty-four a sixteen-year-old chorus girl, Millicent Wilson; how his mother had finally become reconciled to her daughter-in-law at the very moment when Hearst had lost interest in her and taken up with other young chorus girls.

It was clear to Elinor from all she heard about Hearst that he was a very powerful man who was held in some awe, even fear, by his numerous employees. His life-style went against all that she believed in but, nevertheless, she thought that he would be an interesting man to meet.

Then came an urgent summons from Walters in England. He needed Elinor's signature on papers to postpone her marriage settlement once more, and her consent to measures he proposed to prop up Clayton's worsening financial position. Elinor decided to respond to him by making a quick trip to Europe. She was more than a little influenced in this decision by the rumour that the composer Puccini was interested in writing an opera based on her dramatisation of *Three Weeks*. She hoped that she might have an opportunity to meet the composer himself if she sought him out in Europe. In the event negotiations with Puccini came to nothing; he had found a work he liked better and was already engaged in writing *La Fanciulla del West* which would be produced in 1910.

Elinor made the most of being in Paris by replenishing her wardrobe ready for her own foray into the Wild West. At the last moment she had second thoughts about returning to the States when she heard that her mother had been taken ill in Tokyo and that Clayton had decided to journey home not via the Pacific but on the trans-Siberian railway. But her mother urged her not to miss this opportunity and Elinor was easily persuaded to set off once more.

She did not linger in New York this time but boarded the train travelling west. One of her travelling companions was Charles Ponsonby who had been sent to the States by his father to prospect for oil to rebuild the family fortunes after losses made in the brewing industry. He was one of the few Englishmen who had not already read *Three Weeks* but by the time the train reached Nevada he knew it well: Elinor read it aloud to him as they crossed the continent! His enjoyment of the book was a great boost to Elinor's confidence as she faced the prospect of presenting herself to new audiences.

On this second visit Elinor discovered an America very different from New York. The romance she had so much missed in that city she found in abundance in the mining communities in the wilds of Nevada. In that unpromising countryside where there was 'not a single blade of grass' and 'nothing to see but earthy sand and gloomy, greyish sage-brush', where the rough board hotel had bedrooms made of 'cheap ill-fitting plank partitions papered with old newspapers', and where the doors were simply boards nailed together and fitted with a lift latch, she found men whose values she could respect and admire. 'They were full of the chivalry, of the abstract respect for honest womanhood, and of the rough sense of justice towards men, which were the heritage of an earlier time, and which had survived together with the pioneering conditions which had aroused it.'

To her astonishment these men had read *Three Weeks* and appreciated it. She was touched and reminded of how her own family had read books in their log cabin when they had first lived in Canada.

She was an incongruous figure in that community of miners, dressed as she was in as much high fashion as conditions would allow. The men were grateful to her for visiting them and breaking the monotony of their lives and they showed their gratitude in practical terms. They wanted to give her the kind of banquet they thought she deserved. But the resources of a mining town did not run to champagne and flowers. Even drinking water had to be carried in from some distance. Undeterred they arranged for some champagne to be driven in specially and one miner rode ninety miles to find some yellow daisies to decorate the table at her farewell meal.

Elinor was moved to tears by their kindness and gallantry. So when an invitation to visit arrived from one Scottie, a man described by the Governor as a wild bandit and outlaw, she was tempted to accept. She so much wanted to meet a man with this reputation who yet had read *Three Weeks* in his hide-out. The Governor had difficulty in persuading her not to do something as rash as putting herself into the outlaw's hands. He feared that Scottie might abduct her for the sake of a ransom. Elinor could hardly refuse to accept his judgement after accepting his hospitality but she ever after wondered if she had been right to be talked out of such an adventure.

When the time came for her to leave Rawhide the Governor made a formal ceremony of farewell and presented his guest with a silver gun mounted in mother-of-pearl and the badge of a Deputy Constable saying 'We give you this here gun, Elinor Glyn, because we like your darned pluck.' Elinor was more moved by this gesture than by all the attention she had received in New York and she cherished these gifts all her life.

After the unexpected gallantry of these men living such a rough life Elinor was disappointed by her reception in the comparatively sophisticated city of San Francisco. In this place she met with more opposition to her novel than anywhere else in the States. The hostility to the book extended to her personally, as she quickly discovered as she ate a meal alone in a large hotel while waiting for her hosts from Santa Barbara. At another table a group of obviously wealthy women were discussing invitations to a ball to be held a few days later. Elinor was interested to hear them discussing whether a certain person was fit to be invited. When she heard the names of her former hostesses, Mrs Frederick Vanderbilt and Mrs Stuyvesant Fish mentioned, she realised that the discussion was about herself.

Her indignation at their attitude was compounded when she was shown the sights of San Francisco, in particular the damage caused by the recent earthquake. She could not understand how a community which regarded her as immoral could accept without apparent surprise or dismay that many lives had been lost as the result of the collapse of buildings that had been improperly constructed when speculators had failed to use the materials they had been paid for. In her view that was real immorality.

She was introduced to Admiral Long, an acquaintance of Sir Condie Stephen, and expressed her dissatisfaction to him about San Franciscans wrong-headed priorities. The next day she received an invitation to the ball sent by the Admiral. Elinor attended, introduced herself to the ladies who had been maligning her, and to their discomfort thanked them with great sweetness for their kindness in inviting her to their function.

It was not only the post-quake atmosphere and the hypocritical morality which made Elinor turn against San Francisco. She would almost certainly have seen the city in a jaundiced light without these factors for it was there that she received a distressing piece of news. Quite unexpectedly her old friend Condie Stephen had died. Just months before she had dined with him in London and he had been well and his usual lively self. Now she learnt that he had been rushed to hospital with appendicitis and had died shortly after the operation which should have saved his life. He was not the last of Elinor's friends to die in this manner. Elinor mourned the loss of this friend who had always been so kind to her and she wondered if without his help she would, after all, be able to stage *Three Weeks* in London.

Despite her grief Elinor had to continue on her journey. Commitments had been made on her behalf and it would have been out of character and against her grandmother's training for her to have excused herself on personal grounds. She was too preoccupied to pay much attention to Los Angeles. It seemed to her a city like any other with nothing special to recommend it.

She found Salt Lake City in Utah more interesting. She had never been in a Mormon community before nor encountered people who actually practised and advocated polygamy. It was not a practice she admired. She could never imagine herself knowingly and willingly sharing a man with another woman. It was a way of life which went against romance.

In St Louis she met up with James Hackett, a theatrical impresario. He had heard about Elinor's dramatised version of her famous novel and he was keen to see it. To Elinor's delight he liked the script and she was in her turn quite happy to sell him the right to produce it in St Louis.

Back in New York Elinor met Lucy's great friend Elsie de Wolfe who had spent some time in England and had been presented at court by Minnie Paget. But she had not found herself an English husband, largely because her sexual preference was for women. On her return home she had toured the States as an actress. Like Lillie Langtry before her she had made more of an impression with her good looks and her stylish dress sense than with her dramatic talents. Her career had changed direction, however, once she had become involved with the wealthy theatrical agent Elizabeth Marbury. It was as an interior decorator that she had discovered her real talent and with the help of introductions from Bessie Marbury she had built up a successful business.

Elinor, who had her own interest in this activity, was charmed by Elsie de Wolfe's house in Washington Square. She told Elsie about her business arrangement with James Hackett. Elsie suggested that if Elinor really wanted to make money out of the dramatisation she needed an agent and suggested her friend Bessie Marbury. And so it was that in New York Elinor signed the first of many disastrous contracts when she gave to Bessie Marbury all the performing rights to *Three Weeks* that she had not already assigned to James Hackett. Elinor was so lacking in business sense that she did not fully realise exactly what she had signed away in return for only a hundred pounds. Had she fully appreciated both this and the extent of the financial mess which awaited her in England she might, perhaps, have been more circumspect or more demanding.

A chance meeting brought another note of unhappiness into Elinor's life. Throughout her travels she had been unable to forget entirely the young Alistair Innes Ker, as everywhere her readers speculated on the identity of Paul. There were even men who claimed that they had been the model for her hero. Now she learned from the Duchess of Roxburghe something of her son Alistair's life since he had said goodbye to Elinor. He too had been drawn into the American mania for marrying into the English aristocracy and the corresponding English desire to marry into American money. Lacking direction and purpose after the end of his relationship with Elinor, Innes Ker had easily been persuaded by his older brother, who would inherit the family title, that he owed it to his family to marry an American heiress. But it was as loveless and unhappy a marriage as so many other Anglo-American alliances. Elinor grieved for the waste of the young man's life and her letter to Clayton telling him the news held more than a hint of reproach.

However, her mind was taken off Innes Ker by another strange encounter and a proposal for a most unusual Anglo-American alliance.

One evening she was invited out to dinner by Miss McAllister to whom she had been introduced earlier by Mrs Frederick Vanderbilt. This young woman was the daughter of Ward McAllister and came from one of the oldest and most exclusive families in New York. Invitations to social occasions held by Ward McAllister were most sought after and most difficult to come by. Elinor was flattered to be singled out for attention by his daughter. Nevertheless, her hostess warned her in advance that the party had been arranged at the request of a well-known millionaire who was very anxious to meet the author of

Three Weeks. Elinor was surprised when she arrived at Delmonico's at the appointed time that the party consisted of only four people. For, although Delmonico's was the restaurant most favoured by people such as the McAllisters, parties held there were generally on a large scale. What surprised her even more was that the millionaire, a short but apparently strong man who looked uncomfortable in evening dress, had very little to say for himself throughout the evening. He spent most of the time looking at Elinor so closely that she began to feel insulted.

The next day Miss McAllister apologised profusely on behalf of the millionaire. She said that he wished to make up for his unsociable behaviour by holding another dinner party and that he would be greatly honoured if Elinor would accept his invitation. Elinor was as always intrigued by a situation outside her normal experience. However, she might have thought twice about accepting had it been anyone other than the eminently respectable Miss McAllister who was the go-between for this strange man.

On this second occasion, far from being silent, Elinor's dining companion put a series of searching questions to her. She felt as though she were being interviewed for a job. She did not know whether she was amused or annoyed by this unorthodox behaviour. Then came a further surprise when her millionaire, with great correctness and gallantry, asked permission to send flowers to her suite and to visit her there. He made a formal arrangement to be at the Plaza the following day at four o'clock.

The next morning Elinor woke to find her rooms filled with dozens of white gardenias. She was delighted. She knew that they had cost a great deal of money and she appreciated the compliment whilst being puzzled by the extravagance of the gesture.

At four o'clock promptly her admirer arrived. Elinor was just putting the finishing touches to her appearance. She had chosen to wear a negligée of pastel pink satin with matching mule slippers ornamented with silk roses. She looked superb and she knew it.

When she made her entrance into her sitting room she was surprised to find her visitor inspecting a cupboard which her maid had inadvertently left open. It was full of her small, dainty shoes. The stocky man was dressed as for a formal occasion in a morning coat and top hat. Elinor, not at all sure what was coming next, graciously invited her guest to be seated on the sofa.

Then it was his turn to provide information about himself. He told Elinor the story of his life; how he had been born into a poor family in Virginia, how he had run away at twelve and how after many struggles and adventures he had made a great deal of money. Once his fortune was established he had married, but the marriage had been unhappy. Since then he had divided his time between consolidating his fortune and catching up on the education he had missed as a young man. He had always been interested in theories of heredity, he told Elinor. And her novel *Three Weeks* had come to him as a revelation. He confessed that he had looked carefully into Elinor's background. Now he had a proposal for her to consider. He wanted to find, as the Lady in the novel had found, a suitable mate, one who would give to his child characteristics to complement those he would pass on. In Elinor, he declared, he believed he had found what he was looking for. Without giving Elinor time to protest that the situation was not the same, that they were neither of them so young any longer, that they were both married already, he launched into a more detailed description of his proposition. He was fully aware of the existence of Clayton and of Margot and Juliet he said. But from the results of his enquiries he suspected that Clayton did not love Elinor and because he was in debt would probably be willing to be paid off. Elinor was shocked and protested, but her friend pointed out that if Clayton truly loved her, he would never have consented to allow her to travel alone for nine months. If Elinor would elope with him he would settle considerable fortunes on her and on her daughters, whom he would incidentally be pleased to include in his household. Most importantly the son, that he was sure would be the fruit of their alliance, would be his heir.

For once in her life Elinor was flabbergasted. Then she collected herself and pointed out that the arrangement made by Paul and the Lady had not been a business arrangement. They had been passionately in love. Only from such love could a son like theirs be born. She declared herself to be truly honoured at being chosen for such an interesting experiment but that she could not, under any circumstances, give herself to any man without loving him.

The millionaire accepted her rejection sadly but with dignity. He told Elinor that they would probably never meet again and he asked if she would be so kind as to give him her slipper as a memento. Despite the unusual nature of this request, and aware of all the

Cinderella implications, Elinor consented. Only as he was leaving her suite did her rejected suitor turn to her and say, with tears in his eyes, 'Love wouldn't be wanting on one side.'

It was this most unexpected and delightfully flattering and romantic episode that ended Elinor's visit to America.

18 PASSION

At Lamberts Elinor was once more reunited with her family. There was much to talk about after the nine months of separation. Mrs Kennedy was in good health again and Elinor found her daughters more interesting and more attractive as they grew up.

She was, however, shocked by the appearance of her husband. She could not fail to be aware of the terrible deterioration in his appearance, his health and his morale since she had last seen him. He had begun to look fat and bloated. Even Elinor could not now pretend that he was in any way a romantic or attractive figure of a man. He was now obviously an alcoholic and he was weighed down by a depression which even his travels had done little to lift.

He had much to be depressed about. Gradually Elinor pieced together the story of how they had come to reach the situation in which Clayton, like their friend Lord Rosslyn, was bankrupt.

Although Walters had for many years been urging on the couple the need for retrenchment and although he had tried to explain that they were heading for disaster, Elinor does not seem to have fully understood. She did not have a good head for business or figures. If Clayton said they could afford more clothes or more travel, she did not question where the money was coming from. For the first time on her return from America she realised just how unreliable her husband was as a financial mentor. She was all the more aware of his deficiencies after being with money-minded American men. Now she had to face up to the terrible debt they were in.

She began to understand how far back Clayton's troubles went. Long before he had met her he had regularly been in debt. His attempts to halt his progress towards financial ruin by letting first Durrington and then Sheering had been of little consequence in the face of his own and Elinor's continued extravagance. He confided to Elinor now that his doctors had long ago warned him that he must give up all the things he loved such as travel in hot climates, rich food, heavy wines, spirits and cigars. For as long as he had the hope of a son he had curbed his excesses. But the birth of Juliet and the news that Elinor would have no more children had broken his resolve. He had decided that he would enjoy life to the full while he could. He reckoned that his money would last the short life span predicted for him and that then Elinor would find herself a rich husband and his daughters would make good marriages. He had seen Lucy's business go from strength to strength and he was sure that she would provide for Mrs Kennedy's old age.

Did Elinor really believe Clayton's story or did she accept it rather than the alternative possibility that she had been duped into marrying an irresponsible wastrel?

Certainly she did not blame him entirely for their problems. She felt that at the outset she had been generously treated by her husband, that Clayton had done what he could to build up her sister's business and that he had been more than willing to give her mother a home. She knew that she had been as spendthrift as Clayton himself with her love of new clothes and her desire to stay in the best hotels when they travelled. Clayton had also ensured that she would not be too critical of him by subtly suggesting that if only she had produced a son things would have been different, and by implying that she would quite consciously look for a rich husband as soon as he was dead.

Many women of her class put into this position would have been unable to cope. But Elinor had to. She had no parents to fall back on and she remembered how her grandparents had pulled themselves out of a financial abyss by sheer hard work and will power. She determined to do the same.

Remarkably she now took upon herself the entire responsibility for the family's income. She did what she could to settle some of their debts by drawing on her royalty payments and the money she had earned in the States. She wrote off her marriage settlement and she agreed to the sale of Sheering Hall. But there were still pressing debts to settle. Lucy, alerted to the desperate situation by Mrs Kennedy, came to the rescue with generous gifts and loans, so that eventually Elinor felt that she had dealt with the worst of their financial problems. But then there was nothing left on which to live and to maintain the household.

Elinor had to earn money and earn it quickly. She had already planned to write a book based on her travels in the States but for that she needed more time than was immediately available. The only thing she could think to do was to resort to her original plan of presenting her dramatised version of *Three Weeks*.

There were several stumbling blocks in the way of even this plan. Elinor knew that she had to tread carefully with the Lord Chamberlain's office. She was aware that if she started out by applying for permission to present her play in the commercial theatre she might well be turned down arbitrarily because of the misconceptions about the nature of her plot which were still circulating. Her friends advised her that her best hope was to present charity performances of the play first. Once she had convinced select audiences of the true nature of her intentions, and that she had not written a pornographic book, then it should be an easy matter to convince the Lord Chamberlain.

Charles Hawtrey agreed to produce the play and take it to the West End if it was successful. Charles Bryant was cast as Paul and C. Aubrey Smith as Paul's father. After some hesitation Elinor decided to play the part of the Lady herself. Lucy agreed to dress the cast.

The date for the performance was set for the afternoon of 23 July 1908 and the cast went into rehearsal. Elinor worked hard at her part modelling herself as far as possible on the performances of Sarah Bernhardt as Theodora and drawing on her previous acting experience with Lord Rosslyn at Dysart. She knew that many of her peers would find fault with her for acting in such a play. A year later Cynthia Asquith was criticised for acting the part of Ursula in a tableau based on Carpaccio's *St Ursula*. The problem in her case was that she appeared on stage in a bed. When Cynthia was then approached to act in *Priscilla Runs Away* her horrified father refused, saying that it would be better for his daughter to marry a penniless Liberal than become an actress!

Elinor took courage from the knowledge that her hero Louis XIV had frequently participated in ballets and tableaux at court. If it had not been beneath his dignity then it would not be beneath hers.

It was, however, a relief to take a break from the seemingly haphazard rehearsals to attend a ball. Elinor's friend Consuelo, Duchess of Manchester was also back in London after her trip to the States. Perhaps with the notion of promoting an intrigue, Consuelo made sure that Elinor was thrown into the company of her admirer

Alfred Milner. It was an evening when Elinor looked particularly beautiful. She and Milner were delighted to meet up again, and they spent much of the evening in animated conversation.

Also at Consuelo's ball that evening was George Nathaniel Curzon. The beautiful woman with red hair, white skin, glowing green eyes and elegant deportment to whom Alfred Milner was paying an unusual amount of attention impressed him immediately. His curiosity about her was further aroused when he learnt that this was the woman who had written *Three Weeks* and was shortly to perform the leading role in the play of the same name at the Adelphi Theatre. Curzon made sure that he received an invitation to the performance.

Despite Elinor's worries and doubts the cast was ready by 23 July and that first performance went well. The audience were pleased with the play, although the majority of them were surprised to find that it was indeed less than scandalous. This, however, did not prevent the press from taking up the old controversy and describing the play in terms which Elinor considered unhelpful, indeed spiteful and likely to prejudice the Lord Chamberlain's office against her.

She was right. But even so, when Charles Hawtrey decided that the play showed sufficient commercial promise for him to stage it in the West End, Elinor applied to the Lord Chamberlain's office for the necessary permission. She was anxious about the outcome, even though everyone she spoke to said that the application was now a mere formality, that she had proved conclusively that her work was not harmful to the general public. But this optimism proved ill founded. Permission for a public performance of *Three Weeks* was refused.

Elinor was beside herself. She had invested money she could not afford in the production. She had spent time on it which she might have spent on her novel; she had risked her reputation for nothing. The Lord Chamberlain's refusal seemed to her to set the seal on that reputation as a scandalous woman which she was so anxious to refute.

It was, therefore, a great boost to her severely damaged ego when shortly after the performance she received two unexpected gifts. First came a tiger skin from Alfred Milner. Elinor was delighted with this uncharacteristically flirtatious response to her performance.

To her amazement she opened the second parcel to find yet another tiger skin. This, she discovered, was from that seemingly cold and inscrutable yet most attractive of men, Lord Curzon of Kedleston, the former Viceroy of India.

Elinor was extremely flattered to be noticed by Curzon. She had followed his career with interest after her meeting with Mary Leiter who had become his wife. She was impressed by Mary's wholehearted dedication of her life to Curzon and she wondered what kind of man had inspired such devotion. Milner had told her some details of Curzon's career and she knew that at that moment he was less active politically than at any time since he had left Oxford. He had been elected an Irish Peer and was entitled to sit in the House of Lords but he rarely spoke. His superabundant energies had instead been channelled into his responsibilities as Chancellor of Oxford University and as President of the Royal Geographical Society.

From Minnie Paget she knew of another side of Curzon's life. For Minnie Paget was as aware as anyone else that George Nathaniel Curzon was a good catch and that his old friends in that élite clique known as the Souls who had never really accepted Mary Curzon as one of their circle were anxious to secure him a wife from among their own number, or at least one of their choosing.

So far Curzon had responded good humouredly to all the female attention being lavished upon him. He was fully aware of his own potential, as an attractive man of fifty, heir to the beautiful Kedleston Hall and estate in Derbyshire, and comparatively wealthy, at least for the time being, as a result of the money Mary had left him and the royalties from his books. He felt, as others did, that he would yet make his mark on politics and eventually become Prime Minister. Added to this was the sympathy he aroused as a widower with three small daughters.

Already, Elinor had heard, he had established himself as a host at Hackwood House near Basingstoke. In 1907 he had leased the estate with its wooded parklands which were well stocked with game birds. Invitations to his weekend house parties were coveted. One of his regular guests was the young Winston Churchill who observed that Curzon was never happier or seen to better advantage than when he dispensed the splendid hospitality of his various palatial homes. For he was 'a charming, gay companion adorning every subject that he touched with his agile wit, ever ready to laugh at himself, ever capable of conveying sympathy and understanding'.[1]

And yet Elinor had also heard stories about Curzon's stern insistence on a woman's place being in the home and of his harsh treatment of female servants who did not live up to the rigid moral code he considered appropriate to their station.

How, Elinor wondered, should she respond to this man?

She decided to send him a note thanking him for his gift of the tiger skin. She also expressed her appreciation of and admiration for all that Curzon had done as Viceroy of India. Was she aware that in so doing she was touching Curzon's tender spot, his pride in what he had achieved in India and his resentment that he had not received adequate recognition for the service he had done his country? Certainly her note intrigued him and he wrote back suggesting that they should meet.

It was not the first time that Curzon had taken an interest in a female writer. He had been a close friend of Pearl Craigie who wrote under the name of John Hobhouse and when she had died, a month after Mary Curzon, he had arranged for a memorial to be erected to her. As a younger man he had written to the Victorian novelist, Ouida (Louise de la Ramée) asking her to autograph one of her novels for him. He had never met her but he had corresponded with her until she died in 1908.

The July 1908 meeting with George Curzon was a momentous occasion in Elinor's life. She had never met anyone quite like him, this man with an oval smooth-skinned face, high forehead, sensuous and rather cynical mouth, aquiline nose, dark hair flecked with grey and piercing brown eyes. He held himself very straight and Elinor remembered having heard that his spine had been damaged in a riding accident when he was a young man and that since then he had been obliged to wear a leather harness and was often in pain. Elinor noticed his haughty self-confidence and the feeling of energy that emanated from him. He was, in fact, the epitome of the type of man she most admired.

On his part Curzon saw a woman in her early forties, a mature and striking beauty with the red hair he favoured and a wonderful white complexion. Not only were her green eyes unusually beautiful, they were bright with intelligence and curiosity. He had come prepared to admire and patronise and perhaps engage in a little mild flirtation. But he quickly discovered that Elinor was a woman to be taken seriously. For their conversation was not the exchange of bland trivialities with an underlying note of flirtation he had anticipated. Elinor, he learnt with pleasure and amazement, really did know about his career in India. He was gratified that she was suitably thrilled when he told her about the tiger hunt in Gwalior in which he had himself shot the animal whose skin he had sent her. She was interested in his journey to Persia and the Caucasus and the book he had written about it. She wanted to know his view of the Liberal government and of Lloyd George. Then they discovered that they shared a love of the classics.

When Curzon's visit ended it was with the mutual understanding that they had so much more to say to each other that they must meet again very soon.

Curzon had been in love before several times. He had wooed Laura Tennant who had then married someone else; he had flirted with Margot Tennant who for many years carried a torch for him. Sybil Grosvenor, the sister of Millicent, Duchess of Sutherland, had been the object of his desire even after she too had married someone else. But none of these women, except perhaps for Margot, had the sheer strength of character he found in Elinor Glyn. Although they had simply talked at this first meeting, he was powerfully attracted to her physically and he felt that she responded.

Elinor too had been in love before but never with a man like Curzon. In the past the romantic innocence of unconsummated affairs had been enough for her. Now, for the first time, she felt passion and a real conflict between the fidelity she believed she owed her husband and a desire to experience love to the full.

For a while Curzon and Elinor had to be content with meetings over lunch. They met so often at a hotel in Jermyn Street that in later days the room where they had dined was named 'The Elinor Glyn Room'.

Curzon became more and more important to Elinor. She loved to hear him talk about his plans for Kedleston when he should finally inherit it; about how he had decorated Hackwood to which she should soon be invited and about his house in Carlton Street for which his father-in-law had lent him the money. She sympathised when he grew sad and told her about the trouble he was taking with the creation of a memorial for Mary in the chapel he had built onto the church at Kedleston. He showed her the sketches of the tomb that he and his wife had designed and on which they would be portrayed lying together.

Elinor felt no jealousy of the dead woman. She knew instinctively that her relationship with Curzon was quite different. At this early stage in their affair she accepted without protest the need for secrecy. For a while it seemed to her that the romance of their love was only heightened by their pretence in public of being mere acquaintances. She was more than compensated for this secrecy when her lover commissioned a portrait of her by the painter Jacques Emile Blanche who had painted her as Le Chat Nellie in Dieppe just after the birth of Margot and before she had become famous. There was a double compliment in the commission, for to be painted by the Frenchman was in itself to be put into a special category: this cultivated and much sought-after painter now specialised in portraits of writers and artists. Elinor as a subject found herself in the company of Thomas Hardy, Edgar Degas, Aubrey Beardsley, George Moore, Marcel Proust and Jean Cocteau.

When the portrait was finished Elinor was delighted with it but Curzon on seeing it insisted that the ribbon in her hair which had been painted pink should be changed to blue. Far from being annoyed Elinor was thrilled at this masterful attention to the details of her appearance.

Before long, lunches and meetings in public places were not enough for either Curzon or Elinor. This time Elinor did not resist a closer intimacy as she had done with Seymour Wynne Finch. It was not too difficult for them to find a way of being together intimately and for a longer time. Because Curzon's older daughters, Cynthia and Irene, were of a similar age to Margot and Juliet, Elinor had discussed Margot's education with Curzon. He reminded her that Dresden was then the fashionable place to send a young girl before her coming out. Not only would Margot learn another language, she would also be in a beautiful city with many literary and musical associations. Elinor decided to take Curzon's advice, despite the further financial strain it would involve. They arranged that in order to find a suitable place in which Margot and Dixie could live, Elinor should make a preliminary visit to Dresden. Because so many English families had daughters being 'finished' there, it would not be a good place for her to meet Curzon. But on her way home she could stop off at a city less fashionable in English circles. They decided on Heidelberg. Elinor's fidelity to Clayton, maintained in spite of the freer habits of her set, was finally over. For the next eight years it was George Nathaniel Curzon who would be the focus of her intense love and passion.

In the autumn of 1908 the fifteen-year-old Margot and her governess went off to Dresden. But the careful plans for her education were soon disrupted when Margot developed a severe case of scarlet fever. She was immediately put into quarantine in an isolation hospital along with others suffering from the same disease. Dixie was allowed to go with her; having been in close contact with Margot she would have had to be quarantined anyway.

The news of Margot's illness was sent to Elinor who dropped everything and rushed back to Dresden. She was appalled to discover that Margot was in a ward with thirty beds supervised by only one nurse and a helper. Quarantine regulations were strictly enforced and nothing Elinor could do or say would convince the German authorities that she should be allowed to be with her daughter who, she was sure, was close to death. Her only consolation was the obvious devotion with which Dixie was nursing Margot. The time Elinor spent in Dresden was miserable and in complete contrast to the time there just weeks before. She was afraid that Margot would die and she was helpless to do anything for her. She felt an irrational guilt that her affair with Curzon was somehow related to Margot's plight.

Gradually Margot pulled through but still Elinor was not allowed to visit her. And so, once it was clear that Margot would get better and that there was nothing at all that she could do until Margot was declared fit to leave the isolation hospital, Elinor travelled back to England. The new and unexpected expenses associated with Margot's illness made it even more urgent for Elinor to finish writing her new book.

She was not at Lamberts for long. Once Margot was free to leave hospital she went with Dixie to Monte Carlo because she was still not strong enough to face up to the damp and cold of an English winter. Elinor joined them there so that Dixie might have a much needed rest.

It was another time of unfortunate contrasts. It was in Monte Carlo that Clayton had proposed to Elinor. She could not help comparing her excitement and her high hopes at the time of her forthcoming marriage with the subsequent reality. Letters from Clayton and Walters about money only emphasised how little of what she had hoped for had materialised.

Mother and daughter led a very quiet life during those months in Monte Carlo. Margot needed to recuperate, Elinor needed to work and to conserve funds. And all the time she thought about Curzon.

In the spring of 1909 Margot was sufficiently recovered to be able to travel back home.

For the next few months the Glyn family were, for the most part, closeted together at Lamberts. It became very clear to Elinor just how much she was on the fringe of her own family. She had, of necessity, to isolate herself in her 'Trianon' for many hours in order to finish the book which would pay the bills. But when she did spend time with her children organising picnics and games and outings for them she noticed that they would take all their worries, their discoveries, their questions, either to Dixie or to Mrs Kennedy. During the months of travelling they had become accustomed to doing without their mother.

Mealtimes were the worst times. Mrs Kennedy would then preside not only over the children but also over Clayton. Elinor realised that the conversations at table were most often about experiences which she had not shared.

Both Mrs Kennedy and Clayton were very fond of their food. They loved to talk about it and to linger over it. Elinor did not share this interest. How she longed to be able to impose Mrs Fish's rule of short sharp meals. How she missed the lively exchanges of Americans at table and how she missed the kind of conversations she had been having with Curzon.

Instead of reading aloud from Aristotle or Plato after their protracted meals, Clayton and Mrs Kennedy would spend hours playing piquet. Elinor looked back with amazement to her mother's former dislike of playing cards with David Kennedy. For herself she hated card games as much as ever.

She could not escape the fact that Clayton preferred her mother's company to her own and that Mrs Kennedy thought Clayton could do no wrong. Mrs Kennedy still considered that in comparison to the meanness of David Kennedy Clayton's generosity and good nature were to be welcomed and praised.

All Elinor's efforts to introduce household economies met with resistance. Mrs Kennedy felt Clayton should have whatever he wanted and Elinor, who hated to be made to look mean, found herself unable to insist on his spending less on fine food and the best brandy.

And all the time she was trying to write light-heartedly about Elizabeth's visit to America. There is a great contrast between the tone of that novel and Elinor's outpourings in her diary. By now she was obsessed with Curzon and knew it. He was more important to her than her family and her husband. But she struggled against her dependence upon him, for she knew, despite her passion for him, that he was not a man on whom a woman could depend emotionally. And she knew that it was her independence and her strength of character that had attracted him to her in the first place. Her advice to herself which she wrote in her diary this summer was 'Your duty lies in using your brain and force for your sweet ones and your family. It does not lie in undesired and idolatrous obsession over the sun, moon and stars.'[2]

Elinor applied herself with increased vigour and after taking time to arrange for Juliet to go to a school in Eastbourne she finished *Elizabeth Visits America.*

This second novel about the young Elizabeth picks up some years after the previous novel. Elizabeth is now married to her Harry and has children. It is as a result of a quarrel with her husband that she sets off on a journey across America.

The tone is less lively than in the first novel, but that can be explained by the fact that Elizabeth always has at the back of her mind the quarrel with Harry, and because as a married woman she is a little less naive.

When the book was published in 1909 some of Elinor's hosts and hostesses during her visit to the States were surprised and not altogether pleased to find recognisable portraits of themselves in the novel, for Elinor wrote as she found. Mrs Vanderbilt cannot have enjoyed the descriptions of the house of which she was so proud nor of herself loaded with 'forty thousand pounds worth of pearls'. But what the book is primarily concerned with, like the French part of *The Visits of Elizabeth*, is establishing the difference between two cultures and by so doing looking afresh at English society.

The two major differences Elizabeth observes are to do with relationships between men and women and attitudes towards money. The two matters are intimately related. Whilst admiring the energy and industry of the American male, Elizabeth cannot help feeling that 'There is no romance here. I don't see how they ever get in love.' She would not like a husband who was out all day earning money and who was too tired to talk when he came in at night. Almost despite herself she prefers the 'quality of perfect ease and unconscious insolence which for some unaccountable reason is attractive in Englishmen'.

With the payment for *Elizabeth Visits America* Elinor was able to settle most of the household debts. No longer able to bear the stifling atmosphere of Lamberts with Clayton and Mrs Kennedy she took Margot off once more to Monte Carlo. From there she travelled to Carlsbad where she met up with Curzon. Her doubts and anxieties about whether he was as truly committed to her as she was to him were temporarily put to rest by his gift of a Della Robbia Venus which he told her reminded him of her.

A little later that summer Curzon visited Elinor at Lamberts and met Clayton for the first time. He was aware at once that Elinor was living in conditions very different from his own.

Clayton cannot have failed to realise that Elinor loved Curzon and that their relationship was on a quite different footing from Elinor's previous romantic attachments. He knew that Curzon was also wealthier than Seymour Wynne Finch and Alistair Innes Ker. On this occasion he said nothing, but an idea took root in his mind.

Towards the end of the year Elinor took Margot with her on a visit to Count Cahen d'Anvers on his estate at Champs. She had been invited to join what was essentially a shooting party, and at one time in her life Elinor would have been less than keen to accept the invitation. But now anything that took her from home, especially if there was the added bonus of a trip to France, was welcome.

She had not seen her Russian friend the Grand Duchess since their conversation in Paris when the idea of dramatising *Three Weeks* had first been discussed. So she was surprised and her curiosity was aroused when she received a telegram from the Grand Duchess asking if Elinor could meet her in Munich. She had a proposal to make.

19 RUSSIA

When Elinor arrived in Munich she found that the Grand Duchess Kiril was not alone. She was accompanied by her mother-in-law the Grand Duchess Vladimir. This magnificent and stately German woman who had been Princess Mariya of Mecklenburgh before she married the Grand Duke Vladimir, brother of the Emperor Alexander III and uncle to Czar Nicholas, was in deep mourning. Her husband had died the previous year. But she was enthusiastic about her daughter-in-law's idea.

The ladies at the Russian court at St Petersburg had all read Elinor's novels. They were especially interested in how she had depicted the life of the English and French nobility. They were well able to judge for themselves the accuracy of her novels since they spent as much time among the European aristocracy as at home. Their English and their French, like that of all their circle back in St Petersburg, was as fluent as their Russian.

Both Grand Duchesses had married into the Romanov family. They were sensitive to the fact that after 'Bloody Sunday' in 1905 and the subsequent persecution of suspected revolutionaries the Russian aristocracy, and in particular the Czar and the Romanov family, had acquired a bad name in Europe. They knew that the scattered exiles were spreading the word about the plight of the peasants and the industrial workers. They knew what an influence the revolutionary writings of Gorky were having.

What they wanted was for Elinor to write something about how the Russian nobility really lived. Both women had followed Elinor's progress through America. If her book about Russia could excite the same kind of interest as *Three Weeks* had done, they would be well pleased.

Laughingly, Elinor told them about the rumour circulating in the States that she had already written about the Romanovs. It was believed by some people there that the Lady was a portrait of the Czarina. One man had come forward claiming that he had evidence that the Dowager Empress, fearing that there would be no heir to the Russian throne as the Czarina produced daughter after daughter, had sent her daughter-in-law off on a yacht with an Englishman and that the Czarevich Alexis was the result.

Elinor noticed that the Grand Duchesses were less amused by this story than she had expected them to be. She knew how absurd the rumour was. She had seen the Czar and his family for herself at Cowes in 1909. Everyone knew how reserved, prudish and devoted to her family was the former Princess Alix of Hesse-Darmstadt; she had not been Queen Victoria's favourite granddaughter for nothing. It would be difficult to find a woman less like the Lady in *Three Weeks*. Elinor had certainly not had her in mind, and had not even known of the rumours until long after the book was written.

The Duchess agreed with Elinor about the Czarina. But, they insisted, it was exactly that kind of false notion that they wanted her to change. They asked Elinor to be their guest in St Petersburg. They had already decided that she would be more comfortable staying in the Hotel de l'Europe than in one of their palaces. But they would arrange for her to have access to all the people and places she felt she needed to see to write her novel. They offered her further enticements with the prospect of balls and glittering occasions, as it was rumoured that the Czar and Czarina were about to emerge from their country retreat at Tsarskoe Selo and participate more fully in court life. They reminded Elinor that she had already met many of their circle in English country houses. Indeed she had met the Grand Duchess Vladimir's sons Boris and André in Egypt at the Khedive's Ball. Elinor remembered Gritzko and the spectacular Cossacks. She was by no means averse to meeting them again.

Without stopping to consider that this was really quite a strange proposition, Elinor accepted their invitation. As she later said of herself, she had by now crossed the boundary between someone who wrote for her own amusement and the professional writer needing to produce a novel a year to support her family. The Russian trip offered the prospect of desperately needed new material.

It was less uncommon at that time to pay a visit to Russia than it has become since. In 1902 Elinor's friend Millicent had visited St Petersburg along with the Duke and Duchess of Marlborough. Millicent had recorded her impression of Russia at that time:

> It seems to me that this country, with its imperfect education, its Oriental instincts, its appalling number of court officials, combined with the immense power of the church, may have generations to wait before its emancipation. It certainly seems to be ready for nothing but what it has at present – and yet I wonder – Such unexpected things happen.[1]

Millicent had told her friend, Elinor, about her travels in Russia, so she was not entirely in the dark about what to expect there. It was with considerable excitement that Elinor prepared for her trip by, as usual, buying a new wardrobe complete with Reboux hats and fashionable shoes. It was, after all, a different matter to go to Russia as a writer and a guest of the Romanovs from going as an official representative from England. She had to make a good impression on her own account.

On 28 December 1909 she arrived in St Petersburg to be greeted with the news that the Grand Duke Michael, the Czar's great uncle had just died in Cannes. Consequently the whole court was obliged to go into mourning for two months. Elinor was in despair. She had with her only two black dresses and her only black hat was an elegant affair which could not be worn as mourning. Fortunately the wife of the English Ambassador to St Petersburg, Lady Nicholson, was entirely accustomed to the niceties of court rituals and, forewarned of Elinor's arrival, had bought for her a suitable crêpe mourning bonnet with a long veil. For the moment, at least, Elinor's new gowns had to hang unworn in her wardrobe and she had to find other ways of impressing her hosts.

Participation in a state funeral was not how Elinor had envisaged spending her first days in St Petersburg. But by so doing she saw a side of Russia which she might otherwise have missed. She had earlier watched the state funeral of Queen Victoria but she found the atmosphere on this occasion quite different. As the funeral cortège made its way to the Cathedral she felt that the atmosphere was not one of grief, but apprehension and even resentment. The Czarina was huddled in her carriage. The Czar walked in the procession with a pale face and was evidently aware of his vulnerability to would-be assassins. The service in the Cathedral to which she was taken by a Secretary of the British Embassy was interminably long. She had felt that the funeral of Queen Victoria marked the end of an era, and now again she felt that something was coming to an end but that this time violence was in the air.

Once the funeral was over private lives within the palaces went on much as before. Elinor met once again the Grand Dukes Boris and André. She thought that Boris seemed bored, and she was struck by how most of the men despite being tall and slim and fine-looking had unhealthy white complexions. Only André who was in the throes of a passionate love affair with a ballet dancer seemed fresh and alert. The Grand Duchess Vladimir's daughter was introduced to her. Hélène, who was married to Prince Nicholas of Greece, was very attractive and very chic. Elinor liked her immediately. For her part Hélène inspected Elinor very closely and then explained that her brother-in-law, Crown Prince Constantine of Greece, had told her that Elinor had eyes like emeralds. She wanted to see for herself if this was true. Elinor was far from being dismayed to learn that she had been discussed by the Greek royal family.

Because she was the guest of the Grand Duchess Vladimir Elinor found herself being treated with great respect everywhere she went. Word of what she was doing had spread quickly and everyone was eager to help.

Conscious that she was there for a purpose and not just to amuse herself, Elinor made detailed notes of all she saw. She was interested in the richness of the interiors, the lack of fresh air and the oppressive steam heating. At banquets she sampled zacouska, Russian hors d'oeuvres. She found the food too rich for her liking and was surprised by how much alcohol was drunk. The conversation at table pleased her because it was lively and conducted in both English and French. The rigid formality of arrivals and departures was new to her and duly noted.

Prompted by his uncle's widow, the Czar sent word that Elinor was to be allowed to see the Winter Palace even though it was officially closed. Grand Duke André accompanied her on her visit to that magnificent but grim building constructed by Peter the Great. She was impressed by the size and the grandeur but she compared it unfavourably to Versailles. The latter had been a place in which people had really lived their lives, where there had been love, laughter and gaiety. The Winter Palace had no such atmosphere. Since the time of Peter the Great the Czars and their families had taken no pleasure in living there and it was used mostly for State occasions. Once again Elinor had that feeling of déja vu that she had experienced at Paestum and Pompeii in 1902. She seemed to know her way around the Winter Palace. Had she really been there before in a previous incarnation, she speculated aloud, to the consternation of Duke André.

Despite all the local colour she was accumulating, Elinor's novel was not proceeding as quickly as she had hoped. She was first of all distracted by worry about her maid Maria who had accompanied her to St Petersburg. Maria was suffering from stomach pains. At first both women thought the rich food and overheated rooms were responsible. But even when Maria modified her diet the pains continued. Elinor feared appendicitis and decided that she must send Maria home for proper treatment. Reluctantly her maid left for England. In her place the hotel supplied a Russian maid. Elinor could not get on with her at all. They had no language in common and Elinor found her sullen and unco-operative. She was also perturbed when on several occasions she returned to find her rooms in considerable disorder. She was inclined to think that the maid was responsible, but she felt that her hosts might be insulted if she protested, and so remained silent.

A further worry was a letter from England informing her that Clayton had been borrowing money again and that his creditors were pressing urgently for repayment. There was no money to meet their demands. Added to all this she was having trouble finding a focus for her novel. She needed a hero and none of the men she had so far met would do at all as a model. When Princess Hélène took tea with her in her suite and enquired how the novel was progressing, Elinor told her about this problem. Hélène immediately came up with a solution. 'What about Gritzko?' she asked.

Elinor had met Gritzko in Egypt, Hélène pointed out, so she must know what kind of man he was. Since he had recently been killed in a duel there could be no difficulty about using him for the hero.

Elinor did indeed remember Gritzko and the feelings he had aroused in her. She saw immediately that he was exactly the central character she needed.

As soon as it was known that Elinor had chosen Gritzko for her hero she was overwhelmed by people who wanted to tell her stories about him. She had, however, left her Egyptian diary with her own notes on Gritzko at Lamberts. She could not possibly have foreseen that she would need them. She now decided to kill two birds with one stone and return home briefly to deal with the creditors and to collect her diary. She would also turn the journey to further advantage by stopping off to see Moscow.

Even though Elinor had already been pleased with the way everything she wanted was quickly arranged for her, she was amazed at the speed with which the arrangements for her trip to Moscow and then to England were made. The very next day a uniformed official called at her hotel and handed her tickets for her train journey to Moscow and for the night train from Moscow to Warsaw. He explained that it would be necessary for her to spend the night in Warsaw so that she could catch the express to Berlin in the morning. A carriage would meet her at the station in Warsaw and take her to the Hotel de l'Europe. She would find all the reservations for the next stage of her trip waiting for her at the hotel. He added that all officials had been instructed to show her everything of interest in Moscow.

Elinor was delighted with this efficiency. Because she planned to be away only a short time she decided to travel without a maid and with the minimum of luggage.

Moscow made Elinor realise just how untypical of Russia was St Petersburg. The latter had been created by Peter the Great to be as westernised and modern as possible. But Moscow was the old Russia with its blue and gilded onion domes and maze of back streets and at its centre the medieval citadel, the Kremlin. It was there in the Ouspensky Cathedral with its five golden cupolas that Czars were traditionally crowned. On the streets and especially in the churches peasants in a variety of curious costumes mixed with the rich in jewels and furs.

Her mind full of the wealth and poverty, the sophistication and the barbarity she had witnessed in Moscow, Elinor travelled in her sleeping compartment across the frontier and into Poland.

It was evening when she arrived in Warsaw. A little alarmed to find herself alone in this strange dark city where she knew no one and could not speak the language Elinor made her way out of the station. She was grateful and relieved when she was addressed by name as Madame Glyn and motioned to climb into a carriage with two horses to draw it and two men on the box. Silently she thanked the St Petersburg official who had so thoughtfully arranged this for her.

She settled down to watch the unfamiliar passing scene. The journey seemed to be taking rather longer than she had expected. Surely the Hotel de l'Europe could not be out in the suburbs. As signs of all habitation began to disappear Elinor grew afraid. Perhaps there was a misunderstanding. She put her head out of the window and called as loudly as she could to the men on the box, 'Hotel de l'Europe!' Their only response was to whip the horses and speed up the flight of the carriage away from the city.

Elinor thought for a moment of jumping out of the carriage. But even if she escaped injury, which was unlikely given the speed at which they were travelling, what could she do next? Her only hope was to try to attract attention. She was sure now that she was being kidnapped.

Once more she put her head out of the window and this time she screamed and screamed into the darkness. The carriage hurtled on.

But then there were shouts and the carriage jolted to a sudden halt. Looking out fearfully Elinor saw men in uniform arguing with the men on the box. She could understand nothing of what was being said. The man who had spoken to her at the station was ordered down from the box and one of the men in uniform took his place. Still no one spoke to Elinor. The carriage was turned round and this time at a sedate pace made its way back to the centre of Warsaw.

Elinor was glad to be helped out of the carriage in front of the Hotel de l'Europe. Her rescuer said nothing to her. He merely put his finger to his lips, bowed and remounted the box.

At least, thought Elinor, she could recover from her strange ordeal with a good night's sleep in the hotel. But she found to her confusion and dismay that not only was the hotel full, there was no reservation in her name. In great distress she explained that she must have a place to sleep before catching the morning train to Berlin. With growing amazement and fear she learned that the express would in fact be leaving shortly. There was no morning express.

A hastily summoned cab drove her to the station arriving just minutes before the train was due to leave.

Fortunately for Elinor, Sir Savile Crossley, whom she knew slightly, was waiting for the Berlin train. Without her customary care for her dignity and independence Elinor threw herself into his arms. He took immediate control of the situation and arranged for his unexpected travelling companion to have the use of the sleeping compartment he had booked for his valet.

Despite her ordeal, Elinor was sufficiently recovered when she arrived in London to contact Curzon and arrange a meeting. She told him all that had happened in the time since she had left St Petersburg. She was pleased at his anxiety on her behalf and his desire that she should not put herself at further risk by returning to Russia.

While Elinor made a flying visit to Lamberts for her diaries and to find out exactly what was needed to tide the family over financially, Curzon made some enquiries in London in the hope of finding some clues to solve the riddle of the attempted abduction of Elinor. What he discovered simply compounded the mystery. He learnt from Lord Redesdale that it had been through the interference of the Foreign Office that Elinor had been refused permission to perform *Three Weeks* in the West End. Both men speculated as to whether there was any connection between this and the attempted kidnapping.

Elinor returned to London and saw Gerald Duckworth. She asked him to give her an advance on her Russian novel even though it was not yet even begun. He agreed and Elinor used the money to meet the creditors' demands.

When she saw Curzon again he repeated his advice that she should not return to Russia. Lord Redesdale backed him up. Clearly someone in Russia wished Elinor harm and in some strange way *Three Weeks* was involved.

Elinor, however, was not to be persuaded. Laughingly she told her well-wishers that she could not possibly afford to leave her expensive wardrobe behind in Russia. In reality her pride would not allow her to abandon her novel since she had already spent the advance. And so, little more than a week later she was back in St Petersburg where she was warmly welcomed.

No satisfactory explanation for this strange episode has ever emerged. Elinor claimed that she had her own ideas as to who was responsible, but she named no names. Was it a supporter of the Czarina who felt that the rumours that associated her with the Lady of *Three Weeks* were being reactivated by Elinor's presence in St Petersburg? Certainly by this time Elinor had begun to share the view of the other Romanovs that the Czarina was not good for the country.

She had learnt by now of the disaster at Khodynska Meadow the day after the coronation when thousands had been crushed to death and of the ball that same evening given by the French Ambassador which the Czar and Czarina had attended. She had seen for herself how the Czarina held herself apart from the larger family, and from public occasions. She had observed that the Prussian Czarina was still not able to speak Russian though her English was impeccable. Her condemnation of the unfortunate young woman in *Romantic Adventure* would suggest that Elinor did lay blame for her kidnapping in that quarter. She reports that during her time in Russia 'gradually I came round to the general view of her as the evil genius of the country . . . strongly reactionary . . . with a positive hatred for Russians'.

The court was no longer in mourning when Elinor arrived back among her friends. A State visit from the King of Bulgaria provided the occasion for St Petersburg to resume the hectic social life normal there in winter.

There was plenty of opportunity now for Elinor to parade her new Lucile gowns as ball succeeded glittering ball. She was amazed at how low cut were the dresses of the ladies and dazzled by the quantities of jewels they loaded themselves with. She would go to functions which began at five o'clock and continued until the early hours of the morning. And then, instead of returning to bed, the company would wrap up in furs and climb into troikas to ride in the cold darkness across the frozen Neva or to seek out places where gypsies performed. There they would be fired with new energy and excitement by the wild and haunting music of the unkempt performers. They would return to their homes as the workers began to appear on the cold streets, thus underlining the difference between the lives of the two classes. And then they would sleep until midday before preparing for another night of mad pleasure-seeking.

Elinor wanted to set a scene of her novel in a Russian country house. But so far in her visit she had not seen one. All her acquaintances preferred to remain shut up in St Petersburg for the winter. She asked the Grand Duchess Vladimir to describe a typical country house for her. The Duchess promised to do better and to arrange for Elinor to see such a house for herself. The very next day, towards the end of a ball given for the King of Bulgaria – it was about five o'clock in the morning – the Foreign Minister presented a young officer to her. He was to be her escort for a visit to a country house at Peterhof. The house had belonged to Potemkin, the lover of Catherine the Great. The association interested Elinor. She also knew that it was at Peterhof that the Czarevich had been born. She expressed her thanks to both men and said that she looked forward to the excursion. To her surprise her young escort insisted that they must set off immediately if they were to be back before darkness fell again.

It would have been discourteous to refuse to make the journey after so much trouble had been taken on her behalf. So Elinor rushed back to her hotel to change out of her ball gown into something more suitable for a journey by troika in the snow.

It was by no means the first time Elinor had been in a picturesque troika. The one which drew up outside her hotel was particularly splendid with crimson velvet upholstery, a padded velvet rug and a coachman dressed in velvet to match. But she quickly discovered that travelling for a long distance along country roads in such a vehicle was quite a different matter from the short journeys she had made previously. Her escort took the opportunity to hold her in his arms to protect her from the bumps and jolts. Her protests soon turned to gratitude.

At last they reached Peterhof. Elinor, determined to get some results from her uncomfortable morning made the young officer show her every corner of Potemkin's house. It was a great disappointment to her. None of the romance she had expected to find in a house with such associations remained. Instead the house had been renovated and was full of 'horribly mid-Victorian' furniture. Only the sanitary arrangements remained as primitive as they had ever been.

After a quick lunch it was time to return to St Petersburg. As they set off once more in the troika a storm began. Elinor had no choice but to huddle under the rug in the arms of the Russian officer and hope for the best. He murmured endearments in French but broke into Russian to swear as the troika jolted violently. Elinor had already missed one night's sleep and found that even in those uncomfortable circumstances she could not stay awake – even to protect her honour. Only when the troika arrived outside her hotel did she wake up. There was a message waiting for her from the Grand Duchess. Anxious for Elinor's welfare she had summoned her to appear at her palace the next morning to give a full account of all that had happened.

Perhaps only then did Elinor realise how completely she had been at the mercy of her escort. But the risks proved to have been worthwhile for the implications of this episode provided a central incident in the plot of the novel.

Ever since the abortive plot to kidnap her Elinor had been alert to that side of Russian life that her hosts would have preferred her not to see. She was aware of the almost frenzied striving for gaiety that often afflicts a society before a major upheaval. She noted the emphasis on wealth and material possessions, especially jewels, and how starkly this contrasted with the evident poverty of the workers she saw on her way home from various balls. She saw that the coachmen who transported the revellers to and fro were often left outside in the freezing cold for hours at a time. She saw the heavy drinking of the men and then heard snippets of gossip about their brutal treatment of their wives. If she had been critical of aimless young men in English society, what she saw in Russia offended her much more. For there she was a guest of the Imperial family whose male members she felt should be taking a part in the government, instead of which they spent their time in endless pleasure-seeking. One night after returning from yet another splendid occasion she had looked out of her window to see a crowd of poor people dressed in little more than rags being herded along by Cossacks on horseback. Occasionally the riders used their whips to urge the crowd to move faster. Elinor enquired of the hall-porter about the meaning of the scene. She was told that those people, having no work in the surrounding countryside, had made their way to the city. But they had entered illegally, without passports and must be made to leave. The hall-porter gave her this information without comment except for the suggestion that it was unwise to look out of her window in such a treacherous climate. His words seemed a veiled warning. She understood that such questions were most unwelcome, that there were things it would be better not to admit to seeing.

As a novelist this new awareness posed problems for her. How could she write a novel which was both true to reality and pleasing to her hosts? A further, though less important, problem was one of names. Every character in her plot was based on someone she had met in St Petersburg. Clearly the names would have to be changed. Since she did not feel able to invent Russian names the Grand Duke Georgi made them up for her.

In April Elinor was not altogether sorry to leave St Petersburg temporarily. She had had her fill of late nights and excitement and she needed some distance from her subject to work on her novel. But still she had not seen Russia except in the winter and she knew she must return.

In May Edward VII died, so when Elinor, accompanied by Margot, returned to St Petersburg the court was once more in mourning. This time Elinor was better prepared but she had to buy a mourning bonnet for Margot.

The transformation of the city and the surrounding countryside amazed Elinor. Where all had been snow previously, now all was green. She put the last touches to her novel incorporating this new sense of the place and was ready to present her work to her friends who had been waiting impatiently for it.

Rather than pass the manuscript from person to person Elinor decided to read her book aloud to those who were interested. For ten days she held her audience's rapt attention. With great relief she found that she had their approval. She was given the honour of being allowed to dedicate *His Hour* to 'Her Imperial Highness' the Grand Duchess Vladimir.

By a strange coincidence Angela St Clair-Erskine, who had been the model for Elizabeth, visited the city, by then renamed Leningrad, in 1931. Poking around market stalls which offered for sale mementoes of the Imperial family as well as old books she came across this very copy of *His Hour* which Elinor had inscribed to her patroness.

It was June when Margot and Elinor left St Petersburg. Elinor was never to return but she took back to England a souvenir in the form of a Siberian cat.

Gerald Duckworth was also well pleased with the novel for which he had already paid the advance, and in October of that eventful year of her life Elinor's novel *His Hour* was published.

Did Elinor really read the whole of her novel to the Russian court or did she add some paragraphs once she had returned safely to England? For the novel is far from being an uncritical account of the life led by the Russian nobility. Yet the criticism is often hinted at rather than expressed directly. The restrictions imposed on Elinor by the situation may in fact have resulted in a better and more subtle novel. In *Romantic Adventure* she speaks forthrightly, saying, 'But what a strange, sad country is Russia, and what strange sad people its inhabitants must be, thus to endure through century after century this unpardonable, relentless tyranny and heedlessness of human life and suffering.'

In the novel the strongest direct criticism is made by Tamara, the English heroine who is in St Petersburg as the guest of her godmother. She says to the Russian prince Gritzko, who is the hero, 'You all seem as if you had no aim. . . . You are not interested in the politics of your country. You don't seem to do anything but kill time – Why?' She also comments on the lavish spending of money: 'On no occasion was there ever a halt for the consideration of ways and means. They wanted some particular amusement – and had it.'

The explanation that Gritzko gives for the condition of his society does to some extent concede the existence of that savage barbarity that Elinor found so hard to accept.

> 'You must not forget that the country is practically three hundred years behind the time though . . . No doubt quite as great horrors marked others if we look at them at an equivalent stage of development. It is missing this point which makes most strangers and many historians so unjust to Russia and her people. The national qualities are immeasurably great, but as a civilized nation they are very young.'

But even this explanation does not quite justify the behaviour of the hero who, though handsome, masterful, courageous and on rare occasions tender, does behave like an overindulged child whose freedom is a threat to both himself and those with whom he comes into contact. It is only through his love for someone who does not share his frivolous view of life that he may learn to be adult and responsible.

As a picture of Russia at a particular stage in her history the novel could hardly be bettered. The implied but never stated suggestion that this is a society on the brink of a disaster was not understood by all of its first readers. Reading it in the present, knowing the outcome of that wild gaiety, we can see clearly Elinor's depiction of the seeds of destruction.

One reviewer, Sidney Dark of the *Daily Express*, did say

> As one reads, one thinks all the time of Versailles before the

Revolution, with its elegant Voltairean immoral aristocrats dancing while their doom was being prepared. I have always been sceptical about the possibility of a Russian revolution. But Mrs Glyn has almost persuaded me that it is inevitable.

20 WRITING FOR MONEY

In 1935, as she looked through her diaries in preparation for writing her autobiography, Elinor concluded that the years between 1910 and the end of the War were perhaps the most unhappy in her life. There was much to be unhappy about.

Outwardly the family maintained the same routines as it had done for years. Winters were spent in the south of France. In spring they were back in Essex. Then they would spend the season in London, go to the annual regatta at Cowes, spend time in September visiting before setting off once more to Carlsbad and then to France.

But underneath the persistent pattern was turmoil and distress largely created by the two men in Elinor's life.

When Elinor returned from Russia she was more in love with Curzon than ever. But did he feel the same way about her? Sometimes she felt he did and just as frequently she was convinced that he did not. Their relationship offered no emotional stability to Elinor since Curzon would blow first hot and then cold. No one had ever before treated her as inconsistently as Curzon did. She did not like the situation but she felt unable to change it.

In September of 1910 after Elinor had taken Margot to Cowes and then to visit her old friend Billy Grant she met up once more with Alfred Milner in London. He knew all about Clayton, about his declining health, his gambling, his drinking and his debts. How much longer would Clayton be able to survive this life-style? Milner declared himself to Elinor. He told her that he cared for her deeply and that when she needed him he would be ready. So engrossed was Elinor in her own feelings for Curzon that she was unprepared for this veiled proposal of marriage. At one time she would have snatched at the possibility being offered to her. But now she knew that she could never love Alfred Milner in the way she loved George Curzon. She told Milner that she hoped that they would always be close friends but that nothing more was possible on her side.

The next week which she and Margot spent at Crag Hall in Derbyshire with Curzon and his three daughters confirmed her decision. There were picnics and games for the family party and then in the evenings after the children had gone to bed there were times alone with Curzon when he read aloud to her, often from Aristotle. She was happier than she had ever been before.

The return to her real family life at Lamberts threw her into despair, so stark was the comparison. Not only did she share nothing at all with Clayton any more, he was a positive drain on her energy because of the worry he caused her. Night after night she would wake up to see a light burning in Clayton's room at the opposite end of the house. She feared, correctly, that Clayton was sitting up drinking brandy after brandy. Where had the money come from to buy the brandy, or had it been bought on extended credit with his wine merchant?

Her question was answered in October. The excitement of the publication of *His Hour* was overshadowed by Walters' advice that Clayton would be wise to leave the country for a while as his creditors were once more on his trail.

So the whole family, except Juliet who was safely at her school in Eastbourne, made their way to St Raphael, a resort no longer fashionable and therefore comparatively inexpensive. It also offered few opportunities for Clayton to spend money. Once she had seen them safely settled into the Hotel Beau Rivage Elinor returned to England. Curzon and Milner were to speak at a public meeting and Elinor could not resist the opportunity of seeing them together and comparing them. She was filled with pride at Curzon's performance. But her pleasure was short-lived. Did this whiff of public success and the promise of more to come influence Curzon in his decision to break off his affair with Elinor? Ironically he asked Elinor, as Elinor had very recently asked Milner, to remain his close friend even if they were no longer lovers. To soften the blow he presented Elinor with a pair of emerald earrings. Far from mollifying her the gift enraged her. In the past he had given her sapphire earrings and they had sentimentally declared sapphires to be their 'stone of love and faith'. To give her emeralds on their parting was to inflict a double blow. To her diary Elinor poured out all her anger and distress. But in public, by a great effort of her will, she appeared her usual self.

In Paris, where she stayed at the Ritz before travelling on to

St Raphael, it was easier. Many of her Russian acquaintances were there, full of praise for *His Hour*. The French literati too expressed admiration. She had her portrait painted by Marietta Cotton and defiantly posed wearing the contentious emerald earrings. She even had the pleasure of attracting a rich admirer, a man she referred to as 'My American Napoleon', and who may have been Gordon Selfridge the department store owner.

By the time she reached St Raphael in December Elinor was in much better spirits. Her confidence in herself was fully restored when she was approached at the hotel by an elderly man who introduced himself as Professor Bradley. He had read *Three Weeks* with great enjoyment and was delighted to have the opportunity of meeting her and telling her so in person. He could have said nothing which would have given Elinor greater pleasure.

Of all Elinor's admirers Francis Herbert Bradley was the most unlikely. At this time he was sixty-four years old. He had never married, in fact the fellowship he held at Merton College, Oxford, depended upon his remaining a bachelor. As he had spent his entire life in the seclusion of educational institutions, first Cheltenham, then Marlborough and finally Oxford, he had lived almost exclusively in the company of men. His health was not of the best and his annual visits to St Raphael were an attempt to get away from the ill effects of the dampness of the English climate in winter. A man steeped in the classics, he was already famous for his philosophical work, *Appearance and Reality*.

By some strange chemistry the two of them took to each other immediately. They walked together in the surrounding countryside and discussed their common interest in the Greeks and Romans. Although Curzon had been reading Aristotle to Elinor she felt she did not know enough. Bradley was happy to fill in the gaps in her education. They exchanged books. The residents of the Hotel Beau Rivage were astonished to see them sitting together, the elderly scholar happily reading *His Hour* while the glamorous novelist struggled with *Appearance and Reality*.

Elinor had sufficient confidence in her new friend to discuss with him the novel she was developing. It was to be a work quite different from anything she had attempted before. She was taking more time and trouble than usual, and she was using all her knowledge of classical literature to enrich it. Bradley was interested and encouraging. He promised to read the final draft before Elinor showed it to Gerald Duckworth.

Calmness returned to Elinor in the company of Bradley. His racy and sometimes biting humour entertained her. She was able to respond in kind. She began to be resigned to the end of her affair with Curzon.

She was, therefore, greatly disturbed when a letter arrived from Curzon telling her he was tired of the endless parties and that he missed her. She did not know what to make of the letter. Was he suggesting that he wanted to begin again where they had left off or was he just continuing his habit of blowing hot and cold?

When she returned to London in January she decided to telephone him. She then regretted this impulse for she felt that his tone to her on the phone bore no relation to his letter. She was glad that she had already committed herself to a quick trip to the States to discuss the dramatisation of *Three Weeks* with Bessie Marbury. The news that her American Napoleon had booked a passage on the same liner pleased and flattered her. The same news pleased Curzon less and he arranged a meeting before Elinor left. He explained that he did not want to break with her altogether, that he wanted to continue seeing her, but perhaps on a new basis. After the meeting Elinor was no clearer in her own mind as to what Curzon really wanted from their relationship.

Negotiations with Bessie Marbury proved unsatisfactory. Elinor returned to England feeling frustrated and fearing that she had spent money needlessly on the trip. She had not even had the pleasure of flirting with her admirer because she had kept him determinedly at arm's length. As long as there was the slightest hope that Curzon wanted her she was absolutely unable to consider any other man as more than a friend.

She was braced for bad news about Clayton on her return. Had she not faced this situation so many times already? But even so she was not prepared for the trouble that faced her now. Clayton had really surpassed himself. Not only had he taken to borrowing from the money lenders, he had even gone begging from Lucy and Cosmo.

It was Lucy who broke the news to Elinor, and this only added to her humiliation. She was painfully aware of how successful Lucy was and how strongly she was supported by Cosmo's good business sense. Elinor asked Walters to meet with her and her brother-in-law so that together they could review the whole situation and decide what action to take next. Matters were worse than even Elinor's deepest fears had led her to imagine. Unless sufficient money could be put together quickly to pay the moneylenders then Clayton would this time certainly have to declare bankruptcy. Lucy was enraged on her sister's behalf. She wrote to her mother detailing all Clayton's follies and begging her not to encourage him or indulge him any longer.

When Curzon was consulted he told Elinor that she should let Clayton go bankrupt. Otherwise the whole scenario would simply be repeated. But Elinor's pride was too great to allow this. She could still remember the scandal when Lillie Langtry had been forced to sell everything she possessed to pay her debts, and stigma still attached to the Earl of Rosslyn's name after his bankruptcy. With some clever financial juggling by Walters and with money lent by Lucy and Curzon bankruptcy was once more narrowly avoided.

Elinor could hardly believe her eyes when in the middle of negotiations she received a letter from her husband asking for money. He was bored with St Raphael and wanted to go to Algiers. Elinor's sharply worded reply provoked from Clayton a string of reproaches about her personal extravagances, about her trips to the States, her fancy clothes and her newly acquired motor car.

The next thing that Elinor knew was that Clayton had disappeared leaving a note for Mrs Kennedy appealing to her to sympathise with him for having to deal with a wife like Elinor. A few weeks later Clayton reappeared in St Raphael and was then brought home by Margot and Mrs Kennedy.

Elinor immediately took Walters' advice and took various measures to ensure that Clayton had no access to money beyond an allowance she would make him. This involved having Clayton sell to her his remaining interest in the Homerston Estate. Clayton, apparently totally resigned to the situation, signed all the papers that Walters put before him. But as soon as husband and wife were back at Lamberts the storm broke and Clayton bitterly accused Elinor of cheating him. The atmosphere in the house was intolerable. To escape it and to get material for her new novel Elinor set off for Italy with Margot and her maid, Maria, with Maria's husband as chauffeur. For the next few weeks they lived in Sirmione and San Gimignano where the cost of living was considerably below that in England.

But on their return in June Elinor had to face the fact that she still owed money to Lucy and Curzon: the two people she least liked being in debt to. She was desperate to earn some money quickly. She consulted her friend and neighbour, Ralph Blumenfeld, the editor of the *Daily Express*. He told her that he would be happy to buy a new Elinor Glyn novel for serialisation in his paper if she could have something ready in three weeks when he had a vacant spot. Three weeks! Elinor did not know whether to take this as a good omen or a bad one. She accepted Blumenfeld's offer, telling him that she had a half-finished novel already. She did. But it was that novel that she cherished and wanted to write carefully. She was not willing to sacrifice it just to get out of debt. The only thing to do was to start from scratch and work until she had finished an altogether new novel.

It was a real challenge, but Elinor could not afford to fail. Back at Lamberts she took to her bed in her 'Trianon'. Maria was instructed to protect her from the family and any visitors and to supply her with meals when she needed them and plenty of coffee and the occasional brandy.

It took Elinor eighteen days to write the novel. On 3 July serialisation began in the *Daily Express* and in October *The Reason Why* was published as a book.

Of all her many novels this was the one Elinor liked least. Technically she had nothing to be ashamed of. The narrative construction is as good as anything she wrote. What is more, there is a driving force in the book which keeps the reader engaged. It is not only the pace at which Elinor was obliged to write that gives the book its energy but also the intensity of her own feelings of that moment that find their way into the narrative.

The book is ostensibly about star-crossed lovers who make their way through a web of misunderstandings to find happiness together at the end. It is, more importantly, about money and about how the lack of it affects women in particular. The heroine, Zara, is beautiful and, of course, has long red hair coiled in a braid round her head. This is not the only thing she has in common with her creator. At the beginning of the novel Zara has the same desperate need for money as Elinor. She needs it for a sick child and a spendthrift stepfather. It could be said that at the time Clayton was a combination of the two. Zara is full of anger at having to submit to a marriage which she believes to be merely mercenary on both sides just as Elinor was angry at having to abandon the novel she was proud of to write purely and simply for money. Some of Elinor's anger at Clayton and Curzon, who between them had created this situation, finds expression in Zara's words to her uncle on the subject of men: 'I know that they are either selfish weaklings, or cruel, hateful brutes like Ladislaus, or clever, successful financiers like you, my uncle.'

She feels herself to be 'just a chattel, a part of a business bargain'. But like Elinor she had learnt to hide her feelings: 'An iron self control was one of her inheritances from her grandfather.'

Something of George Curzon makes up the character of Zara's antagonist, her uncle Francis Markrute with his cynical attitude towards women. He says: 'There are three classes of the species female: those for the body, those for the brain, and those for both. The last are dangerous. The other two merely occupy certain moods in man. Fortunately for us the double combination is rare.'

And yet the novel is romantic as the repeated references to Tennyson's *Idylls* make clear. It is based on the premise that 'a great love is a very powerful and sometimes a terrible thing, if it is not returned in like measure'. Elinor was painfully aware of this in her relationship with Curzon. In the novel love finally triumphs. The sick child dies and the spendthrift stepfather disappears from Zara's life. Was Elinor hoping against hope that a similar happy ending awaited her?

Once the novel was completed Elinor left Lamberts and took her work to London. This terrible drain on her energy and creativity had resolved one thing in her mind. She could not and would not have Lamberts as her only home. She was tired of having to rely on the hospitality of friends whenever she visited London. Being a guest made it more difficult for her to meet Curzon in the secrecy he continued to insist upon, so she took the reckless step of leasing a small suite at the Ritz. Because she was willing to take it for two years she got favourable terms. It was one more assertion of her independence and one step further away from her marriage.

The coronation of King George V on 22 June passed almost unnoticed by Elinor, so absorbed was she in her own affairs. More interesting to her was Curzon's excitement at his new purchase of Tattersall Castle and his determination to track down the original fireplaces which had been removed and sold by the previous owner.

For Curzon was once more paying Elinor the kind of attention she craved from him. In August he invited her to Hackwood. Once again Margot accompanied her. It was a happy occasion. Margot and Irene, Curzon's daughter, were becoming good friends and Elinor was developing a lasting relationship with Cynthia (Cimmie), Curzon's second daughter.

At this time Elinor was visibly influenced in her political opinions by Curzon. Something of his view of society had already found its way into *The Reason Why*. Now he explained to her why he had led the Conservative peers to create the majority necessary for the passing of the Parliament Bill: he had wanted to avoid the 'pollution' of the Lords by the creation of new Liberal Peers threatened by Asquith with the consent of the new King. Elinor took all he said seriously. She did not understand fully what Curzon's renewed interest in politics threatened for their personal relationship.

At the end of August Elinor accompanied by Margot set off as was her custom to drive to Carlsbad. She had arranged for Clayton to join her there in the faint hope that his health might be improved by the cure. On the way she stopped at Frankfurt. There she and her companions were amazed by the sight of a huge grey cigar-shaped object in the sky. It was the first Zeppelin she had seen. It had been produced by Count Ferdinand von Zeppelin at his Frankfurt base. No one suspected at that moment that they would soon be seeing these objects as sinister threats over London.

In Carlsbad they were delayed by a traffic accident involving the chauffeur. Once the matter was cleared up the party divided. Clayton and Margot went to St Raphael to join Mrs Kennedy while Elinor headed for Versailles. For the next few months she took rooms in the Hotel des Réservoirs right on the edge of the grounds of the Palace. In the shadow of Louis XIV's former residence she completed the work that she had earlier interrupted to write *The Reason Why*. In January she took the completed manuscript of *Halcyone* with her to St Raphael where Professor Bradley was its first reader.

To her relief and gratification he liked this new novel in which she had invested so much pride. She was happy to have him put her right on some matters of classical detail, but he was completely unable to persuade her to correct her spelling. She had every confidence that, as usual, Gerald Duckworth would take care of that.

21 A CHALLENGE TO THE SOULS

As Elinor returned to England at the beginning of 1912 Lucy was preparing to leave for Paris. She had leased a property in the rue des Penthièvres for business and she took a studio apartment for herself at the Rond Point des Champs Elysées. The Fouquet Lemaîtres had always been dismayed that Lucy had gone into trade. They were even less keen to acknowledge her when she started up a business in Paris and, as if to be provocative, made her home just a short distance from theirs on the Champs Elysées. Their desire not to acknowledge her as family soon seemed justified.

Lucy suddenly decided that a trip to New York was imperative and urgent. She persuaded Cosmo to go with her and booked cabins on the new White Star liner, the *Titanic*. Elinor was envious of Lucy's ability at a moment's notice to get first class accommodation on the much-publicised maiden voyage.

Her envy quickly turned to dismay when shortly after the ship's departure she received a phone call from Esmé's husband. He had just heard the unbelievable news that the unsinkable Titanic had sunk. At that time there were no reports of any survivors. Elinor rushed to the offices of the *Daily Express* hoping that her friend Blumenfeld would have the latest news. He was not there but his assistant promised to let Elinor have news as soon as he heard any more.

It was an agonising time. On 15 April the *Daily Express* telephoned to say that in their midday edition they were publishing a list of those who had drowned. Lucy and Cosmo were on the list.

Deeply shocked, Elinor was unable to accept that her sister was dead. Something inside her told her that Lucy was still alive. At one o'clock the *Express* phoned again, this time to say that word had come through that the Duff Gordons were safe. Because this news only confirmed what she had instinctively felt, Elinor was sure that it was accurate and that her sister was safe. Therefore she did not hesitate to take Margot to a ball for which she had a long-standing invitation and then to drive on to Lamberts to share the good news with the rest of the family. The next day she was back in London and attended the memorial service at St Paul's for all those who had not survived the disaster.

As far as Elinor was concerned that was the end of the matter. She was just happy that her family had suffered no losses and distressed for those who had. She looked forward to hearing the full story of Lucy's adventures when she arrived back home.

But the news of what had happened the night the *Titanic* sank reached London before Lucy did. At the best of times Lucy would talk in an unguarded way to newspaper reporters. On this occasion, understandably, she had told her story to anyone who wanted to listen and had even added some embellishments. She spoke with pride of how Cosmo had given money to all the crew members who had shared a lifeboat with them so that they could replace their basic kit lost when the *Titanic* sunk. Little did she know that this act of generosity would quickly be interpreted as Cosmo's bribe for an undeserved place on the boat. She thought that she, Cosmo and her secretary would be treated as heroic survivors both in New York and London. But it was not so. Elinor heard to her horror that Lucy and Cosmo were being referred to as cowards who had bought their lives at the expense of less wealthy women and children.

In early May Lucy and Cosmo returned to London to face a Board of Trade Inquiry into the sinking of the *Titanic* and the events which had followed upon the loss of the ship. Elinor attended the hearing at the Scottish Hall in Victoria. She sat with her friend Lady St Helier, with Margot Asquith and the Russian Ambassador, Count Benckendorff, all of whom were confident that the Duff Gordons had done nothing wrong. But it soon became clear that there were many in the courtroom who had made up their minds against Sir Cosmo and Lady Duff Gordon simply on the basis of class. Even the cross-examination they had to endure was both hostile and biased. It was a long and gruelling day before husband and wife were finally vindicated for the actions they had taken the night of the sinking.

But the disgrace lingered on. Elinor began to believe that this trial was just one aspect of a change that was taking place in society. Class war was now becoming more and more evident and would soon come to a head in a series of serious strikes.

Throughout this distressing time Elinor had been making preparations for Margot's coming out. She had decided that although the suite at the Ritz was an adequate bolt hole for herself it was no place in which to do the entertaining associated with a coming out and presentation at Court. She looked around for suitable premises and took a short lease on a house in Green Street. She immediately started to redecorate it because she wanted to impress not only Margot's fellow debutantes and friends but also Curzon. She had always regretted having to entertain him at Lamberts. This was her chance to show him that she too could transform a house tastefully even if she had to work on a lesser scale than he was doing at Tattersall Castle, Hackwood House and Carlton House Terrace.

It was now that a rift began to develop between Margot and Elinor. Margot was not altogether pleased to see large sums of money being spent on redecorating a house, leaving little for her debutante wardrobe and entertaining. She was unhappy that, although Clayton was ill, Elinor preferred to entertain Curzon rather than accompany her back to Lamberts at weekends. She disliked the way the young men swarmed around her mother and, perhaps, she now understood fully that Elinor loved Curzon and not Clayton. Nevertheless her season was duly accomplished and she was presented at court.

During Margot's season Elinor saw that changes were taking place even in the upper classes. There was less formality and less concern for observing conventions, and that did not please her. She still preferred the old ways. But for the most part she was happy that summer: the Green Street house gave her the opportunity to spend more time with Curzon since she did not have to scheme and contrive to meet him. He gave every sign of being as much in love as she was. He gave her gifts, paid her a great deal of attention and showed an increased interest in her work. In June he presented her with a sapphire and diamond ring to match a pair of earrings he had given her earlier. Small wonder that she began to hope that they had reached a new and more settled stage in their relationship, one that could be sustained in the future.

This was the month that *Halcyone* was published, and Elinor presented her lover with a copy. Only if she had been confident of his love for her would she have done so.

She had known for a long time that Curzon was a leading member of the group known as the Souls. When she had questioned him about exactly why the group had been given this name he had shown her a cutting which he had kept since 1908 from the *Portsmouth Evening News*. It read as follows: '. . . it owes its origin to Lord Curzon, who at dinner one day to the members brought out the essential point that in order to become one of the coterie it was necessary to possess a soul above the ordinary.'

The group of friends which formed a discernible clique within society had been at their closest in 1890. Women were in the majority and they set the tone. They were all women with money or a title or both. They had aspirations to intelligence and wit and at their dinner parties conversation was supposed to be more important than food. They professed to dislike the standard dinner parties of the day where too much was eaten and drunk, where card games were played, often for money, and where racing was a favourite topic for discussion. These friends were so intent on establishing themselves as a tightly knit group that excluded vulgar outsiders that they developed a language of their own. They were possessive of the men in their group and in particular of George Nathaniel Curzon. Margot Asquith, Lady Wemyss, Violet Rutland and Lady Desborough were the core members. All, incidentally, were customers of Lucy, so Elinor knew quite a lot about them from her sister.

Curzon was in the habit of inviting the Souls to Hackwood at Whitsuntide. From there they would all move on to Lady Desborough's home at Taplow Court. Elinor knew with certainty that she would never be invited to join the group at Whitsuntide, and that there would never be a member of the Souls present when she was invited to visit in August. She had to accept that Curzon would continue to compartmentalise his friendships in this way. She knew that Curzon admired these women. He had said of Ettie, Lady Desborough that she was 'always incomparably dressed, and an epicure's feast for the eye'. And it was Lady Desborough who was especially possessive of Curzon and resentful of any woman outside the circle in whom he showed an interest. She appears to have realised that Curzon and Elinor were intimates and she began to do her best to draw Curzon back within the magic circle.

Mary Leiter in her time had been made uncomfortable by these women. Although they had been kind to her before she married Curzon, once she was his wife they were distinctly cooler and made her feel keenly that they had known her husband for longer than she had. She wrote home to her mother shortly after her marriage,

'My path is strewn with roses, and the only thorns are unforgiving women.'[1]

The Souls had far more reason for wishing to exclude Elinor than for their coolness to Mary Leiter. Elinor had no title, she had no land and she was not independently wealthy. The fact that she had earned all that she had through her writing was a mark against her. In their circle it was not even acceptable for a man to be seen earning his living, much less a woman. For all their claims to intellectual superiority, not one of them was as educated as Elinor had made herself and Curzon was not known to read the classics aloud to any of them. And, of course, they could not forgive Elinor for having betrayed their class by holding up certain aspects to ridicule in her novels.

Elinor was sensitively aware of the Souls' growing antagonism towards her, and her novel *Halcyone* is a deliberate challenge to them. If one word appears more than any other in the novel it is the word 'soul'.

Halcyone is a remarkable book. It is at once an expression of admiration and love and a moral fable designed to warn the beloved of following one of the paths she sees opening up before him.

The novel is not simply autobiographical but, like most of Elinor's novels, it draws heavily on her personal experience.

The hero, Derringham, is unquestionably a portrait of Curzon as Elinor perceived him. And it is interesting that, unlike most of her heroes, he is far from perfect.

He first meets Halcyone when she is still a child. Before he ever appears she learns that he is brilliant academically and that he had achieved a double first at university, that 'he is full of ambitions in the political line, and he has a fearless and rather caustic wit. He is a brilliant fellow and cares for no man – following only his own star.'

When he does arrive in person his appearance is exactly that of George Nathaniel Curzon.

> His nose was high and aquiline, his forehead high and broad, and there was something noble and dominating in his fearless regard. His hair did not even grow very prettily, though it was thick and dark, and there was not an ounce of superfluous flesh upon his whole

> person. He never for a moment suggested repose, he gave the impression of a vivid, nervous force.

His arrogant political views echo those of Curzon at this time of popular unrest. He says:

> 'A man may not make a speech but he must choose his words so that uneducated clods can grasp his meaning, he cannot advocate an idea with success unless it can appeal to the lower middle classes. It is this subservience to them which has brought us to where we are. No ideals – no lofty ends – just a means to each one's hand. I will never pretend we are all equals, I will never appeal to anything but the highest in an audience. So they can throw me out if they will.'

To support this arrogance he needs money and he confesses to his old tutor that he can see only one way of getting it. 'I admit that a woman with money may be useful to me by and by.'

Mrs Cricklander, a wealthy American divorcée, is obviously a suitable match: 'Mrs Cricklander was a woman of enormous ability – she had a perfect talent for discovering just the right people to work for her pleasure and benefit, while being without a single inspiration herself.' This lady charms Derringham not only with her money and good looks but also with her apparently brilliant conversation. Little does he know that with the help of her companion she 'gets up' subjects to impress him. Is this Elinor's barb against the Souls, one of whom at least confessed to no breadth of knowledge but just what she had carefully prepared for dinner conversation?

And then quite against his better judgement and despite his long term plans Derringham falls in love with Halcyone just as Curzon fell in love with the unsuitable Elinor.

Halcyone does not have red hair. But she is in many ways like Elinor. She had a lonely childhood which had been brightened by her reading. She has a passion for the classics which, like Elinor, she had come to know through Charles Kingsley's *The Heroes*. She longs to know more and becomes the eager pupil of the old retired professor, Mr Carlyn, whom she nicknames Cheiron, 'the wisest of all things beneath the sky', just as Elinor had sat at the feet first of Lord St Helier to whom the book is dedicated, then of Lord Grey, Alfred Milner and latterly Professor Bradley. Like Elinor, Halcyone has no regard for conventional religion, yet she has a rigid code of ethics based on the notion that 'It is not to whom you give your word – it is to you it matters that you keep it, because to break it degrades yourself . . . You must be honourable to yourself.'

Her dearest possession is a marble bust of Aphrodite. (Curzon had given Elinor a Della Robbia Venus saying that it reminded him of her.) This bust inspires her just as Pallas Athene in *The Heroes* had inspired Perseus, saying, 'from the souls of clay I turn away . . . but to the souls of fire I give more fire'.

Halcyone is, in the words of Carlyn, a woman 'with a soul' and 'a woman with a soul suffers, and brings tribulations'. He warns John Derringham, 'When you meet a woman with a soul you will have met your match, John.'

This proves to be true when Derringham falls in love with Halcyone. But he is no knight in shining armour who braves all for love. Like Curzon he looks over his shoulder to see how such a marriage, such a relationship, would affect his larger career: 'he would not burden himself with a poor, uninfluential girl as a wife, even though the joy of it took them both to heaven.' Eventually he proposes a secret marriage just as Curzon insisted on keeping his relationship with Elinor a secret. Derringham's justification is: ' "It is a curse, this want of money," he said. "It makes a man do base things that his soul revolts against." '

As a result of an accident the secret marriage does not take place as planned. John Derringham is punished for his weakness and desire for secrecy. But all's well that ends well and at the novel's close Derringham says to Halcyone, as there can be no doubt Elinor would have liked Curzon to say to her, 'My darling – my one woman with a soul.'

Apart from this happy ending much of the second half of the book is painfully prophetic as we shall later see.

Halcyone, this novel which Elinor considered her best work, which was admired by friends she respected, and with which she intended to give a different image of herself as a writer than that created by *Three Weeks*, was neither a critical nor a financial success. Elinor's reading public was not accustomed to a hero like Derringham. They did not like him any more than the general public ever warmed to Curzon himself.

However satisfied Elinor was with having finished her novel, she quickly realised that the royalties it would earn would not be enough to keep the family for a year. Once again she had to find a story that she could develop with reasonable speed. At Cowes that August in conversation with the famous political hostess, Theresa, Marchioness of Londonderry, the mother of the woman who was to become one of her closest friends, she heard a story which provided the germ for her next novel. The Marchioness had told her how one of her contemporaries had married a very attractive young American woman. As the couple were leaving the church a woman in the crowd outside had jeered at the bride for being an octoroon. The enraged husband had speedily made enquiries and had discovered, to his dismay, that this was indeed true. In disgust he had left his wife immediately and without ever consummating the marriage.

Elinor considered this story while she and Margot visited Paris, staying at the Ritz, and then in Carlsbad where she took the cure as usual. Then mother and daughter returned to the Hotel des Réservoirs where Elinor had written most of *Halcyone* and where she now settled in to write the novel she would call *The Sequence*. It must have been a dull time for Margot, for once Elinor began to write she had little time for anything else.

But the novel was finished by December so that they were able to return to England once more. After delivering her manuscript to Duckworth Elinor broke with her usual routine and along with Margot made a January visit to Curzon at Hackwood.

In the meantime Mrs Kennedy had set off to establish a comfortable place for the rest of the family in St Raphael. Clayton was to follow in a short time while Elinor and Margot made a more leisurely progress stopping off in Paris and Cannes.

Mrs Kennedy was surprised when Clayton did not arrive at the time she had expected him. She waited for a few days and then contacted Elinor to see if there had been a change of plan. It was then that they discovered that Clayton had again disappeared without a word to anyone. There was some reason to worry as Clayton was a sick man. Margot and Elinor hurried to St Raphael in the hope that Clayton would soon turn up. But he did not. The next news of him came via a letter from Clayton to Dixie, the governess. Clayton wrote asking her to send his clothes to an address in Constantinople.

During February the family waited in St Raphael. They did not think that Clayton could stay away indefinitely as he would be short of money. But Elinor did consider what to do if he did not in fact return. In March she went back to England and to Lamberts. She had never been really happy in the house and she felt that after this latest escapade she no longer had any obligation to consider Clayton's needs. She could well do without the expense of the upkeep of this house. Lamberts was put up for sale and the three women moved into the Green Street house.

Elinor and her mother remembered being in just such a situation after the death of Mr Kennedy. This time there was some financial relief with the publication of Elinor's volume of short stories *The Contrast*. This book is most interesting for the hero of 'The Point of View', a Russian count, who voices many of Elinor's own less than conventional views about marriage and in particular a sentiment of special relevance to Elinor at this time: 'Of what use to chain the body of a woman to one man if her spirit is with another?' There is also a sad reflection of her affair with Curzon in 'The Contrast' when the heroine Pauline expresses anger at having always to meet her lover in secret and then goes on to consider the larger implications of their meetings.

> Her thoughts rapidly reviewed all the subtle changes she had first noticed. The gradual growing anguish which became her daily portion; and yet there were no actual proofs that she could seize upon to convince herself that André no longer loved her. He would be wildly passionate in protestations, and then make excuses not to see her for a week, and each time he returned he would be altered in some way.

There were immediate practical problems to deal with. The Green Street house on which Elinor had spent so much time, money and energy was only on a lease that would shortly expire. Since Clayton had left her, Elinor felt free to make decisions for a future that did not necessarily include him. The question was whether she should have another house in London?

While writing *The Sequence* she had thought a great deal about English society. She remembered the sheer boredom of the social round. Like the heroine of her novel, Guinevere, she also saw contemporary society as 'a sordid, mean, hateful place'. Whilst she had been writing *The Visits of Elizabeth* she had been able to 'glance at it, and laugh and make jest of it'. But she no longer found herself able to do this. The publication of *Three Weeks* and then her affair with Curzon had changed everything for her. She was aware of the continuing influence of the Souls on Curzon. In *The Sequence* the man Guinevere loves is similarly the focus of the attention of a group of jealous women 'who have not the slightest intention of letting him marry outside our circle, if we can prevent it'. Her sister explains the power these women wield:

> 'If ten or twelve women who are his constant companions determine upon a thing, the current is too strong for one man to resist, when he is aware they are plotting and so on his guard – and we have all been so awfully clever, poor Hugh has not an idea that sometimes we lead him by the nose.'

She warns Guinevere to keep her love a secret: 'Never let them – my friends, have a suspicion about it. They would tear you in pieces remorselessly – they would destroy you socially, and make you ridiculous to him – they are all very clever, you know child.'

Guinevere is the first of Elinor's heroines to have a sexual relationship with a lover whilst still married to another man. Like *Halcyone*, the novel ends happily enough but once again Elinor reveals an intuitive knowledge of how her affair with Curzon will end. The tacked on happy ending merely denies the situation as Elinor desperately tried to deny reality in her own life.

For a few months she continued in her usual routine, going to Cowes in August. Then she set off with Margot for Carlsbad. They were still on their way when they learnt that Clayton had decided to return home. But he had fallen ill and was stranded in a hotel in Interlaken. Margot immediately decided that she would go to Interlaken rather than Carlsbad. There she nursed her father until he was able to travel once more and then she took him to England. But Elinor continued on her way utterly exasperated by her husband's fecklessness.

When she did return to England she was forced by Clayton's presence to make some decisions. She knew that she could no longer tolerate living with him and she had little doubt that the feeling was mutual. Her first step was to take a small house in Richmond just big enough for Clayton. *The Sequence* was published in September and Elinor then felt ready to make some decisions about her own future.

She now determined not to stay in England. She was, at least in part, motivated by the need to lure Curzon away from London and the influence of the Souls. And whilst in London society she no longer shone, she knew that in Parisian society she could do so. Would that make Curzon see her as someone worthy to be acknowledged as his partner? At least it was worth a try.

The house that Elinor chose in Paris was No. 5 Avenue Victor Hugo, Parc des Princes, Boulogne-sur-Seine. At that time it was just outside Paris, though we would not consider it to be so now. It was in the Passy area which already had literary associations as it was there that Balzac had owned a house where he could escape from his creditors.

As could have been predicted, Elinor's first consideration was to redecorate her house. She wanted to impress not only Curzon but also the *literati* of Paris and her relatives. No expense was spared to achieve the effect she wanted.

By the beginning of 1914 Elinor was established in Paris. At the same time Grace Duggan, whose husband was seriously ill, took a house in Grosvenor Square.

Curzon did not immediately visit the house in the Avenue Victor Hugo but Elinor was not dismayed. She had to work on the new novel which she had promised to her American publishers Appleton and which was to be published in the States before it was published in England. Her salon was proving successful. Her St Petersburg friends visited her, as well as other writers such as the Duchesse de Noailles and members of the French aristocracy including the Duchesse de Rohan and the new wife of the Comte de Ségur, the man who had taken such an interest in her as a naive young girl on her first visit to her French relatives. It was brought home to Elinor once again how much more respected writers were in France than in England.

She visited Lucy's new acquisition, the Pavillon Mars, a little house in Versailles so called because it had been given by Napoleon to a Mademoiselle Mars.

And then in the Spring Curzon came to stay. It was one of their happiest times together. Elinor took her lover to Versailles, where, like all the men in her life, he refused to be unduly impressed by the palace. But he commissioned a new portrait of her to be done by Philip de Laszlo and he required her to wear his sapphires. Elinor took this as a sure sign of his continuing love for her.

But once Curzon had returned to London Elinor began to look on Paris with a less favourable eye. There was something in the atmosphere she did not like. There was a fever abroad. Life seemed suddenly excessively hectic. She was not alone in noticing the changed atmosphere. Her sister Lucy sensed it and unbeknown to Elinor Edith Wharton was also commenting upon it in the diaries on which she later drew for her autobiography, *A Backward Glance*. In *The Sequence* Elinor had written about the tango as 'alluringly wicked' and 'unmistakably suggestive'. Not that the tango was so very new. In 1908 *Hello Tango* had been a successful musical in London. But suddenly the tango became a metaphor for the atmosphere in Paris. At first Elinor was tolerant of it and in her *Letters To Caroline* she recommends that Caroline (Cynthia Curzon) should learn the tango but that she should be careful with whom she dances: ' "Do not cavort constantly with any creature who may have crept into the houses where you go just because he is a good Tango dancer, if he has no other qualities to recommend him." '

Her sister Lucy saw it as pure madness: 'Just at that time Paris was in grips of a positive mania for the Tango – the post War dancing wave was nothing to it. Everyone was Tango mad . . . It brought in special fashions . . . the vogue for Argentinian bands, and the gigolo.'[2]

Alarmed by the overt sexuality of this dance, 'The archbishop of Paris put out an edict forbidding young Catholic girls to perform the dance. But it was reported that when the Pope had a couple demonstrate the tango for him, his only reaction was: "My poor children! It can't be much fun." '[3]

Looking back at 1914 from the perspective of 1919 Elinor could see the tango as a 'dance macabre . . . a proof of vicious decay, the middle note of the end', that the wild dancing of the tango was in fact a presage of war or cataclysm. Elinor, who had loved the orderliness of French society, indicates in *The Price of Things* her disgust at the sight of 'mothers and daughters, grandmothers and demi-mondaines, Russian Grand Duchesses, Austrian Princesses, clasped in the arms of incredible scum from the Argentine, half-castes from Mexico, and farceurs from New York, decadent male things they would not receive in their antechambers before this madness set in!'

Perhaps it was not, after all, a good time to launch her daughters on French society, Elinor began to think. She made arrangements to travel to London in July. But before that she took the girls to celebrate 14 July at Versailles and then to stay with friends at their château near Paris. No one was thinking about war. Edith Wharton who had been in Auteuil in June staying with the painter Jacques Emile Blanche describes how the house party there reacted to the news of the assassination of the Archduke Ferdinand:

> 'Haven't you heard? The Archduke Ferdinand assassinated . . . at Serajevo . . . where is Serajevo? His wife was with him. What was her name? Both shot dead.'
>
> A momentary shiver ran through the company. But to most of us the Archduke Ferdinand was no more than a name; only one or two elderly diplomats shook their heads and murmured of Austrian reprisals.[4]

It was the sudden and apparently discourteous departure of the Austrian Ambassador from the house party that alerted Elinor to the fact that all was not well. She sent Fielder, her chauffeur, to change some money so that she would have some small bills for her journey home. He returned empty-handed. There were no small bills to be had. Perhaps there was going to be a war after all, he suggested. Elinor hastily looked through all the newspapers available. None of them had anything to say about the possible imminence of war.

Nevertheless Elinor was worried, and with her daughters made her way as quickly as possible to the Channel ferry. They were lucky to have made a booking as there were no places to spare on the crowded boats. They arrived in England on 31 July and were alarmed to see soldiers guarding all the bridges. But nothing was certain. It still seemed that war might be averted and so Elinor and Margot set off for Cowes as usual leaving Juliet at Lennox Gardens, Lucy's London home. They arrived to find confusion. No one seemed sure whether the regatta would proceed as usual.

On 4 August war was declared.

22 ♥ SHARP PRACTICE

As soon as war was declared Elinor realised that her idea of living with her family in Paris had become impossible. She had been lucky to return to England when she did. Suddenly travel became difficult. There were those like Gertrude Stein and Alice B. Toklas who were stranded in England without any money. Edith Wharton, who had just leased a house in England, found herself stuck in Paris without money. There were many such stories.

The declaration of war had the unexpected and unforeseen effect of revitalising the English. There was a new sense of purpose in the air. Everyone had a desire to pitch in and to get the war over as quickly as possible, hopefully by Christmas. Both Elinor's daughters determined to do their bit. As soon as they arrived back from Cowes Margot enlisted as a VAD and began working in the kitchen of a hospital in Park Lane. Juliet suddenly refused to return to school in Eastbourne. Instead she put up her hair and by declaring herself to be older than she was also managed to enlist as a VAD.

All around her women were becoming involved in the war effort. Elinor learnt that Millicent had enrolled with an ambulance unit. Consuelo, Duchess of Marlborough had thrown open Sunderland House for meetings and had set up a maternity hospital. Other friends were manning canteens both in London and in France.

For Elinor the immediate task was to establish a home for her daughters. Clayton was still safe in Richmond, but the girls needed to be in London. As Mrs Kennedy had by now leased a flat in Shelley Court in Tite Street, Chelsea, it was decided that the girls could live with her while Elinor continued to occupy her suite at the Ritz. This arrangement suited everyone. Mrs Kennedy enjoyed looking after her granddaughters, while Elinor had the privacy she needed for working and for seeing Curzon. And anyway she did not expect to be in England very long for she had already been approached by the French to write propaganda articles for the American press in order to encourage that country's participation in the war. All she needed were the necessary permits to travel to the front and then she would set off.

An early sign of how things were changing was the fact that there was no visit to Hackwood that year because Curzon had offered the use of his house to the exiled Queen of the Belgians. When she did see him in London Elinor sensed a change in him. She was used to his swings of mood and had not really expected to find him as relaxed as he had been in Paris. But she sensed that something was going on, something that she was not fully aware of.

And she was right. She might have managed to have Curzon to herself in Paris away from the influence of the Souls, but once he was back in England their scheming had begun again. That summer Violet, Duchess of Rutland, had made a point of having a luncheon party at her house at 14 Arlington Street specifically for the purpose of introducing her dear George to 'that pretty little Mrs Duggan'. Mrs Duggan knew how to charm. She was indeed pretty; she was young, she was lively, she was beautifully dressed and, above all, she had a lot of money.

That lunch arranged by Violet Rutland had been followed by a series of more intimate luncheon meetings about which Curzon told Elinor nothing.

Christmas came and went. Far from being over the war had become more intense. But still Elinor had to continue writing to provide for her family. Occasionally she visited Clayton. He was evidently very ill but still drinking fine brandy in large quantities. Elinor paid his bills without comment.

In March her novel *The Man and the Moment* was published. On the surface the novel reflected little of Elinor's own life at the time. It is about a young American girl and a Scots laird and the confusion in their lives resulting from their secret marriage. And yet it is tempting to see in the contrast between the two central male characters the differences Elinor perceived between Curzon and Milner. Michael Arranstoun, the husband of Sabine, behaves irresponsibly, even brutally: 'He was not a noble hero, you see, but just a strong and passionate young man – with "it"!' It is this undefinable 'it' which attracts Sabine even against her better judgement. Her feelings for him cause her to say 'Love seems to me to be a wild thing, a raging, tearing passion – Can it ever be just tender and kind?' Elinor's diary is sufficient evidence that this is exactly how she felt about Curzon.

Lord Henry Fordyce whom Sabine meets at Carlsbad, just as Elinor had met Milner, is a complete contrast. With him she has agreeable walks. She feels a great affection for him but not the overwhelming passion she feels for the far less admirable Michael. Finally she rejects the better man and is reconciled with her husband. The implications could not have been lost on Curzon.

It was also in March in London that Elinor saw the Zeppelins again. This time they were not a novel means of transport but the bringers of bombs and death. The 'bloody Zepps', as their potential victims described them, intensified Elinor's longing to make her own contribution to the war effort. Frustrated in her attempts to get the permits she needed to visit the front line, she decided to go to Paris anyway to try her luck on the spot.

In July the previous year she had left a Paris hectic with gaiety. It was a very different story just a few months later. There was very little social life; the city of light was now dark at night. Even the Ritz was quiet and sober. And yet Elinor did not feel that sense of purpose and earnestness which had been so striking in England. She was very much aware that had her daughters been young French women they would not have been allowed to work for the war as they were doing back home. Paris seemed to her to be depressed and yet ignorant of the dangers it faced.

Despite her efforts she was still unable to get permits. But she could not bear to leave Paris without achieving anything. She began to make daily visits to the Trianon Palace Hotel in Versailles where a hospital for wounded British soldiers had been set up. She took flowers and cigarettes; she wrote letters home for those soldiers too badly wounded to write for themselves. Just the sight of her in her elegant clothes was cheering to men who had been in the front line. She was immensely touched when back in London she received letters thanking her for her visits and she could feel that she had done something worthwhile.

There had been changes in England while she was away. Asquith had formed a coalition government and Curzon was back in the Cabinet as Lord Privy Seal. He remained attentive to Elinor but she knew that his improved political position was lending force to the Souls' argument that she was not the woman suited to be his intimate companion. But her fears and doubts were a little assuaged when he showed his concern about her difficulties in writing in London at that time by offering her the use of his villa Naldara at Broadstairs. She accepted his offer and throughout June worked on *The Career of Katherine Bush*. She did not know that Curzon had taken advantage of her absence to spend time with Grace Duggan in the house Grace had rented at Burfield.

Katherine Bush was proving to be a longer and more important novel than Elinor had first anticipated. It would be some time before it was ready for publication and produced some income. She was relieved, therefore, when the collection of related essays which she had been working on in Paris the previous year was published in October. *Three Things* is ostensibly about the 'three essentials to strive after in life. Truth – Common Sense and Happiness.' It is actually Elinor's musings on her own personal life and on the changes taking place around her. Once again, whether intentionally or not, she reveals a good deal about her attitude towards Curzon: 'A Woman for instance profoundly desires to retain a man's love when she sees it is waning – but her wounded vanity causes her to use methods of reproach and recrimination towards him, calculated certainly to defeat her ends, and accelerate his revolt.'

His influence is apparent in her unprogressive attitude towards 'hooligan suffragists smashing windows'. This conservative attitude is oddly contrasted with her advanced views on divorce. She expresses the opinion that divorce should be more readily available to the poor than to the rich because they suffer more in unhappy marriages.

When Elinor's lease on her suite at the Ritz expired, she did not renew it immediately. Instead she rented a flat in the building where the rest of her family was living. Her rooms were on the top floor. As usual she took some trouble redecorating them and was pleased that she had done so when she received a visit from King Alphonso of Spain. She knew him through Lucy, as his wife had been a regular customer.

No sooner was she established in Shelley Court than she set off restlessly once more for Paris. She was, therefore, not in London when the long expected death of Alfred Duggan was announced on 5 November. A few days later she received a telegram from Margot summoning her back to England, as Clayton seemed close to death. Elinor journeyed back as quickly as possible, but did not arrive in Richmond until the day after her husband had died. By then Margot had already set in train all the arrangements for her father's cremation and there was not a great deal for Elinor to do.

Although they had long been estranged, Elinor was deeply upset by her husband's death. She still remembered the man she had first married and the contrast with what he had become in his final years. As much as anything she mourned the waste of his life and the unhappiness of their last years together.

She sent a telegram to Curzon announcing Clayton's death and received in return a formal condolence. She could not know that Curzon found himself in the embarrassing position of having both the women in his life suddenly free to marry him within one month.

Not surprisingly, once Clayton's funeral was over Elinor fell ill. She did not know what to make of Curzon's continuing silence. Was he simply observing the proprieties by not approaching her, a recently bereaved widow, or was he signalling to her his intention not to marry her?

It was late November when she pulled herself together and tried to look to the future. Her prospects of getting to France to write seemed no better than they had ever been. She determined to do something of immediate use which would also take her mind off her problems. She volunteered for work at the Grosvenor Street canteen which provided hot meals for soldiers going to and from Victoria Station. Some of the men had come straight from the trenches.

As a newcomer to the organisation Elinor was given the midnight shift. She found herself in good company. She was one of many women who had not done even simple housework before and who now found themselves without even the necessary skills to be a waitress. But even they could do washing up.

In America Elinor had mixed with people of all kinds but she had never done so before in England. She had been surprised to find sensitivity and good manners in the Nevada miners who were living rough. Now she discovered that private soldiers returning home from the appalling conditions of the front also had a code of good manners which she had to admire. Slowly she was beginning to adjust her ideas about the society in which she lived. She had plenty of time to think about what she was daily learning as she walked wearily back to Tite Street through the dark streets in bad weather feeling confident that 'Women doing war work were safe in any places at any hour in those days.'

Then Curzon acquired yet another stately home, the Jacobean house at Montacute. He asked Elinor if she would undertake the supervision of the interior decoration.

Elinor, of course, could not resist this opportunity to do something for him. And she wondered to herself what this request implied. She knew, as all his friends and acquaintances knew, that Curzon was behaving most uncharacteristically. In his relationship with his wife Mary he had never allowed her to take any domestic decisions or to take responsibility for any of their houses. Why was he putting such trust in Elinor now? Could this be his oblique way of telling her that she would one day be mistress of Montacute? Her desire for this to be true made her read all the signs this way.

For the next few months Elinor divided her time between work in the canteen and work at Montacute. Lucy, who was in New York, wrote angrily to her mother about Curzon's exploitation of Elinor's good nature. She who was not in love with Curzon could see more clearly that he would never marry her sister, that he was using her for reasons of his own.

She was right. While Elinor struggled to keep warm in the unheated Somerset house, Curzon was spending a comfortable Christmas with Grace Duggan at Sunninghill.

During the lonely hours at Montacute Elinor thought a good deal about Curzon and her relationship with him over the last seven years. Now, as always, she saw him in a realistic light and she sat down one night to put her thoughts in order. 'Pen Portrait of a Great Man' is a fine piece of writing and shows how well Elinor could judge character. Her description of Curzon's attitude to women is accurate in every detail and is worth quoting at length. First of all she identifies Curzon's attitude towards women in general:

> He has always been loved by women, but he has never allowed any individual woman to have the slightest influence upon his life – it is only collectively that they influence him. He likes their society for entirely leisure moments – they are of no real importance in his scheme

of things. He likes them rather in the spirit in which other men like fine horses or good wine, or beautiful things to embellish a man's leisure, but not as equal souls worthy of being seriously considered or trusted with that scrupulous sense of honour with which he would deal with a man. They are on another planet altogether.

She shows how this general attitude is demonstrated in specific ways in his attitude towards the Souls:

> He must be free and unhampered, and his apparent submission to this group of his friends is probably merely from habit, and because they know his ways and do not give him any trouble, and continually flatter him. His attitude to them is benevolent and affectionate; his language is filled with audacious sallies. He delights in startling them and playing upon their moods, but only so long as they do not love him.

The next passage is indicative of her fear that Curzon could easily be misled by an American woman just as John Derringham in *Halcyone* was:

> He is a most passionate physical lover, but so fastidious that no woman of lower class has ever been able to attract him. Since his habit is never to study the real woman, but only to accept the superficial presentment of herself which she wishes him to receive, he is naturally attracted by Americans, who fulfil all that he requires of women: and even if he were to see how they use him for their own ends, it would only lazily entertain him as one more evidence of the nefarious ways of this astonishing sex!

She goes on to describe her own experience of being loved by Curzon and what marriage to him would entail:

> He could never love any woman with a supreme love – that love which gives body and soul to the loved one without thought but of worship. He could never allow any woman to interfere with him or influence his life, or the unconscious desire to express his own personality in doing his duty. The woman in his life would always have to have the place behind his. Thus he would load her with gifts and benefits, and with the most passionate devotion he would give her love, especially physical love, and spend time with the greatest unselfishness in thinking out schemes for her benefit. If she had sense

enough never to express her own personality in opposition to his, and greatness enough never to realise his almost divine gifts, she would be happy.

But she would have to understand him, and only take that broad splendid view of him which concerns itself with vast and noble aims. His pride would never forgive a woman who wounded it. No woman could have a real influence on him, and could only be either a solace, a servant or a slave, never a real Queen. He has probably never paid real homage to a woman in his life: it is women who pay homage to him. He is so physically attractive that he arouses passion even in the many friendships he holds casually, and it would be extremely difficult for any woman to keep her head or her senses unmoved, even in relations of pure friendship. A sensation of sex would be bound to creep in.

He never gives a woman a single command, and yet each one must be perfectly conscious that she must obey his slightest indirection. He rules entirely, and when a woman belongs to him, he seems to prefer to give her even the raiment which touches her skin, and in every tangible way shows absolute possession, while in words avoiding all suggestion of ownership, all ties, and all obligations, upon either side. It is extremely curious.

Her concluding comments are of a more general nature describing the public man:

He is Olympian, not Dionysiac. The noblest ruler ever since August Caesar elevated Rome.

His will is of iron. His nerve and resource never fail him. The necessity for activity dominates him to such an extent that it has obscured somewhat the line between actual duty and pleasure.

He is arrogant, and this is one of his great charms. Because his arrogance is unconscious, it is of the true and real aristocrat . . .

His own manners are those of the greatest grand seigneur, polished, courteous and aloof in general company, and stern and icy when he is preoccupied. He can withdraw into himself, and then he is unapproachable even by his children. But he has charm, and can convert an enemy into a friend by one of his beautifully expressed sentences and his rare smiles. He has a loveableness, and at times a childishness and playfulness.[1]

The style and quality of this essay on Curzon is quite different from all that Elinor had written and continued to write about him in her diary. Only in *Romantic Adventure* does she again achieve this kind of objectivity. She was on this occasion putting the facts clearly to herself as she struggled to come to terms with the affair and its possible, if not probable, conclusion. What she had written before had always been in response to Curzon. Here she was responding not to a specific encounter, but trying to look clear-sightedly at the man she loved. What she in fact told herself was that she could never be this man's wife. Although in her diary she used terms like 'Idol', 'Lord' and 'god', in practice she is unlikely to have been able to live comfortably in the shadow of such a dominating man. When she was a young woman she could, perhaps, have adjusted herself to Curzon's demands just as Mary Leiter had done. But at her age, a woman who had supported a family for some years, who had travelled and socialised alone and on her own terms, she would not have been able to subordinate her personality as completely as she recognised Curzon would have required.

From this point on a new note enters into everything she says about the relationship with Curzon. She now knew what she should do; her only difficulty was in putting this knowledge into practice.

Early in the new year Curzon was again spending time with Grace Duggan, this time at Ratton in Eastbourne. When she was asked to move from this coastal spot because she was an alien, Curzon intervened on her behalf and she was allowed to remain.

Without having any real evidence Elinor was fairly sure that Curzon was less whole-heartedly in love with her than he had been. At the very least his new position in the government was causing him to withdraw from her. She wrote in her diary, 'The moment might come when you would again think only of what was best for you, and then what would become of me? Should I die, or simply go to hell?' On another occasion she expressed her inability to stop loving Curzon despite her knowledge of his real nature: 'I care not whether you are selfish, as everyone says, or no. I care not if you are famous, or no. Nothing can change my absolute love.'[2]

Curzon continued to see both women. Grace Duggan may have heard rumours about Curzon's earlier relationship with Elinor, but at Montacute, cut off from the rest of the world, Elinor did not know of Curzon's increasing attentions to Grace Duggan. In other circumstances she would almost certainly have heard from Minnie Paget about Grace Duggan's visit to Hackwood at Whitsuntide.

If Curzon had any lingering doubts about what course of action he should take, these were dispelled entirely when his father Lord Scarsdale died and he inherited Kedleston Hall in Derbyshire. Curzon was passionate about the house. He had already poured a good deal of Mary Leiter's money into its restoration and improvement and he had begun to use the money left by Mary, in trust, to their daughters. He knew that source of income would dry up the minute the girls came of age. He absolutely needed a rich wife if he was to continue the work on Kedleston on which he had set his heart.

In August he took Grace to see the newly acquired Bodiam Castle and then at Winchelsea he proposed marriage. After some hesitation Grace accepted and they became secretly engaged. The engagement had to be secret for two reasons. First of all Grace Duggan's husband had been dead for less than a year. She did not wish to flout convention by marrying before the prescribed year of mourning was over. Secondly, though Grace was unaware of this consideration, Curzon had to decide what to do about Elinor, who was at that very moment working on Montacute and dreaming of becoming mistress there.

Grace sailed for Argentina in September to see her parents-in-law whom she had not seen since their son's death and to oversee her financial affairs in that country. The couple had decided to announce their engagement on 11 December in *The Times*. Grace would return on 20 December and they would be married on 22 December.

While Grace was away Curzon wrote to her lovingly, professing his absolute devotion to her. At the same time he was regularly visiting Elinor at Montacute. When Elinor asked him point blank if he had fallen in love with someone else, he denied it. She wrote in her diary:

> I know that all is transient, nothing lasts at its zenith. The zenith of my worship of you, my heart, is passed – at least, I hope it has passed, but I never know . . . Sometimes I have felt it can only be because you have grown to love some other woman that you are so cruel to me. But you yourself, when I asked you, told me it was not so, and you would never lie to me or try to deceive me. You said it was nothing I had done and that you loved me the same as ever, only it was circumstances and your life . . . For even if you are ruthless, you are pure and noble and I know you would never stoop as other men do to women. I have at least that complete trust in your word

and your honour, so I must comfort myself with that and try to grow completely numb.

Having failed to break the news of his engagement to Elinor, Curzon returned to London. He summoned Consuelo, Duchess of Marlborough, to visit him and in floods of tears he put his problem before her. But still he did not tell Elinor the truth.

It would, perhaps, have been small comfort to Elinor to know that she was not alone at this time in being deceived by Curzon. His behaviour politically echoed his behaviour in the matter of his marriage.

Asquith too put trust in Curzon's words and he was shocked to be abandoned by him when Curzon joined Lloyd George's coalition government and was given a place in the Cabinet. Robert Blake's words about Curzon's treatment of Asquith are just as relevant to his treatment of Elinor: 'It is difficult to acquit Curzon of a considerable measure of sharp practice in all these transactions.'[3]

Curzon's engagement was announced as planned in *The Times* on 11 December. Elinor was at Montacute where there was no telephone. It was only on 17 December that the newspaper reached her and she became aware of Curzon's treachery. She wrote in great distress to a friend, 'Oh, that he whom I adored, whose nobility I treasured, whose probity I worshipped, could prove so faithless and so vile!'

At last Elinor had Curzon's true measure. She left Montacute never to return.

In the midst of her misery about Curzon Elinor received yet another blow. She had taken to court Weston Feature Film Company alleging that their film *Pimple's Three Weeks (Without the Option)* was a violation of her copyright of *Three Weeks*. Early in November both sides had presented their cases but it was not until 21 December that written judgement was given by Judge Younger.

Whatever Elinor had hoped for from this case she certainly did not anticipate that she would receive a public reprimand for having written a 'grossly immoral' novel.

The judgement is an extraordinary document, for the judge takes it upon himself to offer a plot summary and a critical analysis of both the novel and the film. *Pimple's Three Weeks* he describes as 'frankly farcical', 'vulgar to an almost inconceivable degree' and 'indecently offensive'. The film makers who had consciously made a 'screaming farce' were not likely to have been worried by such criticisms.

But for Elinor to have her novel described in print as follows for everyone to read was almost intolerable:

> . . . a glittering record of adulterous sensuality masquerading as superior virtue . . . calculated . . . to mislead into belief that she may without danger choose the easy life of sin many a poor romantic girl striving amidst manifold hardships and discouragements to keep her honour untarnished.

The judge concluded by saying that 'to a book of such cruelly destructive tendency no protection will be extended by a Court of Equity. It rests with others to determine whether such a work ought not to be altogether suppressed.'[4]

In other words, because he considered *Three Weeks* to be immoral the judge decreed that it was not entitled to the copyright protection normally available to literary works.

Not only did Elinor fail to establish her entitlement to copyright she was ordered to pay her own costs. Far worse even than the financial loss, in Elinor's view, was the disgrace of having her novel once more held up as an example of gross immorality and the subsequent loss of her much prized dignity. All her old wounds on this score were once more re-opened.

Elinor thought her life could hardly be more miserable but she was to suffer yet one more humiliation when on 2 January Grace Duggan was married from the Ritz, the place that Elinor considered her second home.

Recognising fully that she would never again be close to Curzon Elinor burnt the five hundred letters that she had received from him. After that symbolic gesture she then looked about her for ways of starting a new life.

23 WAR

'There is not one that hath been transported to the mad degree of love, which shows that great spirits and great business do keep out this weak passion.'

These words from Bacon are quoted in *The Career of Katherine Bush.* Elinor now set about proving their truth. Her first task was to finish the novel. It was not easy to give the book the happy ending she had planned. For the career of Katherine Bush, unlike that of Elinor, culminates in her being happily married to a charismatic Duke and with her giving birth to the longed-for heir. Perhaps this is why the ending is the least convincing part of what is otherwise a sharply acerbic novel.

In many other aspects it is a book ideally suited for the times in its depiction of a young woman who does not allow her lower middle class origins to prevent her from acquiring an education, establishing herself in a successful career and marrying into the upper classes. So many women who, because of the war, were doing jobs which would have been considered impossible a few years earlier, wanted to read this kind of story which mirrored their own best hopes. The war had meant the casting off of many old attitudes and gentilities and Katherine Bush's unabashed honesty and ambition were greatly appreciated.

In these years there was also a greater frankness about sexuality, though perhaps few young women would have gone quite so far as did Katherine Bush in setting out deliberately to lose her virginity because 'she decided her experience must be more complete'. And, although Katherine is not a suffragette, she likes 'women to advance in everything', and for herself has reached the radical conclusion that 'For a woman to throw over her future for a man was to her completely contemptible.'

The aristocracy as seen through this ruthless young woman's eyes does not appear to advantage. True there are two whom she greatly admires, Lady Garribardine who is modelled on Theresa Lady Londonderry, and the Duke of Mordyn who has many of Curzon's qualities but none of his faults. But the sense of class responsibility exhibited by these two simply shows up the general idleness and irresponsibility of the majority of their peers.

The book was generally well received and by some critics declared to be Elinor's best novel to date. There were others, Anthony Glyn being one, who found the heroine 'the most dislikeable of all Elinor's heroines'. Another man who found Katherine Bush hard to take was William Randolph Hearst. He preferred quite another type of heroine as his predilection for chorus girls indicates. He had planned to serialise the novel in *Cosmopolitan* but wanted some changes which would soften the nature of the central character.

Although Lucy had been writing for the Hearst Press for some time, this was Elinor's first direct contact with William Randolph Hearst himself. She flatly refused to change her story and even risked losing the sale altogether. Hearst was eventually won over and *The Career of Katherine Bush* was serialised in *Cosmopolitan*. It was not the last time that these two strong willed people would come into contact.

Fortunately, as soon as *Katherine Bush* was safely in production, Elinor's long awaited permits to go to the Front as a journalist became available.

In April, the month in which *Katherine Bush* was published, Elinor made the increasingly hazardous journey to France. On this occasion the passengers on the channel boat were required to wear life jackets for the whole of the crossing which took a day and a night.

She decided not to live in her house in Boulogne-sur-Seine at this time as she needed to be closer to the centre of things. She was also influenced by the fact that in that hard winter fuel had become scarce. She did not want to waste her time on housekeeping. She took a room on the rue Cambon side of the Ritz which was less fashionable and so less expensive than the Place Vendôme side. In the Ritz she could at least be sure of heat and food.

From this vantage point she was well able to assess the quality of life in Paris. To her astonishment the Parisians were behaving as though there was no war. The depression she had witnessed on her previous visit had been replaced by what seemed to her a vicious gaiety which contrasted harshly with the wartime spirit in England. Whereas food was controlled in England, in Paris there did not appear to be shortages. There was a disturbing sexuality in the air emphasised by the obvious presence in numbers of women from the demi-monde. Elinor noted, 'The women have a sex-urge, but they are vicious with over-civilisation. They want men, they do not want children.'

In England Elinor and her daughters had worked alongside all classes of women for the war effort. In France, even at this late stage of the war, young women of good family were not allowed to do such work. Apart from some notable exceptions such as the Duchesse de Rohan who had turned her house into a hospital and the Comtesse de la Berodière who had opened her house in the Parc Monceau to British officers on leave, the French aristocracy in general was holding aloof from war work.

Elinor was shocked. Her belief in France and its civilisation was suddenly shaken. 'What has become of the proud old French race?' she asked, and concluded, 'So much of the aristocracy here in Paris seems to be just *fin de race*.'

Some of the bitterness and bewilderment she felt at this time appears later in the novel *Man and Maid*. There are the three young Frenchwomen who ask,

> 'After all, will it be as agreeable if peace does come this summer? – one will be able to dance openly – that will be nice – but for the rest? It may be things will be more difficult – and there may be complications. One has been very well during the war – very well, indeed.'

In the novel criticism is not confined to the behaviour of the French. There are English and Americans in Paris who take the war just as lightly. The Duchess who has turned her house into a hospital rages, 'France is full of sensible kind Americans and English – but those in Paris – they make me sick! Quarter of an hour twice a day – to have the right to a passport to come – and to wear a uniform – Pah! Sick, sick!'

Elinor, however, was in France for a serious purpose. She had a uniform made for herself in elegant khaki. There were good practical reasons for wearing khaki and she wanted to present herself as business-like but attractive. She knew already from her hospital visits how good for morale was a well-dressed woman. When she was advised to make her will before setting out to do her job, Elinor realised fully just what she had undertaken.

Her first day as a war correspondent was very nearly her last. A young American driver turned up at the Ritz in a Red Cross car to drive her to Compiègne. He was surprised when she chose to sit in the back rather than next to him but put it down to some British snobbishness. Elinor herself was not sure why she made this decision. But then the driver misjudged the width of a tram and the front side of the car where Elinor should have been sitting was badly damaged. Any passenger would have been killed, and both she and her driver felt she had been saved by a premonition.

She continued her journey with a French officer and a chauffeur and by nightfall was at Compiègne where she had a meal at French GHQ. Some of her faith in France and the French was restored by her contact with these hard-working and serious officers. And then, as she began to tour the battle lines close to Compiègne the full horror of what French troops, British troops and ordinary French people were experiencing came home to her.

She wrote after seeing Bailly where a large village had been reduced to a 'series of huge stones' and where fruit trees in bloom had been wantonly hacked down by the Germans, 'I had not understood the actual hideousness and cruelty of wars until that moment.'

She was deeply moved in Forêt de L'Aigle to see in the midst of devastation lilies of the valley in bloom. Then there were the trenches.

> I had seen photographs of trenches, of course, but no picture gives the impression of the real thing, for the colour – and the stench – are lacking. I could imagine the sheer horror of going down into this terrible place, with its foul smell and its cramped space, and of having to crouch there for hours and days.

Although Elinor had been in London while bombs were dropped from Zeppelins, she found being close to the front line and hearing guns quite a different matter. 'It is a solemn moment when one first hears the sound of guns – guns not firing volleys in honour of some public rejoicing, not exploding empty shells at reviews, but guns deliberately aimed at human beings with the intention to kill.'

Elinor was not safe from danger herself. On one occasion near

Soissons the car she was travelling in was pursued by a German aircraft. The French officer who was driving pushed her out of the car and dragged her into a gravel pit by the road. There they ate sandwiches and drank a bottle of white wine until the danger was past. His gaiety and courage in such circumstances impressed Elinor. It was exactly the kind of behaviour she most admired.

Even more uncomfortable was the day when the shelling was so bad that the French general with the 3rd Army made Elinor and all the other war correspondents take shelter with him in a deep dug-out. Elinor's claustrophobia almost overcame her. She realised that to be brave was to control fear rather than to feel none. She summoned up all her grandmother's training, and no one else in the dug-out knew the terror she felt. But she never forgot what it had been like to feel buried alive and she used the experience to brilliant effect when she came to write *Six Days*.

At Péronne she witnessed the devastation of the village. At first it seemed that no one had been left alive. Then they discovered a family living in a cellar. They had been there for some weeks. The family was starving and they were grateful for food except for one of the young women, who Elinor discovered was named Fleurette. She was reluctant to be brought back to life and the misery of all around her. Much moved by her distress, Elinor wrote about this incident to Lucy who immediately saw its potential for raising money. She put on a performance of 'Fleurette's Dream in Péronne', and indeed did raise quite a lot of money which was given to Secours Franco-Américains Pour La France Dévastée.

There were many nights that Elinor did not sleep in a bed. A car or even a ditch sometimes had to suffice. On one occasion she was arrested as a spy, for she did look the most unlikely war correspondent. She produced all the permits which validated her position so close to the front, but the soldiers insisted on searching her bag. For some inexplicable reason it was the sight of her pink satin nightdress which convinced them that she was genuine.

She had no need of that particular garment on the night she watched St Quentin being bombarded. At nightfall the elderly French officer who was accompanying her on her tour and their chauffeur decided that they must take shelter. All that was immediately available was a house in a ruined village. This had received a hit which had blown its front off so that it looked like a child's doll's house. With real gallantry the Frenchman insisted that Elinor should sleep on the one remaining bedstead in an upstairs room with the car rug to cover her while they slept where they could downstairs. But there was no sleep that night. As if in the front row at a theatrical spectacular Elinor watched the destruction of St Quentin.

> The livid sky above reflected the scarlet flames that leapt upwards as the fire swept through the town. The bursting shells hurled great masses of earth and masonry into the air, while the gaunt, magnificent old cathedral stood out black against the glow, as if defying the forces of evil.

It was quite shocking to return to Paris and the comparative luxury of the Ritz to find herself, after all she had been through, upset at the trivial matter of a squashed Reboux hat. It brought home to Elinor that people were only surviving the horror of it all by assuming an 'extraordinary callousness and indifference to suffering and death, even one's own'.

Her close involvement with the war had made her more or less indifferent to a matter which would have been cause for rejoicing and triumph only a few years earlier. Her agent, Hughes Massie, had decided to try once more to get a production of *Three Weeks* mounted on the London stage. He felt it necessary, however, to present the Lord Chamberlain with a completely new script. Roy Horniman was commissioned to do the work with the result that on 12 July 1917 *Three Weeks* opened once again, this time at the Strand Theatre. Had Elinor been present she would not have recognised the play as having much to do with her novel. But in its softened and changed form it managed a three month term in London and was then taken on tour.

The money was useful but more important for Elinor's financial well-being was Duckworth's agreement with Jonathan Cape to bring out a cheap edition of her books at a shilling each. Suddenly a whole new readership of women who had not been able to afford the hardback editions of her work was created.

She continued, however, to view Paris with a jaundiced eye. Even though regular bombardments by Big Bertha had begun it seemed to Elinor that no one in Paris had the slightest doubt that victory was inevitable. She was horrified when people used the petrol which was in such short supply to drive out, just for a frisson, to see the damage done by Big Bertha. When she became Vice-President of Secours Franco-Américains with Mrs Prince of Boston as President, her disillusionment only increased. She was put in charge of resettling the area of Noyon which she had only recently visited. Temporary shelter for the original inhabitants had to be found, and they had to be helped and encouraged in that war-torn place to plant new crops as there were terrible food shortages. But Elinor found herself frustrated and thwarted every step of the way by chaotic committee meetings and the unwillingness of the French members to take matters seriously.

When the Americans began to arrive in December they provided a great contrast. They were serious, well-organised, well-equipped and healthy. Like Winston Churchill, Elinor found the very sight of the young American soldiers rejuvenating. She was, therefore, all the more horrified by what she saw as the ungrateful response of the Parisians. Edith Wharton, who was also working in Paris at the time, was less surprised. She saw, as Elinor did not, that, at least initially, the Americans' calm conviction that they could quite quickly sort out the backward French was deeply offensive. She wrote a book *French Customs and Ways* to try to help both sides understand and appreciate the differences between them.

At New Year Elinor decided that something had to be done and so she organised a party for American officers. She wanted to give the impression that it was a French welcome and so she enlisted the help of the Comtesse de Sainte Aldegonde and persuaded her to allow her house on the Avenue du Bois to be used. Along with Mabel Malet and the Comtesse de Luart she press-ganged French women from Secours Franco-Américains into appearing as 'hostesses'. But the party did not bring the French and the Americans closer. If anything it emphasised the coldness between them and made Elinor's French co-workers increasingly suspicious and resentful of her.

At about the same time as the Americans began to arrive Alfred Milner appeared in Paris in his role as a member of the War Cabinet. He took a room at the Ritz and was glad to spend his free time with Elinor. She attracted him as much as ever. She, for her part, was grateful to him for his continuing devotion after the terrible betrayal by Curzon. Not that she was short of admirers in Paris. She struck up a friendship with the American Provost Marshal, General

Allaire, and she was frequently joined at her corner table in the Ritz dining room by the British military Attaché Colonel Le Roy Lewis and his friend General Spears. The latter was of particular interest to Elinor as he was embarking on a passionate love affair with the American heiress and novelist, Mary Borden.

From the conversations which took place at her table Elinor was pretty well aware of how the war was progressing. Even the Parisians could not fail to be aware of the approaching German army. One night when the warnings sounded Elinor heard a knock at her door. There was Henry (Chips) Channon who had taken the trouble to cross the Ritz from one side to the other to escort her to the hallway where all the guests were being assembled. Elinor in her pink negligée, fluffy mule slippers, lace cap and fur coat was one of the least strangely dressed in that oddly assorted gathering. For example, the former Russian ambassador to Stockholm, with whom she whiled away the hours until it was possible to return safely to her room, wore a heavy leather coat over a nightshirt; on his head was a slouch hat, his legs were bare and on his feet were slippers that were rather too large for him. Only determinedly respectable elderly American women, clutching their jewel cases, and staff officers who had not yet gone to bed when the alarm sounded were dressed in their normal day clothes.

The hectic and sometimes dangerous life Elinor had been leading for some months began to tell on her health. In the spring of 1918 she fell ill first with influenza and then laryngitis. Clearly she could not be a useful worker until she was well again and so she was persuaded to leave Paris for a short stay in St Raphael. Just before her return to the capital she visited Nice. The contrast between the atmosphere of gaiety, the abundance of food, and luxury goods, and the suffering she had seen elsewhere appalled her. Her disgust hastened her on her journey back to Paris and comparative reality. There she found conditions had worsened rapidly. The city was now under constant attack. One night she attended a concert at which the pianist could hardly be heard above the sound of falling shells. That was the night that the gardens of the Tuileries were struck and also the Ritz.

British personnel in Paris were becoming alarmed for the safety of civilians like Elinor and she was urged to leave for England. She consulted Milner and told him that she was reluctant to leave France. He suggested that the best way for her to remain and at the same time to be useful was for her to respond to the request made by the Americans that she should visit the troops, many of whom were admirers of her work. So on 12 June she set off for the American base camps at St Nazaire. Once again she was impressed by the sheer competence of the Americans. She toured camps and drill huts and was everywhere received with gratifying warmth. She took her role seriously and in each place would stage a recitation of the piece she had written after visiting Bailly, *Destruction*. She would dress in black and stand on an improvised stage in front of the American flag with a single spotlight highlighting her pale face and red hair. She moved many of her audience to tears.

All the time she was doing this work she was working on a new novel, *The Price of Things*, and taking notes which she subsequently used for a series of letters from Elizabeth's daughter travelling around the American base camps in France in the company of a red-haired, green-eyed writer, the authoress of an infamous novel entitled *Nine Months*. These letters were later serialised in a Hearst Press journal, *Novel Magazine*, but they were never published as a book.

Elinor had not seen her mother and two daughters for almost a year. But in July she managed to make a brief trip to England. Both girls were prospering. Margot was secretary to the Deputy Chief of Air Staff and Juliet to Admiral Richmond. Mrs Kennedy was happy looking after her granddaughters.

What surprised Elinor when she was back in Paris once more was a new and growing hostility on the part of the French towards the British. Even people she knew quite well who had always been polite and pleasant previously were now calculatedly insulting to her. She never really understood how it had come about. The unpleasantness continued until the announcement of the Armistice.

That November day in 1918 was a memorable one. Paris had become a quiet city during the war years. The loudest and most persistent noises had been the roar of Big Bertha and the sound of airplanes fighting overhead. On this day the quiet was broken by the sound of church bells. Gradually more and more joined in until Paris was alive with the sound of the exultant bells and the clamour of excited voices.

The war was over.

24 INTERIM

With the end of the war came a flood of visitors to Paris. At the Ritz Elinor found that the new social life was distracting her from her work, and she could not afford to stop writing. She had to write a series of articles commissioned by several magazines; she had to polish up *Destruction* for publication, and there was her novel to finish. She did not give up her rooms at the Ritz but in addition rented a modest apartment over what had once been stables in the rue Peintre Le Brun. She was only slightly further away from the Palace than she had been at the Hôtel des Réservoirs. Inevitably she spent some time redecorating before she moved in and started work.

But the war had changed a great deal. Elinor's whole-hearted admiration for Louis XIV and his court was tempered by her sense of what it had all led to. The attitude towards Versailles expressed in *Man and Maid* is almost bitter:

> The architects were great, the King's thought was great – but only in one way – and everyone – the whole class – forgot the real meaning of noblesse-oblige and abused their power – and so the revolution swept them away – they put false values upon everything – false values upon birth and breeding – and no value upon their consequent obligations, or upon character.

Revolution was very much in Elinor's mind after the events in Russia the previous March. And, although she felt the Czarina had been a hard and haughty woman, she was distressed at what was happening to those people she had been close to quite recently. It was not mere coincidence that one of the central characters of the novel she was just finishing was a Russian noble.

The germ of the narrative of *The Price of Things* had come from gossip passed on to her by Lucy some time ago. The story was that a certain aristocrat, desperate for an heir, had casually remarked to his wife that she should find a man who could get her pregnant.

Taking him at his word she had done just that only to be met with the husband's appalled anger.

Elinor gave the story an added piquancy by having the husband persuade his look-alike cousin to do the deed. The wife Amaryllis discovers the plot only after she has conceived and the whole plan is thrown into disarray when she falls in love with the father of her child.

The novel is set in wartime and is an indication of how much the war had changed Elinor's attitudes. It would have been unthinkable for her to have written the following when she was still under the influence of Curzon: 'If the politicians could have that dogged, serene steadfastness which the Tommies and almost every man has in the trenches, how supreme we should be.'

And he certainly would not have approved of the view that 'Every man and woman who works should have the right to a good home.'

In fact Elinor had Curzon very much in her mind when she was writing this novel. For she knew only too well that one of the disadvantages that she had suffered when Curzon was thinking about marrying was that she could not conceive and provide the heir he was most anxious to have. She probably relished the irony that, although the woman he did marry had already had sons and although she gave up her gay social life for a year, she had not and would not provide an heir.

A letter from Curzon's daughter Cimmie at this time added to the irony of the situation. For Cimmie had written to Elinor rather than to her stepmother for advice. Cimmie at twenty wanted a life very different from the one her father had envisaged for her. She had developed a new sense of society as she worked as a clerk in the War Office and then as a land girl. She wanted to lead a useful life and, if she had to go into politics to do so, it would certainly not be as a Conservative.

Elinor's reply to Curzon's daughter was not one he would have approved of. Elinor supported Cimmie's desire to do something with her life: 'You were born with great beauty, great position, charm, riches, a certain amount of talent, a strong will – what huge gifts! What are you going to do with them? Drift on, doing no particular harm, but certainly no good?'[1]

She even went so far as to advocate socialism of a kind: 'The true socialism should be to help change conditions so that every child has an equal chance until it comes to fifteen, say, and then sift the chaff from the corn.'

Closer to home Elinor had concerns about her own family. Lucy, who had been in the States for the duration of the war, much to the disgust of her daughter and husband, had tried to get Elinor to side with her in a business battle with Cosmo. She had wanted to sign over most of the business to an American, John Shuloff, whilst Cosmo had been adamantly opposed to this move. At first Elinor had agreed to support Lucy but then, even with her poor business sense, she had realised it was not a good idea. She knew from previous experience that Cosmo was more likely to be astute in such a matter than Lucy, and so she withdrew her backing. Lucy had, however, got her own way. The result had been just what Cosmo had predicted and Lucy suddenly found that she no longer not only had no place in the American business but that her London branch could only continue to trade under the name Lucile with permission from John Shuloff.

It was a discontented Lucy who had left America and an even more discontented woman who had left London and arrived in Paris. She installed herself at the Ritz. Elinor had the job of telling her that her beloved Pavillon Mars had been used as a billet for officers during the war and would need to be completely redecorated.

After an initial period of sulking Lucy set to work on a new collection to present in Paris. Elinor attended the showing but she was aware that Lucy's clothes were no longer fashionable or even suitable for everyday wear. Her long stay away from Europe had made her out of touch. What particularly worried Elinor was that the income Mrs Kennedy relied on from her initial investment in Lucile was now at risk and that she, Elinor, would have to make good the difference.

These gloomy thoughts were pushed aside temporarily by Milner's return to Paris and his growing possessiveness in relationship to her. When she planned to visit London briefly in April he asked her to wait a few days so that he could be there at the same time. He saw a good deal of her on that occasion. When they were both in Paris once more, he staying at the Majestic and Elinor at the Ritz, he was addressing her as 'My dear Elinor', and planning a timetable which meant that he would be with her for part of every day during one week.

17. Prince Gritzko Wittgenstein who was the inspiration for the hero of *His Hour*. Elinor first met him in Egypt in 1902 and for ever remembered him as 'the most physically attractive creature whom I have ever met'.

8. Grand Duchess Kiril, who ıvited Elinor to Russia in 1910. he had a 'peculiar unconscious harm, a downright honest ıanner'.

19. Elinor in love. Her portrait by Philip de Laszlo commissioned by Curzon.

20. In this second portrait by Laszlo Elinor presents herself as The Lady of *Three Weeks*. She wears the jewellery given to her by Curzon.

21. Elinor with her two daughters, who are now in uniform, in 1918. They survey a devastated area near Compiègne in France.

22. Elinor in Paris in 1919 wondering whether to follow Lucy's advice and 'deliberately marry a millionaire . . . and never have to work any more'.

23. 'Madame Glyn' the scriptwriter with Gloria Swanson in 1921. Elinor described Swanson as 'a very remarkable actress, extremely intelligent, and filled with strong personal attraction'.

24. Following Elinor's instructions, Rudolph Valentino as Lord Brackendale in *Beyond The Rocks* kisses the palm of his leading lady, Gloria Swanson.

25. Elinor in Hollywood in 1923. 'Self-centred, callous and addicted to money' is her description of herself at this time.

26. A publicity photograph of Elinor and Aileen Pringle in 1923. Elinor was delighted that the girl selected to play the Queen in *Three Weeks* looked so much like her younger self.

27. Elinor with her mother Mrs Kennedy in 1933. Elinor said that her mother 'successfully laughed at Father Time all her life'.

28. Elinor in 1936. 'I thank God daily for my unimpaired faculties and unwrinkled skin'.

29. Elinor with her cats named after Voltaire's characters, Zadig and Candide.

30. Elinor, the by now legendary author of *Three Weeks*, complete with her tiger skins, in Connaught Place in 1936.

It was especially flattering to Elinor's ego to be seen around so much with Milner, as at that very time the new Lady Curzon, accompanied by Cimmie, was in Paris. Elinor heard through gossip that already there was trouble in the marriage and that Grace Curzon was said to be ' "fed-up" with George Nathaniel'.[2]

Although most of the foreigners in Paris that summer were there for the serious purpose of negotiating the terms of the Peace Treaty at Versailles, they managed to have a lively social life. There was dancing at the Majestic most nights and there were many dinner parties. Elinor was invited frequently to parties given by Lord Riddell, who was there as the Press Liaison Officer. His dinners were good and the company interesting. On one of these occasions Elinor met Sir William Orpen who was there to paint the signing of the Peace and who was busily employed in doing individual portraits prior to embarking on painting the group. He and Elinor enjoyed each other's company. Then Elinor learned with horror that Lucy had also met the famous painter. She had come across him at Versailles working at his easel. Because his appearance was unprepossessing Lucy had assumed he was a poor old man trying to scratch a living together by copying the work of more famous painters and had tried to tip him.

One of the people in Paris at that time whom Elinor was eager to meet was the Prime Minister, David Lloyd George. Although Curzon had accepted a Cabinet position from him Elinor knew that the two men did not like each other and were not politically close. Her own political views were undergoing a change and she was curious to meet the man who had for so long been represented to her as the enemy. Her opportunity came when she was invited to dinner at the apartment in rue Nilot where Lloyd George was at that time living. The apartment was furnished with valuable French antiques such as Elinor herself loved. But she found that they were less of a pleasure than an unwanted responsibility to Lloyd George who was too worried about damaging them to be comfortable.

Before long she was involved in an intense conversation with her host. She found she was greatly impressed by him. He was smarter and better dressed than his newspaper photos had suggested, and his voice charmed her. When he was conversing with her she found his eyes had an almost hypnotic effect upon her, especially as he gave her his entire attention to the apparent exclusion of everyone else in the room.

Unwittingly Elinor antagonised Frances Stevenson, who played the piano that evening, by her attention to Lloyd George. She was not to know that Miss Stevenson was not simply Lloyd George's secretary but also his lover, and that she was tired of seeing him monopolised by society ladies.

In her diary Elinor recorded the meeting. Her pen portrait of the Prime Minister is as fine a piece of writing in its own way as her description of Curzon. She made other fine portraits of the politicians assembled in Paris including an unfavourable one of the American President, Woodrow Wilson, which she concludes with the comment, 'I feel that no one believes in him less than he does himself.'

The Peace was to be signed in the Hall of Mirrors at Versailles on 28 June 1919. Elinor was anxious to witness this historic occasion and Lord Riddell made sure that she got a press pass which would allow her to attend the signing. The only other woman privileged to be present was Frances Stevenson.

Despite the grandeur of the setting in that long Hall of glittering glass and twinkling chandeliers with the paintings of Louis XIV's military victories on the ceiling as a reminder to the Germans of France's earlier glory, the occasion was not at all what Elinor had expected. First of all the press had to be in place hours before the signatories arrived. Because Elinor was so much smaller than most of the press present, she had to stand on a bench and was all the time fearful of falling. But her account of the actual signing shows her characteristic ability to catch the significant detail and bring the scene alive for the reader. This is the account she submitted to the *News of the World* (a very different and more responsible paper in those days) for publication on 29 June.

> A hushed hum of voices, the grave faces of the statesmen and delegates silent at their table. Clemenceau's jaw set firm, dark coated press men at one end of the Hall of Mirrors, guests at the other, the only note of brightness the helmets of the National Guard, and here and there a uniform of khaki or blue.
>
> That was the first impression.
>
> Then waiting, waiting, waiting, with the increased tension of nerves and at last, from the end by the Queen's apartments, five depressed looking men emerged, frock coated, spectacled, unprepossessing. These are the Germans. Look at them well.

> The fair one's lips are trembling, and the tall, thin man, with his eyes close together, frowns. But they are very quiet and very pale, only there is some cynical look in the fourth man's eyes. Is he thinking of the scrap of paper which perforce the five must sign? Who knows?
>
> They rise suddenly believing their moment has come, but subside again when the ringing voice of France's saviour begins his short harangue. Crisp and trenchant and powerful the words fall on our ears: 'An agreement of peace between the Allied and Associated Governments and the German State.'
>
> 'The German State.'
>
> Not the proud Kingdom of Prussia, or the Empire of other days, but just a newborn republic which, tomorrow, may be gone. No splendid Hohenzollerns, in brilliant uniforms bursting with pride sit there, but huddled in their places, five plebian German men. Then, when the short statement is ended, and its translation in English proclaimed, the five rise reluctantly and walk forward to sign. How quickly it all passes, this for ever historic scene. They affix their signatures hurriedly as though in haste to be gone, and then the ignoble figures file back to their places again and the thin upright form of President Wilson is seen moving forward to sign. How he smiles as he returns to his place at the table, followed by Colonel House. Is he thinking that a burden has fallen from his shoulders, and that he can now go home?
>
> How slowly they walk the Englishmen, and how unmoved they are. Mr Lloyd George seems grave and solemn as he bends to take the pen. Then Mr Balfour stately grey can be seen advancing and Lord Milner, Mr Bonar Law and Mr Barnes. What are they all thinking also? Shall we ever know? The silence grows denser than ever, and the Frenchmen rise in their turn. Clemenceau, Pichon, Lotz Tardieu and Clambon each bends down to sign. After this come the Italians, and then the smaller nations. And so at last, an end. But the climax has passed with Clemenceau, and the great deed is done. Sic transit gloria Mundi.

The signing over, there was the same feeling of anticlimax in Paris. The delegates began to leave. Now was the moment when Elinor thought that Alfred Milner might propose to her. She did not love him but she had a strong affection for him and she could imagine herself living with him on harmonious terms.

Milner, however, was having second thoughts. It was not that he did not care for Elinor, as he explained to her. Rather it was that he cared too much. She aroused in him a physical passion which alarmed him. He was very conscious that while he had been in Paris he had found himself spending more and more time with Elinor and less time than he felt proper on his work. He was a serious politician, dedicated to the service of his country. He feared that his career was not compatible with his passion for Elinor. He did not altogether rule out marriage eventually but he did not feel ready to commit himself at that moment. He left Paris.

Elinor was convinced now that the moment was past and that he would never marry her. She wrote home to her mother in some bitterness about Milner's decision.

Lucy, whom she visited once a week at Pavillon Mars, suggested that Elinor should return to the States and marry a millionaire. The advice was a little cynical for Elinor's taste but she could see its advantages. What, after all, was she going to do now that the war was over? She must, of course, continue writing. At that very moment she was collecting essays together to be published as *The Philosophy of Love*, and she was plotting the novel *Man and Maid*, which would use some of her wartime experiences. But the thought of returning to England did not appeal to her. She knew that life there could never be the same again. She was inclined to feel as did Lady Angela Forbes that 'The war had accomplished in England what the revolution failed to do in France. There the aristocracy starved behind locked doors rather than admit equality with the nouveaux riches.'[3]

What place could she occupy in the new society? Her daughters did not appear to need her. They had careers as assistants to high-ranking civil servants which would outlast the war, and it was clear that they would not be content to stay at home waiting for suitable husbands to appear. Mrs Kennedy was quite happy to continue to provide a home for them both.

For the time being Elinor divided her time between Versailles and Paris, writing and entertaining friends including Marie, the Queen of Rumania. She continued to quarrel intermittently with Lucy, particularly after she absentmindedly left her chow alone for some hours with Lucy's miniature dog, Fleurette, and the large dog ate the small one.

Casting about for an activity on which to focus her energy, Elinor decided to re-open her house in Passy, and it was while she was there supervising the repainting of her salon that she received a visit from the King of Spain. She had only enough warning from the

Ambassador who telephoned her to enable her to hurry the painters out.

The King was in a flirtatious mood and made all his attendants wait for him in another room while he talked to Elinor in the freshly painted purple salon. In response to his amorous words Elinor told him that she found the love of kings too passing. She preferred their friendship. She had no intention of following in Lillie Langtry's footsteps. The King was not offended as he made clear by inviting Elinor to make a visit to Spain. And Elinor was both amused and flattered by his attentions.

At the turn of the year came an invitation from Lady Congreve whom Elinor had come to know during the war when the former was running a hospital in France. Lady Congreve was in Egypt where her husband was the General Officer Commanding the Forces in Egypt. Milner wrote to say that he too would be in Egypt at that time. Remembering the delights of her last visit and thoroughly bored by post-war Paris, Elinor accepted the invitation.

But like almost everywhere else Egypt had changed and not for the better. She found the atmosphere 'bleak and troubled'. And, despite parties given by Prince Hussein for Milner and for Crown Prince Carol of Rumania, the glamour had gone. Even an attempt to repeat the magic of a moonlight visit to the Sphinx was a failure spoilt by 'hateful tourists, dirty Arabs and banal jokes'.

There was no joy to be had from Milner either. He was busy and often frustrated and had little time to spend with Elinor. Perhaps he had been right to avoid marriage, Elinor reflected. After four weeks she was as glad to leave Egypt as she had been to leave Paris and to set off for Spain where she was to be the guest of the King and Queen.

It was Elinor's intention to use this visit in much the same way as she had earlier used her visit to Russia. She wanted to write a novel, but in the meantime she was content to write up her impressions of the country in such a way that they could be published separately as a travel book.

If Egypt had been a disappointment, Spain was ample compensation. Elinor was there for the Easter ceremonies of Holy Week. In a world in which so much had changed so fast Elinor was especially moved by the continuities represented by religious and court ritual. The France of Louis XIV might be lost for ever, but here in Spain everything was done according to the conventions established by

Louis XIV when he sent his grandson to be Philip V of Spain.

In England and France everyone had become shabby during the war. In Spain the festivities were remarkable for the beauty and splendour of the clothes being worn. It was a feast for Elinor's eyes, long-starved of colour.

Elinor soon realised that the Alphonso she knew in London and Paris was a man on holiday, freed of the expectations of his court. But in Spain he was King and there was complete formality in his dealings with everyone including herself. Nevertheless her description of him in *Letters from Spain* makes it clear that she still found him an extremely attractive man. She was intrigued, of course, by the ways in which Spanish men differed from those of other nationalities. She found them passionate, jealous, sometimes cruel and often unfaithful. They were men who adored their mothers, respected their wives but did not hold women in general in very high esteem. Marriage customs also interested Elinor. Marriages were for the most part arranged as in the upper classes in England and France. But that was the only resemblance. Once married, women were faithful to their husbands and, as a result, were kinder to and more interested in other women. The men might be unfaithful but it would never be with women of the same social class as their wives. There were none of the elaborate intrigues such as Elinor was familiar with in London and Paris.

What struck her very forcibly was the absence of homosexuality. In Paris it was ubiquitous and overt. In Spain it appeared not to exist. As Elinor put it, there were just two sexes – men and women.

She was entertained a great deal in private houses and country villas. But two things in particular made a deep impression on her.

The first was bull and cock fighting. She went to two bull fights determined not to be squeamish and to observe what she saw meticulously. She was surprised by her own reactions and the 'wild, tigerish and primitive' emotions aroused in her. She had conflicting feelings about this which she wrote about in *Letters from Spain*. On the one hand she was 'sure that such sights arouse emotions in human beings which in the end cannot be good for the advancement of civilisation in the race'. She felt this especially keenly as a result of what she had seen in the war. 'All living things, animal or human have a vein of cruelty in them if they are strong, and custom deadens any horror after a while, as all those men who fought in the War know well.'

But she could also see a positive value in the existence of such rituals: '. . . at the present stage of the world's unrest, a legitimate outlet for fierce passions may be a safety valve in that particular country where the War did not reach, and keep it from worse things.'

Her actual description of the two fights she saw are masterly, both in her descriptions of what took place in the ring, and her assessment of the crowd's reactions. The quality of this writing impressed Gertrude Stein, a true aficionado of the bull fight, sufficiently for her to recommend Elinor's descriptions to that connoisseur of the sport, Ernest Hemingway.[4]

In complete contrast, the second important experience of those months in Spain was a visit to Seville and in particular a visit to the Garden of Alcazar. There she saw 'a riot of orange trees in full bloom, of roses, of jasmine and every voluptuous sweet-scented thing' offset by little fountain sprays cunningly placed on the tiled walks and the cool of the bath of the ladies of the Harem. If the whole of Seville was 'passionately romantic', the Royal Garden was 'the concentrated note of it'. It was in this garden that Elinor planned to set her novel. But this was a plan that never came to fruition.

Elinor had been restless before she went to Spain. After her visit there she was even more so as she contrasted Spanish life with that in Paris and London. So a letter from her agent, Hughes Massie, about a new possibility was most timely and welcome. He had been trying to sell the film rights of *Three Weeks* and had met for discussions with a Miss Mayo, a representative of Famous Players-Lasky, who was then in Europe. Miss Mayo expressed a desire to meet Elinor, and Elinor, always ready to promote *Three Weeks*, was quite willing.

When the two women met in Paris, it turned out that they were talking at cross purposes. For Miss Mayo was less interested in *Three Weeks* than in Elinor herself. Her proposal was that Elinor should go to Hollywood, learn the business and write at least one film scenario.

The idea had immense appeal for Elinor. She loved the States, she was at that time thoroughly tired of her way of life and she needed the money. The fact that she knew nothing about film-making, had rarely even seen a moving picture, did not at all deter her. Nor did the fact that she was now almost fifty-six dampen her enthusiasm for beginning something entirely new. She authorised Hughes Massie to negotiate a contract for her.

In the autumn the formal invitation came from Jesse Lasky for Elinor to start work in Hollywood. The terms of her contract were for her to travel to Hollywood, all expenses paid, spend some time learning the technical aspects of film-making and then write a script. If this arrangement worked to everyone's satisfaction the contract could then be renewed on better terms. For this initial contract she was to receive £10,000.

Without thinking too hard about what it would mean to put a great distance between herself and her family, Elinor accepted. She packed up her apartment and set sail on the *Mauretania*, ready and eager for another adventure.

25 HOLLYWOOD ADVENTURE

Elinor was determined to make a success of her new career in Hollywood. She knew precisely why she had been invited there. It was because she was a very English writer, a promoter of romance, a woman who was known to move in the best circles, who could name among her friends royalty and aristocrats and who had, therefore, a certain snob value. These were the attributes she had to exploit, and by so doing bring a touch of class to the new film industry.

She remembered how important it had been to Lucy's business to be able to use the name Lady Duff Gordon. In democratic and republican America Elinor had found to her surprise that titles of any kind gained respect. Unfortunately Elinor had no title. As things stood she would be just plain Mrs Glyn. So she decided that her first step should be to change her name in some way. In France throughout the war she had quite naturally been called Madame Glyn. Outside France this sounded much more impressive than Mrs Glyn. She could see no reason why she should not continue to use this title in America. It was, therefore, Madame Glyn that Jesse Lasky met when the ship docked in New York.

She was pleased with the compliment implied by the head of the film company's coming in person to meet her. She knew also that it was Lasky who was responsible for her being offered a contract in the first place and that he would have the final say about its renewal. If she wanted to stay in Hollywood for any length of time she needed to make a good impression on him.

Lasky was waiting for Elinor with his limousine, as he planned to drive her from the docks to see her safely to her hotel. But Elinor had other ideas. As soon as they reached Fifth Avenue she put her secretary in charge of all their luggage and then insisted that Mr Lasky accompany her on foot the rest of the way as a celebration of her being back in New York. She would not be persuaded that walking on a New York street was a very different matter from walking down Regent Street or the Champs Elysées. She did not care that the occupants of passing cars craned their necks for a better view of the small but striking figure with her bright red hair and fashionably short skirt, tottering along on her high heels, accompanied by Jesse Lasky, elegant in his spats, with his pince-nez and cane, looking as if he belonged where he longed to be, back in his limousine.

Although Elinor loved New York, she did not stay there long. She was anxious to begin the adventure of her new career as soon as possible. The only sensible way to travel from the east coast to the west coast was by train. The journey took five days but the time could be passed pleasantly by anyone who could afford to travel first class as, of course, Elinor did. (Though she could not yet emulate Lillie Langtry whose admirer had given her her own special luxurious coach for her acting tours across the United States.) Already movie people regularly alternated working in Los Angeles with working in New York and the trains were well equipped with sleeping cars, observation cars, dining cars, drawing rooms and even libraries. The route across the continent took them through country which was familiar to Elinor from her previous travels in the States. She had many happy memories of that time but she had not been impressed by her short visits to San Francisco and Los Angeles and she was prepared to feel the same way about them on this occasion. What she did not fully realise until she arrived was that she was not going to San Francisco or Los Angeles anyway, but to somewhere quite different.

On her last visit to the States, Hollywood had been a relatively unknown place and no one had thought it worthwhile to take her there. Like most people who were not actually involved in making movies, she assumed that Hollywood and Los Angeles were one and the same city.

But by now Hollywood had developed its own identity. Elinor first began to be aware of this when she was advised to get off the train not at Los Angeles Central as she had planned, but at Pasadena, the station closest to Hollywood itself.

Hollywood had begun as a genteel place largely inhabited by well-off retired people who were there for the climate and the tranquillity. Ironically, it was in an attempt to preserve that gentility that the small township had opened the way for 'movie people'. Hollywood city fathers had placed a prohibition on liquor in the town long before prohibition became a federal law. They had hoped in this way to prevent the wrong kind of people from settling there. As a result the town's one roadhouse had been forced out of business at just the time that two brothers, David and William Horsley, on the run from the law, were looking for a place to house their newly formed Nestor Film Company. One of the advantages of Hollywood as far as they were concerned was its helpful proximity to the Mexican border. If the law became too pressing they could leave the country quickly.

Once they were established, others were quick to see the potential of Hollywood for film making. But initially the newcomers continued to live in Los Angeles while working in Hollywood. This situation only changed when they realised that the road between Hollywood and Los Angeles could be made impassable by rain. Since everyone had to be on location at six in the morning, it made sense to live in Hollywood as well as work there. So the movie people descended on the peaceful town where there were still plenty of orange groves, where pepper trees and palms lined the streets and where grass grew down the centre of Sunset Boulevard.

At first they were far from welcome because they were very different from the staid and genteel original inhabitants. Because tourists rarely visited the town, hotels were few and far between. In fact there was really only one place for the newcomers to stay until they began to build and buy houses of their own, and this was the Hollywood Hotel. It was to the Hollywood Hotel that Elinor was taken on her arrival at Pasadena, and it was in this unlikely setting that she was to make her home for the next few years.

After the Ritz in London and Paris and the Plaza in New York the Hollywood Hotel was something of a come-down for Elinor. It was a rambling wooden building with pepperpot towers and a verandah all round, more like a large house than an hotel. In earlier days the verandah had been occupied by retired men and women enjoying the sunshine and the quietness. But when Elinor arrived in Hollywood it was movie people who sat in the rocking chairs watching the world go by, giving and receiving the latest Hollywood gossip.

Immediately upon her arrival Elinor learnt that she was going to have to adjust to a very different lifestyle. In London, Paris and New York she was accustomed to having a suite of rooms whenever she stayed in an hotel. Her request for this kind of space at the Hollywood Hotel met with incomprehension. No one else in Hollywood had asked for this unusual privilege, and anyway the hotel did not actually boast a suite. At first the eighty-year-old Miss Hershey, who ran what was then little more than a theatrical boarding house, advised Elinor to find a place in Los Angeles. Elinor was not anxious to move and so she overcame her misgivings and set out to charm Miss Hershey into giving her what she wanted. Miss Hershey succumbed. She liked the fact that Elinor was rather older than most of her guests. More importantly, she was obviously that rare breed in Hollywood, a lady, with genuine titled connections. She could not offer her a suite when none existed but she did the best she could and Elinor was given two adjoining rooms instead of just one. By this fact alone she established her difference from all the other hotel guests right away and her 'suite' of rooms was the subject of much discussion.

The style of the rooms did not suit her, so she immediately set about transforming them to create the kind of ambience she felt at home in. She did this in a manner reminiscent of the Lady in *Three Weeks*. She scattered purple satin cushions everywhere; she hung exotic fabric drapes; she put her own pictures on the walls and set out her framed photographs; she set up a table with an incense burner, and, of course, she put a tiger skin on the floor. The rooms became as different from the rest of the hotel as Elinor was from her fellow boarders.

Despite its unprepossessing appearance, the hotel provided Elinor with the best possible introduction to the way of life in Hollywood and to the people who worked there. It was the nerve centre of the movie community. What didn't actually happen there was quickly reported to the boarders, most of whom were associated with the film industry. Nowhere else could Elinor have found out so quickly what life in Hollywood was like.

She learnt that it was here that Rudolph Valentino had spent the first night of his honeymoon, only to find himself locked out of the marital bedroom before he could consummate the marriage. It was here that another actor brought his blushing bride only to kick her down the stairs a few hours later. There was obviously plenty of scope for the introduction of the kind of romantic ideals Elinor believed in.

When Elinor settled into the hotel she found Somerset Maugham, Maurice Maeterlinck and Edward Knoblock already there on the same kind of contract as she had signed. Also staying in the hotel were

Anita Loos, Fatty Arbuckle and Virginia Rappe. Marion Davies was installed there briefly by William Randolph Hearst but she was quickly removed when Hearst saw how the young male actors flocked around her.

Although the town was officially dry, strong drink was regularly smuggled into the dining room. Miss Hershey, who was unaware that this was being done, was often puzzled by the wild hilarity of her guests for which there was no obvious cause.

There was little to do at night in Hollywood: when darkness fell everything closed down. So the regular Thursday night dances in the Hollywood Hotel were popular and always very well attended. Miss Hershey tried to police these affairs by attempting to see that prohibition laws were observed, and she desperately tried to prevent members of the opposite sex ending the evening by sharing rooms. Her concern was not misplaced. Many young would-be actresses were under age and willing to exchange sexual favours for parts in movies. On the occasions when such relationships were discovered there was always a great scandal. Miss Hershey did not want her hotel involved in anything illegal or immoral.

Everything about the Hollywood Hotel was foreign to Elinor. She found herself living at close quarters with people such as she had never encountered before. When she had been in Nevada and living among miners she had felt that they lived according to some kind of moral and social code which made sense to her. She had certainly never been offended by their behaviour. In Hollywood she discovered that there was no formality of any kind, there was little privacy and a complete disregard for good manners. Elinor, who in 1914 in *Letters to Caroline* had set out her notions of the kind of conduct suitable for those dining in public places, stressing the importance of quiet and unobtrusive behaviour, found herself now sharing a dining room with someone like Fatty Arbuckle. To her horror he insisted on demonstrating his favourite party trick. He took a pat of butter from the table and with his napkin deftly flicked it up onto the ceiling. Then he waited and watched as the butter began to melt and drip down onto the head of the unsuspecting diner below. The distress and surprise of his victim reduced him to helpless laughter.

It was hard for Elinor who was so fastidious that she even found elbows on the table at mealtimes offensive and who believed that 'in public, true distinction is shown by the quietest and most dignified bearing', to accept this kind of practical joking. In the *Letters to Caroline* she had observed that the whole tendency of modern society was towards rowdiness and vulgarity. In Hollywood she saw her worst fears being realised. She did not, however, hold herself aloof from the small community, as might have been expected given her views. She expressed her horror at the way people in Hollywood lived in no uncertain terms in her letters to her mother and in a series of articles she wrote for *Photoplay* entitled 'What I find wrong with Hollywood'. But she was not entirely repelled by the crude and youthful society she found in Hollywood. She admired there what she had always admired in America, an energy, a willingness to work hard, a strong sense of purpose and the possibility for women to work and to earn as much money as men.

Although she was one of the oldest women living in the Hollywood Hotel at that time, she found she had something in common with her younger fellow boarders in her love of dancing. And so she joined in the Thursday night gatherings with enthusiasm.

Now that she had seen the place for herself she felt even more strongly than before that she had been brought to Hollywood for a purpose, and that it was her responsibility, her mission even, to introduce a note of culture and refinement into that philistine community. Her grandmother had done it in the wilds of Canada; she would do the same thing in Hollywood.

She began by holding a Sunday tea-time salon. A salon such as Elinor envisaged had never been heard of in Hollywood. But, according to Anita Loos, the salon was well attended. This was not because Elinor was suddenly satisfying a long-felt need in the community; in fact the reasons were ones she would not have cared to admit to herself. Her occasions were attractive partly because most of the guests were recovering from their Saturday night hangover, the result of too much bootleg liquor; partly because there was no real alternative entertainment available in the town on Sundays. And of course everyone was curious to see exactly what the eccentric English woman would do in the rooms about which rumours had already begun to circulate.

Elinor presided over her salons in pastel-coloured silk lounging pyjamas, and really did serve tea, much to the amazement and disappointment of some of her guests who had hoped for something a little stronger. To the astonishment of those who had accepted her invitation to tea, she would arrange herself gracefully on the tiger skin and then read poetry aloud to them, often inviting them to read also. She did not make many converts to the art of poetry reading or to tea drinking but she did establish for herself a reputation as a forceful and distinctive personality in that community of enlarged egos.

When Elinor met all the other eminent writers Lasky had lured from Europe by the promise of easy money, she found that they were already, for the most part, disillusioned. Somerset Maugham was the first to decide that, despite the money to be made, Hollywood was no place for him to work. He preferred working alone to working in a group and he liked to have the last word on his scripts rather than be answerable to a director and a censor. He fulfilled the bare essentials of his contract and then left.

By contrast, the Belgian poet Maeterlinck worked enthusiastically on his script. He threw himself into the life of Hollywood with such energy that his wife, alarmed by reports of a love affair, speedily joined him.

There are differing accounts about Samuel Goldwyn's response to Maeterlinck's first finished script. One observer reports that Goldwyn rushed from his office after reading the script shouting in bewildered consternation, 'But the hero is a bee!!'[1] When asked to produce something a little more earthy Maeterlinck obliged with a sizzling sex drama which the company had no hope of getting past the censors. Disappointed that neither of his scripts had found favour, Maeterlinck, urged on by Madame Maeterlinck, decided that Hollywood was not for him.

For a while Edward Knoblock, who had earlier co-written plays with Arnold Bennett, survived by writing scripts for Douglas Fairbanks, but this work had its limitations. He became bored and then he too left.

Elinor also found it difficult to make the adjustment from novelist to script-writer. When she had signed her contract with Famous Players-Lasky, she had expected to work on a script for *Three Weeks*. Instead, when she arrived, she was given instructions to write a completely new script suitable for the talents of Gloria Swanson. Hoping that this was merely a preliminary to her real work on *Three Weeks*, she accepted the situation, albeit reluctantly. First of all she had to meet her new star. Gloria Swanson was then working under the direction of Cecil B. de Mille making the film *The Affairs of Anatol*.

Before she ever met him Elinor had learnt from talk at the Hollywood Hotel something about this director. Already in 1921 he had established a formidable reputation. Of Dutch background, he had begun in the film world as an actor, but quickly realised that he had more talent as a director. He was also attracted to the greater power of a director. Some of his success came from new ideas he had introduced into the business. Unlike most other contemporary directors he did not rely on the old formula of boy meets girl in a romantic setting. Love between older couples, sometimes even married couples, was a feature of his films. He was quick to see the possibilities of bathroom scenes and partial nudity. He managed to avoid offending the public and the censors by entertaining them with thrilling sin whilst appeasing their sensibilities with conventional moral conclusions.

De Mille was considered by many working in Hollywood to be a difficult person to deal with. He always consulted the wishes of his mistress, Jean MacPherson, so that it was always necessary for anyone working on a film with him to please and satisfy her as well as the director. He was known for falling into almost insane rages. Everyone who worked for him learnt to recognise and fear the signs of de Mille's increasing impatience. When he began to jangle silver dollars in his pocket it was almost certain that trouble was on the way for someone. His appearance was as striking and idiosyncratic as Elinor's. He did not attempt to compete with his young handsome actors on their terms. He was bald and proud of it. On the set he habitually wore sporting puttees and breeches and carried a silver whistle.

His working methods were unusual. He never gave his actors and actresses a script, but instead told them the story they were to depict in general terms and then let them get on with it. Each night actresses, actors, crew and director met together to see the rushes. In this way everyone could judge the successes and failures of the day's work and discuss any changes that needed to be made. Such occasions could be nerve-racking if the director seemed displeased with what he saw.

When Elinor first met de Mille in his office at Famous Players-Lasky studios on Sunset and Vine, she was immediately aware of him as a sympathetic person. He too had taken pains to express his personality in his surroundings. His office was unlike any of the others at the studios as it had panelled walls, stained-glass windows and a polar-bear skin on the floor.

De Mille, for his part, recognised in Elinor qualities to match his own: a self-confidence that was at times arrogance, a sense of purpose and a determined wilfulness. He was soon to show his appreciation of her in a practical and helpful way.

The first meeting between Elinor and Gloria Swanson established their relationship for the future. Elinor at once scrutinised Gloria's face and after a few moments declared her to be Egyptian. When Gloria protested that she did not have a drop of Egyptian blood, Elinor explained why that was irrelevant: she must have been Egyptian in another incarnation. She then went on to explain her theory of karma and reincarnation. She was taken with Gloria's petite figure and her undeniable magnetism, but was less delighted with the way Gloria was dressed and the way her hair was done even though she knew that these were the studio's responsibility.

Gloria Swanson was twenty-two when she met Elinor. She had been in Hollywood since she was sixteen. For a short time she had worked for Mack Sennett but had found she detested working in his slapstick comedies. Like Elinor she took herself very seriously and she had ambitions to be a serious actress not a comedienne. At seventeen she had married Walter Beery and after an horrific abortion she had started divorce proceedings against him. Her career had begun to prosper when she began playing bad-but-good girl parts under the direction of Cecil B. de Mille. She had married for the second time in 1919 and a year later given birth to her daughter. By 1921 her second marriage was coming to an end. She confided to Elinor that she felt that all the romance in her had been crushed and that she was beginning to have qualms about her career.

Elinor saw Gloria's potential as a disciple and began to work on her immediately. First of all she reassured the younger woman that marriage and having a baby had not damaged her screen image. Gloria Swanson quotes her as saying, 'Miss Pickford, perhaps, might have problems with public acceptance, but you're the new kind of woman altogether – daring, provocative, sensuous – I'm sure religious-minded people will be reassured to learn your life takes a normal course.'[2]

What Elinor saw in Gloria, in fact, was a young woman much like she had been in her youth. She set about improving Gloria's diction, her hair-do and even sent her to seek the advice of her own dress designer.

On this first occasion, however, Elinor herself had much to learn about movies and how they were made. To give her first hand experience of what was involved de Mille gave her a part as an extra in *The Affairs of Anatol*. She quickly learnt how unpleasant it was to work under the harsh mercury lights still in use at that time. She began to appreciate the garish make-up used by everyone on the set. To her embarrassment, she discovered that the harsh lights changed the colour of certain substances. Her teeth were false but no one would have known this under normal circumstances. Under the mercury lights, however, her gums turned a deep purple. She was horrified by the amusement this change caused and by the threat to her dignity. As a result, she was always very self-conscious under the lights and in all her brief film appearances of this time she keeps her mouth firmly closed.

After this brief initiation into the practicalities of film making, Elinor set to work on her own script for Gloria Swanson. If she had hoped to have de Mille as a director she was disappointed but she learnt a lesson in the way the studios put economic considerations before all else. Because any film directed by Cecil B. de Mille was sure to be a box office draw and because any film starring Gloria Swanson was also guaranteed to pull in a crowd, the studios concluded that it made more financial sense to have them work on different films. That way they could be certain of having two financial successes not just one. Since Gloria was to be the star of Elinor's film, it followed that the direction could be safely left to an assistant director, Sam Wood, without any fear of losing the audience.

Elinor was irritated and considered that she was getting second best in her director. Sam Wood had none of de Mille's temperament or genius. For him, directing was a job like any other, one which he found slightly less lucrative than his side-line business of making real-estate deals. It was not until later when he began to work with the Marx Brothers that he really found his work interesting and congenial. He was impressed neither by Elinor personally nor by her reputation. In his view the importation of writers from Europe to Hollywood had been a mistake. The studios had managed very well before such writers arrived and he felt that they could continue to do so. He was determined to make no concessions to the middle-aged, aggressively English woman who had been foisted upon him.

Writing a film script was a very different matter from writing a novel, Elinor found. Like Somerset Maugham she enjoyed the total control over her work that novel writing gave her. As a novelist she was rarely asked to make many changes apart from corrections to spelling and grammar. On the occasion when William Randolph Hearst had asked for changes in *The Career of Katherine Bush* she had been uncompromising; she had got her own way and the book had been published as it stood.

She was not pleased when she gave Sam Wood her script, *The Great Moment*, and he failed to be delighted with it. On the contrary he told her it lacked drama and that it was old-fashioned. Her humiliation was complete when he advised her not to worry since, with the help of his continuity writer, he could lick it into some sort of shape.

Elinor found it too painful to witness the way in which Sam Wood and his assistants transformed her romantic story into slapstick comedy. She felt that the whole point of her being in Hollywood was called into question by such drastic changes to her work. For a while she kept away from the studio and caught up on her correspondence. Sam Wood put the word about that she was sulking but that he was glad to be rid of her so that he could get on with his work. This was just the kind of challenge to provoke Elinor, and besides she could not for long resist the temptation to see what was happening. She determined to visit the studios again and attempt to regain her lost authority. She was delighted to find that Sam Wood had reached an impasse. After all the changes he had made to Elinor's script he could no longer see a way to end it satisfactorily. Elinor chose her moment. She waited until Cecil B. de Mille was in the studio and then when he was in earshot she commented with icy British dignity to Sam Wood that perhaps she might be able to suggest an ending since it was, after all, her script. Cecil B. de Mille was vastly amused by her supercilious manner and her willingness to fight back against Sam Wood. Writers usually behaved quite differently. He intervened on her behalf to the extent that she once more had some say in how the script would be developed. It was an important moment both for Elinor and for other writers. For the first time a writer had managed to exert some authority, however slight, over a script. The incident did not go unnoticed.

Everyone in Hollywood heard the story and Elinor's reputation was greatly enhanced.

However, the difficulties between writer and director were far from over. Some of them arose from circumstances over which neither had any control. During Elinor's first year in Hollywood there had been several scandals which had shocked smalltown America. There had been the painful death of Virginia Rappe. This bit-part actress, whose lover worked for Mack Sennett, had been staying at the Hollywood Hotel. Fatty Arbuckle had been there at the same time. Although Fatty Arbuckle had many admirers in the movie world, Virginia Rappe was not one of them. She had disliked his loud, vulgar antics and had not troubled to conceal her antipathy. Both of them had been present at a drunken party in San Francisco. It was alleged that at this party Arbuckle had raped Virginia Rappe, ruptured her bladder and left her bleeding to death. The sensational trial of Arbuckle was the focus of American attention. Arbuckle was finally cleared of the charge of manslaughter but his name and that of Hollywood was besmirched by the whole affair. For even though the court's verdict was that Virginia Rappe had died of natural causes, the public now knew that wild parties with drink, drugs and sex were attended by Hollywood stars.

Then there had been the death of Wallace Reid, the handsome hero of many silent movies. He, it emerged, had become a drug addict and died of an overdose. His wife laid the blame for his addiction on the studios. She claimed that Reid had suffered a painful injury in the course of filming. When it had seemed likely that the completion of the film would be delayed by his inability to work, the studio management had urged Reid to take morphine to deaden the pain and enable him to complete the film. In this way his addiction had begun.

The studios feared that the growing unsavoury reputation of Hollywood would frighten off movie audiences. Several measures were taken to restore the appearance of respectability to Hollywood. The most important one as far as Elinor was concerned was the introduction of a degree of voluntary censorship.

In Elinor's script the heroine finds herself alone in the Nevada desert with the hero. She is bitten by a snake. The hero recognises that the only thing to do in such circumstances is to cut the wound and suck out the poison. There was no dispute about the inclusion of this dramatic scene. What was disputed was the location of the snake bite. Elinor insisted that the girl be bitten in her bosom. Wood wanted her to be bitten on the wrist. Despite his earlier accusations that Elinor was too old-fashioned, he now felt her script to be too daring in this matter, and was terrified that the censors would demand the film's withdrawal.

The argument moved into the public domain as Elinor asked all her acquaintances for their opinions. As it happened, the publicity was not bad for the film: cinema managers were intrigued and began to order copies long before it was released.

Eventually a compromise was reached. The heroine was bitten on the shoulder. This allowed for the audience to be titillated when the hero cut away the girl's clothing to treat the wound. But no one would be too shocked.

Always a stickler for detail and accuracy, Elinor drove everyone working on the film mad with her repeated requests for changes in the set and in the clothes worn by her heroine. While Elinor strove for authenticity, everyone else involved with the making of the film was concerned with what they regarded as glamour. But in this last matter she was unlikely to find a champion in de Mille since it was he who had established the idea that glamour was synonymous with elaborate clothes. He had required Gloria Swanson to wear ever more extravagant dresses trimmed with fur and jewels and embroidery. She had begun to feel that she was more of a clothes horse than an actress. Sam Wood was only following de Mille's lead when he insisted on scenes whose principal objective was to show Gloria Swanson in a series of exotic gowns. Elinor wrote bitter complaints about this excess to her mother but there was nothing she could do to prevent it. She did find an opportunity for revenge, however, when she came to write the novel based on the script.

In a letter to her mother, written in August 1921, she had singled out with particular scorn the boudoir scene in Washington. She described it as being in 'vile bad taste and muddled . . . Miss Swanson's awful hair in that scene, with two Chinese fans in it!!!' She had denied responsibility for 'the fearfully vulgar get up when she looks like a cook as she becomes engaged to Hoppner' and 'the vulgar plush curtains'.

Yet, when she came to write the novel, rather than cutting out the above details, she used them to great effect to underscore how far the heroine had fallen from her former standards of good taste and how totally enmeshed she had become in the vulgarity of her companions. Even the despised Chinese fans have a place in achieving this effect. When the hero sees his beloved decked out in her finery he is appalled. She suddenly sees herself through his eyes and realises how grotesque her appearance is. She rips off the cumbersome train of her jewel-encrusted dress and pulls the Chinese fans out of her hair before setting off in pursuit of the man she loves.

The Great Moment was a huge financial success. Elinor had established herself. It was a great satisfaction to her that for the first time in Hollywood the name of a writer was almost as much of a box-office draw as the name of the star. With Elinor, at least, Lasky's policy of bringing in writers with a reputation outside the movies had been justified.

Elinor's social success equalled her success on the set. Her very appearance attracted attention. Most of the women in Hollywood at the time were young. All the good female parts in the movies were for young attractive women. Mary Pickford, for example, just could not afford to grow up. She was 'America's Sweetheart', and that she had to remain. So Elinor in her late fifties, still glamorous with a good figure, bright red hair, pale skin and false eyelashes, was a vivid exception to the general rule. Her clothes were always of interest. She never followed fashion, but chose to set it. For formal occasions, which she loved, she had her own designer create a series of elegant evening gowns and she still had Lucile designs in her wardrobe.

One mark of her success was the way in which she was taken up by Mary Pickford and Douglas Fairbanks and regularly invited to their home, Pickfair.

The marriage of these two Hollywood stars had all the elements of romance that Elinor could wish for, as long as she was prepared to overlook the fact that to achieve it they had both had to go through divorces.

It was well known in Hollywood how Fairbanks had wooed his lady. He had formed the habit of going to bed as usual with his wife Beth. Once she was safely asleep he would climb down from the verandah of their bedroom. As the house was at the top of a hill he could let his car roll down silently without starting the engine. He would spend stolen time with Mary and then return home. Unfortunately the only way to get the car back up the hill as quietly as it had come down was to push it. Then there was the climb back up on to the verandah and into the bedroom. Fairbanks found these midnight excursions gave him a tremendous appetite and he had to remember to leave himself cakes and milk to sustain him on his return.

Pickfair itself was a suitably romantic setting for the newly-weds. It had been little more than a hunting lodge in the wilds when Fairbanks had bought it. He had proceeded to transform it into a Tudor style home suitable for 'America's Sweetheart'. In 1921 it was one of only two houses out in the mountains that were inhabited throughout the year and not just in the summer. It was reached by driving down Sunset Boulevard, past the Beverly Hills Hotel, north through the Benedict Canyon and finally on a dirt road up San Isidoro Canyon.

In this romantic setting stood the large house with its well-lit, spacious rooms. There was even a swimming pool surrounded by a sandy beach.

Elinor appreciated being a regular guest at Pickfair because it was acknowledged that the marriage of Mary Pickford and Douglas Fairbanks had set a new tone in Hollywood and that only the best people were invited to their home. For Elinor it was refreshingly like the old days in England to go to dinner at Pickfair. Douglas Fairbanks insisted on the kind of formality that Elinor appreciated but found nowhere else in Hollywood. There were, for example, printed invitations and printed menu cards for every dinner party. Like Elinor, Fairbanks was against alcohol. His was one of the few homes of movie stars where alcohol was not served. Both husband and wife were fanatical about their appearance and their fitness since their livelihoods depended upon them. They had this in common with Elinor, and she approved of the simple food served at their dinners.

Fairbanks loved a title just as much as Elinor did. This weakness of his was something of a joke in Hollywood. On one occasion Charlie Chaplin arrived for dinner and asked Fairbanks in an offhand manner, 'How's the Duke?' Fairbanks replied 'The Duke? What Duke?' Chaplin responded, 'Oh come on, Douglas. Surely there must be at least one Duke dining tonight.'

Elinor herself was regarded by Fairbanks as something of a social asset. He knew her sister was Lady Duff Gordon because Mary had first modelled and then bought Lucile dresses. Samuel Goldwyn recalls in his autobiography how he first met Elinor at Pickfair. He had been told in deferential tones that she was one of the guests at dinner that night. He felt he had been accorded a special privilege when he was taken outside to meet her. Fairbanks introduced him to a 'Circe looking woman in sea green chiffon seated on a stone bench gazing at the water'. When she spoke to him he found her voice just as strange as her appearance. 'She has the trick, so I found, of convincing you that her voice is some far-away, mysterious visitant of which she herself supplies a humble and temporary instrument of escape.'[3]

At this time Samuel Goldwyn had recently left Famous Players-Lasky, the Lasky part of which he had helped to found. He was about to set up a new company, Metro-Goldwyn-Mayer. He was smitten by Elinor. He regarded her as the most spectacular of all the writers to have made an impression on Hollywood. Her appearance in her 'exquisite gowns' delighted him and he found her to be a most entertaining dinner companion as 'her narratives and comments usually keep a whole roomful of people in an uproar of mirth'.[4] He always felt that she was playing a role and he admired her for it.

> I myself believe that she plans her personality as carefully as she does her stories. When for instance, arrayed in the most superb evening attire and accompanied by the handsomest man she has been able to find in the assemblage, Mrs Glyn sweeps slowly through a ballroom; when she murmurs soulfully, 'Orange, orange, how I love it! Often I sit in a room by myself and think orange. I fill my whole soul with its beautiful, warm rays – I drink them down into my heart – ah, orange!' – then she is showing her supreme ability, not only as a writer who can tell a popular tale, but as the writer who knows how to get herself constantly before the popular mind. I once said of her that she was a great showman, and when she heard my comment she was exceedingly gratified.[5]

That Goldwyn's admiration was whole-heartedly genuine he was later able to prove.

26 NEW FRIENDS

Although at first Elinor held herself aloof from much of what went on in Hollywood, her increasing circle of friends gradually changed her position from that of an observer to that of a willing participant.

There is some dispute about the occasion when Elinor first met Charlie Chaplin, a fellow English exile, but from the opposite end of the social scale. Whilst Elinor had been doing the rounds of English country houses, Chaplin had been living in extreme poverty and misery in London. Chaplin claims that he first met Elinor in her sitting room at the Hollywood Hotel. He had been invited for cocktails prior to a dinner party for ten people. In his version of this first meeting Elinor had greeted him effusively: ' "Ah," she said cupping my face with her hands and gazing intently at me. "Let me have a look at you. How extraordinary! I thought your eyes were brown but they're quite blue." '[1]

She went on to comment that Chaplin did not look nearly as funny as she had expected. 'Neither do you,' was Chaplin's prompt reply.

Another version of their first meeting suggests that it was at Samuel Goldwyn's house after a dinner and a showing of Chaplin's *The Kid*. Elinor had enthused over the film to Chaplin telling him how she considered it to be far and away the best of his films. Chaplin's response had been to ask Elinor which of his other films she had seen. To Chaplin's huge delight Elinor had to confess that *The Kid* was in fact the only one of his films that she had seen.

Whichever account of the meeting is the most accurate, both demonstrate the nature of the relationship between the two of them. Chaplin, though feeling rather overwhelmed by Elinor's grand and dramatic manner, was always able to prick the bubble of her pretentiousness. Far from resenting him for this she became very fond of him and her affection was returned. Chaplin recognised, as did many others, including the maids at the Hollywood Hotel, that behind Elinor's elaborate façade there was great kindness. In the next few years Chaplin was to become involved in various affairs and scandals of which Elinor must have disapproved, but the friendship remained strong.

Early in 1921 Margot and Juliet both married. Margot married Sir Edward Davson and Juliet married Rhys Rhys-Williams, a barrister. Elinor's earlier attempts at matchmaking had failed. Both girls had chosen husbands for themselves from among the men they had met during their war work. In both cases they had chosen to marry men older than themselves. Elinor was at first disappointed, and she did not attend the weddings. She gave as her excuse the need to be on the spot when work began on her new film, but her daughters were not convinced that this was the real reason, and were hurt by her apparent lack of interest in their futures.

Also in this year Milner made the final break with Elinor when he wrote to announce that he was about to marry Violet, the widow of Sir Edward Cecil. Elinor cannot have been too surprised by his announcement for she knew that for some time Lady Cecil had been advising and assisting Milner on matters such as buying and furnishing a house.

Milner was quite aware that he was choosing safety rather than adventure and the unexpected which marriage to Elinor would have meant. He wrote to her:

> I hope the Tiger may not look upon the Elephant as now so domesticated as to be quite uninteresting, but that we may still have many opportunities of exchanging ideas about books and men in that free spirit and with that mutual understanding which always made us such good company to one another.[2]

All these matters seemed very remote to Elinor, involved as she was in the quite different life of Hollywood. Her social life was increasingly full. She had discovered pleasures beyond the weekly dances at the Hollywood Hotel. Her favourite place for dancing was now the Patent Leather Room in the Ambassador Hotel in Los Angeles. Her companion was often a young, good-looking actor from Oklahoma named Dana Todd. He was just one of a sequence of handsome young men who were only too glad to be seen dancing with the well-known and influential writer.

By now Gloria Swanson had left her husband and was living apart from him in the Silver Lakes area. Frequently she and the young director Marshall Neilan would make up a foursome with Elinor and her young man of the moment. Elinor had by now entrée to all the interesting parties in Hollywood and at the Patent Leather Room a table would always be found for her however full the room appeared to be. The lovers were happy to enjoy the benefits of Elinor's social success.

The way in which Hollywood was taking a hold on Elinor is shown in her attitude towards Gloria Swanson at this time. She would once have disapproved of this young woman who at twenty-two was about to part from her second husband. Instead she encouraged her in her affair with the good-looking Neilan.

She did, however, attempt to maintain a dispassionate view of Hollywood life. She tried to counterbalance the pace of the life she was leading by regular readings of Plato and Herodotus, both of which she kept by her bed to read before she slept. She must have been the only person in Hollywood to do so.

It was through Marion Davies, William Randolph Hearst's young mistress, that Elinor finally met the man whose press she had written for over a period of years. Once again she was becoming involved with people with whom she would have had nothing to do in her earlier years in England.

William Randolph Hearst had been born in the same year as Elinor's sister Lucy. In 1921 he was fifty-nine to Elinor's fifty-seven. His blonde, pretty and vivacious mistress, was thirty-three years his junior, that is about the same age as Elinor's daughter Margot. Hearst had first been married in 1903 to Millicent Wilson, a Gibson girl who had already been his mistress for some years. The couple had two sons but by 1915 when Hearst met Marion Davies his marriage was one in name only. Marion Davies, born in Brooklyn as Marion Cecilia Douras was a successful showgirl when Hearst first met her. He was already a very rich man with his burgeoning newspaper empire, but the death of his mother in 1917 had made him a multi-millionaire. He became obsessed with the idea of making Marion into a movie star and set about forming his own company, Cosmopolitan Films, specifically to promote her.

When Marion had first come to Hollywood she had stayed at the Hollywood Hotel like everyone else. Hearst quickly realised to his displeasure what a magnet she was to all the young men. He moved her to an isolated bungalow on the coast but she was soon bored and refused to stay there. Eventually he rented a house for her in Beverly Hills where she established herself by holding huge dinner parties: sometimes there were as many as a hundred guests.

Hearst had decided that he approved of Elinor Glyn as a companion for Marion. His hope was that the older, more experienced and respectable woman would be a steadying and restraining influence on his vivacious and over-exuberant young mistress. It is open to question whether Elinor influenced Marion or vice versa. Certainly Elinor was soon attending Marion's parties which were as different as could be from the civilised and restrained gatherings at Pickfair. The company at Marion Davies's house was not select. There was often a mixture of 'actors, actresses, senators, polo players, chorus boys, foreign potentates'[3] along with members of Hearst's executive and editorial staff.

At Pickfair Fairbanks and his wife treated each other with affectionate courtesy. But in the Davies household there was often tension. More than one witness describes a scene in which Hearst, surrounded by his staff, was doing business whilst Marion reclined on a couch on the other side of the room surrounded by her guests. Her anger at the situation grew until she yelled at her elderly protector, a man much feared by his employees, 'Hey! You!' When Hearst acknowledged her call she spoke to him angrily saying, 'Do your business downtown. Not in my house. My guests are waiting for a drink, so hurry up and get them one.'

At Pickfair no alcohol was served. William Randolph Hearst would have liked to have been able to say the same thing about Marion's house. The best he could do was to try to limit the amount of alcohol consumed by refusing to serve it before a specified hour.

Between these two very different establishments Elinor moved freely, apparently unaware at the time of how completely she was compromising her own principles by so doing. When Hearst gave Marion her own beach house at Santa Monica, Elinor appears to have been oblivious to the vulgarity of the seventy-roomed Georgian style house with its three hundred foot wide and three storey high façade, its gold-leaf gilded ballroom and dining room. She did not at this time object to the mixture of paintings by Reynolds and Lawrence, among which were some obvious fakes. Even the oak-panelled library in which when a button was pressed a section of the floor rose and became a screen for movies, the swimming pool of Italian marble with its venetian marble bridge and convenient bar-room and dance floor did not unduly upset her. In earlier days she would have found this ostentatious show of wealth ready material for satire and mockery.

Perhaps she had some inkling of how far her values were being changed by Hollywood, for in September she exercised the right which was written into her contract to spend some time in Europe each year. Douglas Fairbanks and Mary Pickford were about to set off on their belated honeymoon little suspecting the enthusiastic crowds that awaited them. Elinor decided that it would be more interesting to travel with her friends than alone. So the three of them took the train across the States to the east coast and set sail from New York to France on the *Olympic*.

Elinor's stay in Europe was not a lengthy one. She gave this as a reason for not seeing her two recently married daughters. But there is no doubt that had she really wished to see them she could have done so. She did, after all, manage to spend time with Lucy and Esmé in Paris. She wrote to her mother enquiring about whether Margot was in France. She was, but Elinor did not take the opportunity to meet her. She knew that Juliet was pregnant but even this did not affect her decision to stay away from England. Behind all her flimsy excuses was the simple fact that she was not ready to face her daughters and the husbands they had chosen for themselves. For some time she had not played the role of a mother and after spending time in Hollywood she was even less able to do so. She had entered with gusto into the kind of life that Margot and Juliet knew nothing about and she was now used to being treated as a single woman with responsibility only for herself. She almost certainly anticipated questions and criticisms which she did not care to deal with at this time. Perhaps she felt a certain amount of guilt about the way she had, in effect, abandoned her children and involved herself in a life in which they could have no part.

Being with Lucy was easier. She had treated her own daughter in a similar manner when she had spent the years of the war in the States. And Lucy knew about life in America; she was less likely to criticise Elinor for taking the opportunities it presented. But even so absence had changed little in the relationship between the sisters. They had hardly exchanged greetings before they began to quarrel about who was wearing the correctly fashionable skirt length.

Elinor checked up on her apartment in Versailles and her house in Passy. But she was not tempted to linger. The excitement of Hollywood had begun to work on her and she was eager to be back to her two rooms in the Hollywood Hotel and her work at the studio.

Elinor's short stay in Europe, far from reinforcing her initial doubts about staying in Hollywood, had confirmed her decision to make a new life for herself in the States. Her resolve was strengthened when it became clear that her first film, *The Great Moment*, was a commercial success. In her by now famous, pithy comment Anita Loos summarised how completely Elinor had made a place for herself in what had seemed the unlikely setting of Hollywood. 'Elinor never allowed anyone to forget she was a lady to the core, but for all her pretensions to a Mayfair background she belonged, body, heart, and soul to Hollywood: in fact had Hollywood never existed, Elinor Glyn would have invented it.'[4]

The success of *The Great Moment* had an immediate effect on Elinor's status in Hollywood. She was now given more influence over the making of her second film. This time she did not write a completely new story but adapted her novel *Beyond The Rocks*. The leading roles were given to Gloria Swanson and Rudolph Valentino.

Valentino who had come to Hollywood in 1917 after working first as a 'taxi-dancer' at a *thé dansant* and then as the partner of Bonnie Glass doing exhibition dancing in New York, was twenty-six years old when he met Elinor. It was in the role of Julio, the playboy, in *The Four Horsemen of the Apocalypse* that he had established himself as a leading actor. His previous experience as a dancer, his remarkable ability to act with his eyes and his Latin good looks had all come together to make the tango sequence in that film an overwhelming success with audiences. Other successes had followed so that when Elinor first met him he already had a following of devoted women. The qualities which made him so compelling were exactly those which Elinor had always stressed in the heroes of her novels and in her writing about the relationship between the sexes. He gave the appearance of being simultaneously masterful and tender.

Writer and actor struck up a friendship immediately. They had a great deal in common. Both had a strong sense of their European backgrounds; both laid doubtful claim to some distant aristocratic connections; both believed in the transmigration of souls. They shared a similar taste in interior decorating; they both enjoyed making money and both were careless in their spending of it. And they both loved to dance.

Despite his fame and good looks, Valentino was often lonely. His marriage to Jean Acker had ended almost before it had begun and he had not yet persuaded the designer, Natasha Rambova (born Winifred Shaugnessy de Wolf), to marry him. Before long he and Elinor were frequent dance partners.

Elinor had by now reconciled herself to Sam Wood's direction and he had come to terms with working with a writer who knew her own mind. There were lunch-time script conferences in which Elinor, Valentino and Sam Wood worked closely together. Elinor had learnt a great deal from the making of her first film. She could see that costume dramas did have an appeal to the movie-going public. So this time she was prepared to make drastic alterations to her original novel in order to incorporate flashbacks which enabled her two young friends, Gloria and Rudolph, to show themselves at their best in glamorous historical costumes. Her complaints about the unsuitable extravagance of some of the clothes were now confined to letters to her mother. On the set she was prepared to co-operate. She even introduced a tango scene, which had little to do with the narrative line, simply because there was nothing more calculated to bring audiences flocking than the combination of Rudolph Valentino and the tango.

Gloria Swanson remembered the heady days when this film was being made:

> Everyone wanted *Beyond The Rocks* to be every luxurious thing Hollywood could serve up in a single picture: the sultry glamour of Gloria Swanson, the steaming Latin magic of Rudolph Valentino, a rapturous love story by Elinor Glyn, and the tango as it was meant to be danced, by the master himself.[5]

Even in this film Sam Wood was conscious of his need to be careful of the censors. One of the rules he had to observe was that kisses should run no longer than ten feet of film. Each kiss had to be shot twice so that the short kiss could be included in the version for the American market and a longer, seemingly more passionate kiss included in the version to be released in Europe.

It was, however, with a sense of relief that Sam Wood moved his actors and crew to Catalina Island to shoot the shipwreck scenes. Elinor had decided not to go to the island and remained behind. Director and writer needed a break from each other and the strain of working amicably together.

Work on *Beyond the Rocks* came to an end in February. Even while she had been working on the film Elinor had not neglected her writing. She had written a series of pieces for *Photoplay*, so that when Valentino was asked to write for the same magazine she was able to ghost parts of the article for him. She slanted his material so cleverly, stressing his commitment to romance, that his fan mail was immediately greatly increased.

She had begun her novel about France during the closing stage of the war in 1919. She finished the work while in Hollywood and it was published in the spring of 1922. She also worked on making her screenplay for *The Great Moment* into a book. It would be her first completely American novel.

Elinor's contract with Famous Players-Lasky came to an end in March 1922. She could have left Hollywood at this time feeling that she had successfully achieved what she had set out to do. Various unsavoury events taking place around her could well have persuaded her that it was time to leave. There was the death of fellow Englishman William Desmond Taylor in circumstances which were never fully explained, though he appeared to have been murdered. In the ensuing scandal, in which it was suggested that Taylor had been involved in a ménage à trois and dealing in drugs, careers of the two actresses named as conspirators were irretrievably damaged. Her good friend Chaplin divorced his young wife Mildred Harris and embarked on a spectacular and well-publicised affair with the much-married, wealthy and flamboyant Peggy Hopkins Joyce. When the German film actress Pola Negri arrived in Hollywood from Berlin in a blaze of publicity she too began an affair with Chaplin and their engagement was announced and called off several times. Rudolph Valentino divorced his wife Jean Acker. He married Natasha Rambova and was immediately put in prison for bigamy. He had not waited long enough between divorce and marriage to comply with the law. Only by making known that his first marriage had never been consummated did he manage to gain his release.

There had been a time when Elinor would have looked on these events with dismay and turned her back on the place where they were happening. Her letters to her mother are full of complaints about life in Hollywood, about the delays, the cheating and lying and general uncertainty. But far from being ready to leave Hollywood and its scandals, she was eager to remain.

Famous Players-Lasky was willing to negotiate another contract. Elinor, however, had a new sense of her own value as a writer after her successes. She wanted Famous Players-Lasky to film her recently completed novel *Man and Maid*, but she was not prepared to accept the terms they offered. Mary Pickford and Douglas Fairbanks showed interest in having her write for their company, United Artists, but once again Elinor's demands could not be met. Suddenly she realised that she had created a situation from which she could not easily retreat with dignity. She was beginning to think that she would have to leave Hollywood after all. She toyed with the idea of going to New York and concentrating on her writing. A return to England seemed an unacceptably dull alternative after the excitement and activity of the last two years.

At the last moment she was saved from having to make a decision by the offer of a contract from her two staunch admirers at Metro-Goldwyn-Mayer, Samuel Goldwyn and Louis B. Mayer. The terms of the contract they offered were not particularly good, as Elinor was forced to recognise. But the bait that secured her signature was the promise of the chance not only to write the screenplay of *Three Weeks* but also to have a major part in the directing of the film. It was an opportunity which Elinor was unable to resist. She still regarded *Three Weeks* as one of her best novels and she still smarted from its original reception. To make a film of the novel would go some way to vindicate and compensate her. The contract was signed and Elinor set off in some triumph for her annual visit to Europe.

27 A HECTIC AND ABNORMAL LIFE

Any differences there had been between Elinor and her daughters were smoothed over on her visit to England. Elinor stayed in Shelley Court and was able to see for the first time her two new grandchildren. As in the old days she took Margot off with her for a visit to Cannes before going on to Paris where she re-opened her house in the Avenue Victor Hugo.

Intending to make the most of her time in Europe Elinor was off on her travels at the beginning of 1923. She had been invited to make a lecture tour of Scandinavia by the Anglo-Swedish Literary Society. She was pleased by how well she was received and thoroughly enjoyed herself lecturing on such topics as 'Women's Place in Modern Civilisation', and 'Marriage Customs'. Later in the year she was to turn this newly discovered talent for lecturing into a profitable enterprise when she undertook to deliver a series of ten-minute talks in a vaudeville theatre in New York for good pay.

In February she was back in Hollywood, her confidence in herself greater than ever. Goldwyn and Mayer were anxious to please her and prepared to indulge her. As an indication of her new status in their company and their concern and admiration for her, the two men met Elinor when her train arrived and escorted her to her new home in the Ambassador Hotel in Los Angeles. This time she did not have to bargain with the equivalent of a Miss Hershey for the use of an extra room. The company had engaged a five-room suite for her. Before long Elinor had transformed the rooms to provide a suitable ambience. Her sitting room was decorated in shades of blue, green and orchid. She brought in her own furniture – Chinese lacquered pieces also in green and orchid.

This flattering beginning to her new relationship with Metro-Goldwyn-Mayer was, however, deceptive. Goldwyn and Mayer merely wanted to create the illusion that Elinor had unlimited powers. Elinor wanted the actuality. Whilst Elinor began the difficult job of writing a screenplay from her novel the company started the search for an actor to play the leading role. Elinor mistakenly thought that she could have the final say. In her mind's eye she knew exactly what Paul should look like. She had, after all, created him. When she found a young man who matched her idea in every respect with the exception that his hair was dark not blonde, she persuaded him to dye it. She presented Eric Glynne Percy for a screen test, confident that he would be given the part despite his limited acting experience. Goldwyn and Mayer had other ideas. They could not afford the risk of giving the starring role to an unknown and largely untried actor. They knew that any film Elinor was involved with would be expensive to produce. They needed the certainty of a box-office star in order to be sure of making their film profitable. The actor they favoured for the part of Paul was Conrad Nagel.

From Elinor's point of view it was quite bad enough that they had turned down her protégé, but when she discovered that Goldwyn and Mayer had chosen a young man of German background for this very English character she threw a fit. She was not favourably disposed towards Germans at the best of times and she could not understand how her producers could possibly have been so insensitive as to choose a German to play the part of a hero who is supposed to epitomise all that is good in a young English gentleman. She feared that the whole spirit of her work would be ruined by this unfortunate choice for the leading actor.

Goldwyn and Mayer stuck to their decision. No amount of raging, cajoling or sulking by Elinor could change their minds. What they did offer, however, as a consolation was to let her work more closely with them in the search for an actress to play the part of the Lady.

The publicity surrounding the choosing of the Lady has only been equalled since by the search for an actress to play Scarlett O'Hara. Hundreds of young women were interviewed. Everywhere Elinor went she talked about the search and surveyed all the young women present in the hopes of spotting a potential Lady. Anita Loos was an observer of the whole performance. In *A Girl Like I* she reports the comments of her current escort, the vaudeville actor Joe Frisco. To him she attributes the following remark: ' "You want to find some tramp that don't look like a tramp, to play that English tramp in your picture. But take it from me, that kind of tramp don't hang out in Hollywood." '[1]

Undismayed Elinor continued to look for her ideal Lady. To her delight Aileen Pringle was chosen to play the part. There were several reasons why she favoured this young woman. First of all, she could see in her some resemblance to herself when younger. And, of course, in Elinor's mind by now the Lady was herself. To reinforce the point and gain even more publicity, profile photos were taken of Elinor and Aileen Pringle in which the resemblance between them is unmistakable. An added bonus in Elinor's eyes was her new star's background. She turned out to be the daughter-in-law of Sir John Pringle, the Governor of Jamaica.

The director, Alan Crosland, and the art director, Cedric Gibbons, were not men Elinor had worked with before. Then at the last moment Crosland was replaced with King Vidor. Fortunately Elinor got along well with the two men, in great part because she was allowed a good deal of her own way. She had firm ideas about everything in the film. When she felt it to be necessary she would even play the part of the Lady herself to demonstrate exactly what she intended Aileen Pringle to do.

The sets and costumes were lavish and, as anticipated, the production costs were very high. But the success of the film when it was released justified the expenditure. Its success, especially in the States, was the result of its 'teasing morality'. The audience was allowed to enjoy all the pleasures of sensuous sin without feeling guilty about the blatant and 'heavily anguished transgressions of Victorian morality. After all, in the end, morality prevails and everyone get their just desserts.'[2] Elinor had succeeded in making her point at last.

Throughout her time in Hollywood Elinor had been pleased at the amount of money she had been able to earn. Increasingly she became careless of exactly what sums were involved. She assumed that she had all the money she needed and she spent without any thought about what she could or could not afford. In her own words she became as 'addicted to money' as she had once been to romance. For a long time she had believed profoundly in the power of thought to determine the course of life. While in Hollywood she narrowed this belief to the idea that by thinking forcefully about material objects she could enable herself to acquire them.

She did not, however, give sufficient attention to the way her money was being managed. The men she chose to advise her were chosen more for their good looks and charm than their business acumen. At times William Randolph Hearst gave her advice but she was capricious about acting upon it. She made some disastrous investments including the purchase of shares in an unprofitable gold mine. She found herself a Hollywood agent to prevent her from being cheated by the film companies but was completely unaware that he in turn was cheating her by getting her to sign a contract which gave him fifty per cent of all her earnings. Either she did not trouble to read her contract or she assumed that she was earning so much that it hardly mattered.

Fortunately her family was gradually beginning to understand her total inability to manage her money. As a result, when she visited Europe that year her son-in-law Rhys Rhys-Williams asked if he might look at her contracts. The confusion he found was even greater than he had feared. He suggested that in return for his help in negotiating a better contract Elinor should allow herself to be made into a Limited Liability Company. Glad enough to have anyone sort out her increasingly tangled affairs, Elinor agreed without really considering what this might imply for the future. A board of directors was established which included all the family members; Juliet was the secretary. Elinor's first indication of what was happening came when she realised that she alone did not have a seat on the board of the company which bore her name. On 1 March Elinor Glyn Ltd was formed. The company was to hold the copyright of all Elinor's works and to receive her royalties. Elinor herself would then receive the money she needed from the board. In this way Margot and Juliet hoped to protect their mother from herself. Rhys-Williams made some investments which Elinor could not have immediate access to in the hopes of providing for her when she was no longer able to earn money in such large quantities.

For the first time Margot and Juliet learned how much their mother had been earning and how much she had been spending. In Margot's mind this knowledge started to create a resentment which was to erupt at a later stage.

In order to deal with the contractual problems Elinor had created for herself, Juliet and her husband decided to visit Hollywood. Rhys-Williams managed to talk Louis Mayer into giving Elinor a better contract. He found the agent harder to deal with. Elinor had, after all, signed the contract of her own free will. Rhys-Williams abandoned his attempts to make the agent behave more honourably. Instead he adopted another tactic. He agreed to let the contract stand but said that he would make the terms of the contract public. In this way he would ensure that the agent got no further business. Realising that the profits from Elinor would not compensate for the loss of potential earnings from other gullible Hollywood writers, the agent finally agreed to the contract being torn up.

Juliet found that Hollywood agreed with her almost as much as with her mother. When work on *His Hour* began she took part in writing the continuity. Elinor was very proud to have her daughter taking such an active part in her work, and she regarded her with new respect. She was also pleased that Aileen Pringle was to play the part of her heroine, Tamara. An unknown actor, John Gilbert, was chosen for the hero. It was the part which launched him on a very successful career in movies. Elinor was equally lucky in having the versatile and talented Alan Crosland as her director once more. Not only was he good at his work he was also adept at handling difficult personalities and he succeeded in achieving what he wanted without once ruffling Elinor's feathers. He even let her direct the Wedding Scene. Once again she had to be warned about provoking the censors when she described how the love scene beneath the furs on the speeding sleigh which drew on her own experiences should be played. In fact before the film was edited Louis Mayer showed this scene to a meeting of MGM film directors as an example of 'the varieties of passion *not* permitted in an MGM production'.[3]

It was Elinor who had introduced Charles Chaplin to Marion Davies. She had arranged a small dinner at which the two of them met. Marion Davies was always interested in flirtation and Chaplin was not averse to responding, despite his many other entanglements at that time. Indirectly, therefore, Elinor could be said to have had some responsibility for the much-discussed events which took place on the yacht *Oneida* in November.

The yacht belonged to William Randolph Hearst. When he had set up Marion Davies in Hollywood he had sailed the *Oneida* through the Panama Canal to have it available for entertainment in California.

The accounts of the November cruise vary and it is now unlikely that the exact truth can be uncovered, given the web of lies and intrigues which was created in the immediate aftermath. The following seems to me the most plausible sequence of events.

Hearst had become aware of the growing friendship between his mistress and Chaplin, and was not pleased about it. Not only was he jealous but he also had information about Chaplin's part in yet another potential Hollywood scandal. Starring in the film Chaplin was currently making, *The Gold Rush*, was Lita Grey. When she had been given the part she had lied about her age, as the studios were more and more anxious about the problems which arose when they employed girls under the age of consent. According to Lita Grey and her family, Chaplin had seduced the girl whilst they were away on location and made her pregnant. Only when he learnt about the pregnancy did Chaplin also learn that Lita Grey was under age. If his guilt was proven, he faced a jail sentence and a serious threat to his career. His alternative was to marry the girl and fake the child's birth date. Although this seemed the only way open to him, he was reluctant to take it because he did not want a second child bride. Hearst did not want Marion mixed up in such a scandal. He saw the cruise as a way of observing at close quarters Marion's attitude to Chaplin.

Chaplin, for his part, was prepared to go on the cruise because it offered a temporary respite from his problems. Also invited were Elinor, Tom Ince, and other guests including a woman reputed to be Ince's mistress, Marion's sisters and Louella Parson, Hearst's gossip columnist, and other members of his staff.

The party assembled on Tuesday 18 November. After a dinner party the first night, they were due to set sail in the morning to San Diego. Because Hearst was the host, water was served with dinner. Tom Ince proposed a toast to his son's birthday but Elinor refused to drink, saying that it was bad luck to drink a toast in water. Elinor's comment coupled with her reputation for being psychic cast a damper on the party.

It is what happened after dinner that remains unclear. According to one version Tom Ince was up all night vomiting. Fellow guests suspected food poisoning and recommended that he be taken off the yacht and driven immediately to hospital. In this version acute indigestion was diagnosed; Tom Ince returned home and died some days later of a heart attack.

The other, more dramatic version of the story, suggests that late that night Marion was talking on deck with Ince. Hearst saw the couple, and is said to have mistaken Ince for Chaplin and shot him in a fit of jealousy. Before daylight Tom Ince was taken off the yacht and rushed to hospital. Chaplin, fearing to have his name linked with this affair, left the boat at the same time. He was met by Kono, his discreet secretary, who later said that he had seen Tom Ince being taken off the yacht with a bullet wound in his head.

Ironically it was the smoke-screen Hearst attempted to throw around events that made the public interested in knowing exactly what had happened on the yacht that night.

In the papers which Hearst controlled there appeared the dramatic headline, SPECIAL CAR RUSHES STRICKEN MAN HOME FROM RANCH. In this piece it was claimed that Tom Ince, his wife and two children had been staying on the Hearst ranch when he had been taken ill.

By 20 November rival papers in New York and Los Angeles were asserting that Ince had been on the yacht and that he had died within ten hours of his removal.

There was apparently no inquest, and none was requested. The death certificate was properly signed and the body was examined by the LA Chief of Homicide before it was cremated on 21 November.

When those who had remained on the yacht disembarked after the planned cruise to San Diego, they were bombarded with questions. When Elinor was asked for her version of events by Elinor Boardman she replied that everyone on board had been sworn to secrecy.

Why would this have been necessary if Ince had simply died of natural causes? In his autobiography Chaplin claims to have visited Ince at his home shortly before he died. This is certainly inaccurate. And in letters home to her mother Elinor tells the story using a time scheme which does not fit with what is known of the events.

The whole incident is a clear example of how far Elinor had travelled in compromising her own earlier strict principles. She says little about the cruise in her autobiography but she does make much of another occasion on which she, Chaplin and Marion Davies all witnessed a murder. The next day the hotel staff denied absolutely that anything untoward had happened in the night. Only a blood stain on the lobby carpet remained to convince the three that they had not dreamt up the whole thing. Is it possible that Elinor transferred some of her feelings about the incident on the yacht to this other more anonymous happening?

For whatever reason, Chaplin was jolted into action in the matter of Lita Grey and on 23 November he married her. His relationship with Marion Davies reverted to simple friendship.

Elinor, Marion and Hearst continued to be friends even after Elinor left Hollywood. It has been suggested that the guilty conspiracy bound them together. But as Elinor maintained friendships with other Hollywood stars until the end of her life, there is no reason to put such a sinister interpretation on this particular relationship.

These events were not allowed to interrupt work. Elinor was intent on making a screenplay from her novel *Man and Maid.* Shooting began at the end of 1924 and the film was released in 1925. In the same year she wrote the screenplay for *Love's Blindness.*

It was a year with many reminders of the past and of a world and a way of life so very different from that of Hollywood.

She had heard that in 1923 Curzon had been passed over for the position of Prime Minister in favour of Stanley Baldwin. Knowing well just how ambitious he was, she knew what a major disappointment to him this had been. She appreciated the irony that it was because he had been at Montacute, cut off from the larger world, that he had not been aware of how events were shaping in London. She knew painfully how that felt.

Grace had not given him the heir he longed for and what is more, once all hopes of his ever being Prime Minister were dashed, she had begun to lead a separate life. All this news had filtered through to Elinor. What she could not have known is that Grace had written to Curzon as follows: 'As our feelings are what they are, the only possible thing is that we should lead our separate lives as much as possible. I shall always play any part where I am needed, and do all I can to help your public position.'[4]

Consuelo Vanderbilt Balsan describes Curzon's visit to her in France just before his death. She was saddened by his poor health and loneliness.

Back at Kedleston Curzon had collapsed whilst supervising work in the gardens. He had spent two days on his own there and then, despite feeling very ill, he had returned to London and from there he had gone to Cambridge to make a speech. But a serious haemorrhage prevented him from carrying out his intentions. His London doctors found his condition alarming and urged an operation to save his life. But his recovery was temporary and he was told that he was near death. At this news he immediately fell into a deep sleep from which he never woke. He died on 20 March at his home in Carlton House Terrace. After a service in Westminster Abbey his remains were taken by train to Kedleston where he was interred along with his beloved Mary.

Hearing about his life since he had betrayed her and knowing how unhappy he had been at the last, Elinor was now able to think of Curzon without bitterness or rancour. She wondered, though, if he might not have been happier, after all, if he had married her rather than Grace Duggan.

By an uneasy coincidence, this was also the year in which that other long-time suitor, Lord Milner, died. His end was very different as he was living contentedly in his house in Sturry along with his wife. He had willingly given up his political ambitions before he married.

Visits from the Duchess of Alba and Penaranda were further reminders of Elinor's past. Even more so was the arrival of Millicent, Duchess of Sutherland. The two women had seen many changes since they had last met at the peace conference in Paris. Since then Elinor had developed a new life in Hollywood while Millicent had bought a château in France and embarked on a third disastrous marriage. After the war she too had been restless just as Elinor had been. In 1924 she had decided to divorce her husband and to set off with her maid on an overland crossing of South America. She was now on her way back to England and breaking her journey by staying with Douglas Fairbanks and Mary Pickford.

Millicent and Elinor made a striking couple. Both were still very attractive and were taking care to remain so. Both dressed very elegantly and shared a fondness for the company of handsome young men and dancing. Elinor's young man of the moment was John Wynn. She was trying, without much success, to get Rhys-Williams to pay him an enormous salary from the company as her business manager. In the meantime he was her dancing partner. She found another good-looking young man to partner Millicent, and for a few days the two women threw themselves into dancing and party-going. At Marion Davies's house Elinor had Valentino, partnered by Pola Negri, demonstrate for Millicent just how the tango should be danced.

When Millicent left there were other social excitements. One occasion which made a great impression on Elinor and which she recorded in unusual detail in her autobiography was what she ironically described as the 'Great Mexican Scandal'.

One of Hearst's many properties was a vast estate in Mexico close to the border. He had invited a party of actors and actresses there for a visit, including Elinor, Chaplin and his wife Lita. Elinor travelled with the married couple in a car which was at the rear of the convoy headed for Mexico.

At nightfall they found that a portion of the road had been washed away. It seemed dangerous to continue in the dark but out there in the wilds there was nowhere to spend the night. They found a run-down place with several dilapidated shacks. It was agreed that the men would sleep in the cars and the women would share the shacks. By the time Elinor's party arrived there was just one place left, a cabin with a double bed and a smaller bed for a child. There was nothing for it but to settle there for the night. Chaplin and his wife had the double bed, which left the child's bed for Elinor. Although she was not a tall woman, the bed was a little too short even for her, so a box, which proved to contain broken crockery, was found and put at the end of the bed as a footrest. Chaplin and Lita made themselves as comfortable as possible on the double bed.

Elinor made a cursory inspection of the shack before she went to bed, and announced that she intended to keep all her clothes on, and not for reasons of modesty. She put back on her hat and gloves and lay rigidly in the dark listening to the whispered bickerings of Chaplin and his wife. None of them could sleep. Then Chaplin got to thinking about what Hearst's newspapers could make of this situation. The headline could be, ELINOR GLYN AND CHARLES CHAPLIN. THREE-IN-A BED SCANDAL IN NEW MEXICO. Carried away by this he gleefully elaborated upon how each newspaper would develop this story. Before long the two women were convulsed with laughter. And then, just before dawn, Chaplin discovered for himself what Elinor had suspected all along, that the place was alive with bugs. His mournful response to this and to the bites he found all over his body again reduced the women to helpless laughter.

Suddenly the cabin door burst open and in rushed the rest of their party. The two groups stared at each other in bewilderment. The noise in the cabin had been so loud and so alarming that everyone else had been woken up. Convinced that they were hearing cries for help, they had rushed to defend the three against what they felt sure was an attack from bandits.

The estate in Mexico was not the only large tract of land Hearst owned. He also had a property at San Simeon. A visit to this residence was a real test of Elinor's ability to put out of her mind all her European notions and to accept her Hollywood friends on their own terms.

For a more vulgar, ostentatious show of wealth and bad taste than San Simeon would be hard to imagine. To Elinor, accustomed to English stately homes, it must have been a nightmare to equal any of the film sets she had so roundly condemned in her early days in Hollywood. Here under one roof was a priceless collection of paintings, furniture, fireplaces, silver, porcelain, tapestries, carpets, and *objets d'art*, all collected, as if by a magpie, by the acquisitive Hearst. His taste in individual items may well have been good but the final assemblage showed no sensitivity to anything beyond the pleasure of ownership.

The façade of this amazing building was described by Chaplin, who was also a frequent visitor there, as 'a combination of Rheims cathedral and a gigantic Swiss chalet'.[5] This edifice, which would house thirty guests, was surrounded by five Italian villas in each of which six guests could be accommodated. The villas were furnished in Italian style complete with baroque ceilings and carved seraphs and cupids.

It was in the main château that Hearst's passion for collecting had run riot. The dining room had been constructed to look like the nave of Westminster Abbey and it was hung with a mixture of fake and genuine Gobelin tapestries. It was here that guests were required to assemble every evening at seven-thirty for cocktails. It was a house rule that guests should not drink in their rooms and that no alcohol was to be consumed before six o'clock. This was not a rule that perturbed Elinor, but other less abstemious guests would meet secretly in Marion's rooms where she kept her own supply of drinks. Dinner was eight o'clock sharp and Hearst expected all his guests to be there. After dinner movies were shown. For the rest of their stay the guests saw little of Hearst: they were expected to entertain themselves. This was not difficult to do as swimming, horseback riding, tennis and even a zoo were available.

The first time she was invited Elinor visited the zoo. Among his collection of rare animals Hearst had a chimpanzee called Jerry. For some reason this animal would become enraged at the sight of Hearst or anyone else dressed in bright clothes. Elinor did not know this and was unlucky enough to attract his attention. His manner of showing his displeasure was to defecate and then hurl excrement at the person unfortunate enough to have aroused his dislike.

Hearst was appalled when he learnt that Madame Glyn had been subjected to this treatment. Much to the distress of Marion, Hearst decided that Jerry had to go. He was shipped out to another zoo.

Although like everyone else in Hollywood Elinor had been intrigued to be invited to Hearst's castle, it was always with some relief that she left it.

Love's Blindness was filmed in 1925 with Antonio Moreno in the lead. But after this Elinor's career as a film scenarist and director seemed to be coming to an end. Elinor herself was aware that the kind of romance she was accustomed to writing was no longer so popular with the public. Her contract allowed her to make one more film for Metro-Goldwyn Mayer. There was no talk of giving her another contract. She published the book based on the film *Love's Blindness* and then she wrote a script called *The Only Thing*.

Her former director, King Vidor, had agreed to make a film for Hearst's Cosmopolitan Films. The film, as always, was to star Marion Davies. *Show People* is a film about Hollywood. In it Marion Davies plays a part closely based on Gloria Swanson's rise to stardom. Everyone well known in Hollywood at that time appears in the film, including Elinor who has a brief walk on part as herself. The heroine gasps with pleasure at gaining a glimpse of this world famous writer of romance.

No picture about Hollywood at this time would have been complete without the inclusion of Elinor. But her role in the community was much less forceful than it had been. A photograph taken at the time provides a visual clue to this. The occasion was the wedding of King Vidor to Elinor Boardman. The ceremonies took place at Marion Davies's home in Santa Monica. A double wedding had been planned, as John Gilbert had expected to marry Greta Garbo. But Garbo changed her mind and did not turn up. John Gilbert blamed Louis Mayer for interfering; he picked a quarrel and before long the two men were fighting. Once they had been separated the marriage was solemnised. The wedding group was photographed after the ceremony. There at the very back, peeping over the shoulder of Samuel Goldwyn, is Elinor.

In August Irene, Curzon's daughter, now Lady Ravensdale, came to visit Hollywood. Her title was a recent acquisition. When Curzon had realised that he was not going to have a son he had arranged matters so that his eldest daughter would inherit his subsidiary title, though it would revert to the male line after her death.

With her Irene brought news from England, particularly about Cimmie. She confirmed that when her father had died he had not been reconciled with Cimmie after a dispute about Cimmie's inheritance. Now Cimmie's husband, Oswald Mosley had been elected as the Labour MP for Smethwick and Cimmie herself had just agreed to stand as the Labour MP for Stoke on Trent. Although Elinor's own political views were gradually changing as a result of the war and her life in Hollywood, this news about Cimmie startled her. She remembered the picture she had painted of the Labour MP in *Halcyone*, the radical Mr Hanbury-Green, an unpleasant, uncouth opportunist who marries Mrs Cricklander for her money. In her novel she had contrasted him with the conservative Derringham, based on Curzon himself, to the latter's distinct advantage. How strangely things had turned out.

Irene herself had not changed politically like her younger sister. She still belonged to the old country-house circles. She spent a lot of money on clothes and travel and gambling. She was still unmarried. Once Elinor might have envied this apparently carefree young woman. Now she was just aware of how Irene's life lacked purpose and a centre especially in comparison with the lives of the young men and women with whom Elinor was in daily contact. They might play hard and get into trouble of various kinds, but they also worked hard and had ambitions.

While Irene was in Hollywood the news came of Rudolph Valentino's death. He had been in New York for some time after having separated from his wife. He had been taken to hospital with appendicitis, but because the operation was delayed until a suitably prestigious surgeon could be found to operate, peritonitis had developed. On 22 August the thirty-one-year-old star had died. In New York there had been hysterical scenes as thousands of women struggled to see their hero lying in state. There was a memorial service in Hollywood on

30 August which Elinor and Irene attended.

She was shocked by this sudden death of her young friend, but in true Hollywood style she continued with the arrangements for a party she had planned for Irene, consoling herself with the thought that Valentino would have wished it.

Increasingly Elinor considered leaving Hollywood. She had already written to her mother saying that she was 'getting so fed up with everything here, the uncertainty, the delay about everything, the cheating and the lying, that I am going to just write stories and not bother to supervise any more'. She did not need to be in Hollywood to write.

Then suddenly something happened which turned her plans upside down and began a new phase in Elinor's Hollywood career.

28 THE 'IT' GIRL

*I*n a last ditch attempt to keep her place in Hollywood Elinor had attempted a new kind of film. In 1925 she made *Ritzy* for Paramount. Reluctantly she had moved out of the world of high romance and given her story a contemporary setting and a certain raciness. But the film was not a success. Elinor was casting about for new ideas when she received an unexpected offer from B.P. Schulberg.

Benjamin Schulberg was also working for Paramount at this time. He had returned to the company after some years working as an independent producer with his own company, Preferred Pictures. Although Zukor had been responsible for his original dismissal from Paramount, he had invited him back for a specific reason.

Whilst he was running Preferred Pictures Schulberg had signed up Clara Bow. She had been sent to him as an unknown Brooklyn actress shortly after she had won the Brewster Publications Fame and Fortune award which guaranteed her a screen test.

When she arrived in Hollywood Clara Bow was just eighteen. Although many other actresses came from poor backgrounds Clara Bow's home life had been worse than most. She had been born an unwanted child in the slums of Brooklyn. Her mother, who was little more than a teenager herself when her daughter was born, suffered from bouts of madness. At such times she would try to kill herself and her daughter. When Clara was seventeen her mother was confined in a mental asylum where she died. Robert Bow, Clara's father, has been described by her biographer David Stenn as 'a man stunted not just physically but emotionally'; women 'he regarded as objects put into existence for the same reason as liquor: so that he could abuse them'.[1] It seems highly likely that he sexually abused his daughter.

Nevertheless when Clara Bow settled in Hollywood she sent for her father and the two of them, together with Clara's first lover, had set up house together.

Schulberg soon discovered that Clara Bow was an excellent actress. He turned her abilities to good account and by exploiting the 'loan system' he had his protégée make sixteen movies in eighteen months. She was nominated one of the Baby Stars of 1924.

It was to capture Clara Bow for Paramount that Zukor was prepared to employ Schulberg again.

In 1926 Schulberg read a novella being serialised in Hearst's *Cosmopolitan*. He immediately recognised the potential of both the story and the writer, Elinor Glyn. The story entitled 'It' was about the kind of animal magnetism that is more than simply sex appeal and which some people are born with. Elinor had identified this phenomenon even in her early novels.

What attracted Schulberg to the notion was that he felt that this was exactly the quality which made Clara Bow so charismatic. He decided to buy the rights for the story from Elinor even though he had every intention of radically rewriting it. As an important part of the deal he made with Elinor, she had to agree to promote Clara Bow as the personification of all that she meant by 'It'. Wisely he secured Elinor's agreement to this arrangement before he introduced her to Clara herself.

Elinor knew all about Clara Bow even if she had not previously met her. (Their social circles definitely did not overlap!)

At a time when most Hollywood stars were intimidated by the morals clause in their contracts and were trying desperately to keep their public images untarnished by scandalous gossip, Clara Bow made no secret of her hectic and promiscuous sex life. Just before she met Elinor she had been engaged to two men at the same time and had married neither of them. Elinor, however, was sufficiently keen to keep her place in Hollywood and sufficiently intrigued by the girl herself to agree to Schulberg's terms.

The two women made a startling contrast when they did meet. Elinor, in her sixties now, was draped in purple chiffon. Her manner was kindly but patronising. Clara Bow was dressed in the uniform she was wearing for the film *Wings*. She had all the energy and youthful confidence to be expected in a twenty-one-year-old star. She was not particularly impressed or intimidated by Elinor. She continued, as was her habit, to chew gum, and made no attempt to modify her Brooklyn accent.

Instead of being deterred, Elinor saw Clara as a challenge.

She was predisposed to like her because Clara really did have the magnetic quality Elinor admired and because she had chosen to dye her hair a brilliant red. Elinor always favoured redheads like herself.

She soon realised, however, that Clara Bow had a will of her own. She would not or could not change her accent. She would not accept Elinor's criticisms of her clothes and was just as likely to turn up at a formal dinner wearing a bathing suit as she had ever been.

Schulberg's plans for publicity required the two women to be seen about together. Elinor found herself being driven about in Clara's red Packard accompanied by her red chow. Since Clara had no respect for traffic lights or speed limits, these appearances were a sore trial to the older woman.

When she visited Clara's home she faced a muddle to equal that at San Simeon. But whilst Hearst lacked taste in putting together individually beautiful and priceless objects, Clara lacked any discrimination even in the choice of the objects themselves. In a contemporary biographical article about Clara Bow, 'The Playgirl of Hollywood', her house is described as follows:

> A gaudy doll in frowsy skirts and wig leans against a wonderful Ming lamp. A huge fuzzy teddy bear with a pink bow round his neck occupies a corner of the luxurious brocaded davenport. The center table is a fine thing of carved oak and the rugs are awful imitation Chinese. The lamps look as if they had come from the five and ten cent store, but the shawl on the piano might be work by a Spanish Infanta.[2]

Clara's pride and joy was her 'Chinese room'. This room with its colour scheme of predominantly red and gold with its monstrous lacquer god on a carved pedestal and its brass incense burner seemed to Elinor like a nightmare parody of her own Chinoiserie rooms at the Ambassador.

The studio had finally persuaded Clara to hire a cook and a chauffeur. She rarely let the chauffeur drive her. But at least guests were now spared macaroni-cheese dinners cooked by Robert Bow at which it was not unknown for father and daughter to engage in bitter arguments which ended with them throwing food at each other.

To add to Elinor's discomfort, Clara had begun yet another affair, this time with Gary Cooper who had a minor role in the film. Elinor was herself enthusiastic about the young man's looks, but she was not happy when Clara Bow described in detail her passionate sexual relations with her new lover.

Surprisingly she did not condemn Clara's behaviour altogether. She took the attitude that other stars in Hollywood had relationships which would not stand close scrutiny. The only difference was that women like Marion Davies were secretive whilst Clara Bow was not. Elinor believed that Clara's sexual openness in 1926 had something in common with her own exposure of hypocrisy in her early novels. Her own social ostracism on the grounds of immorality after the publication of *Three Weeks* made her more sympathetic to Clara's position as an outsider in the seemingly free and easy environment of Hollywood.

But it was seeing Clara on the set that convinced Elinor that she had not made a mistake in promoting her as the 'It' girl. Everyone who worked with Clara Bow in these years was impressed by her talent. When Clarence Badger was directing *It* he simply explained a given scene to her and then let her make of it what she would. Elinor was in complete agreement with this policy. Her respect for Clara as an actress survived all the many inevitable difficulties of their association. Even after word reached her that Clara Bow had been calling her a 'Shithead', and even after Elinor had long since given up her early attempt to make her behave and dress more correctly, that respect remained. She saw in Clara something that Clara herself was aware of when she said, 'All the time the flapper is laughin' and dancin', there's a feeling of tragedy underneath . . . she's unhappy and disillusioned, and that's what people sense. That's what makes her different.'[3]

Elinor supported Clara's efforts to get the studios to give her more serious and demanding roles than those Schulberg was prepared to offer. Schulberg was only interested in money. He had found a star and a format that for the present made a lot of money. He saw no reason to take risks by presenting Clara to the public in a new kind of role and he was not interested in Clara's long-term career as an actress.

For a while the two women went their own ways. Once Elinor had filmed her bit part in *It* she went about the country promoting the film by giving talks about *It* and about Clara Bow. She had less to do with the actual making of this film than with any other based on her writing. By the time it was finished, in fact, Elinor could scarcely recognise the script as having anything to do with her story, as Schulberg had employed Louis Lighton and Hope Loring to rewrite it and shift the emphasis so that Clara's part was absolutely central.

The film was a great success. But even so Elinor was surprised when Paramount bought *The Vicissitudes of Evangeline* for $50,000 as another vehicle for Clara Bow. How could this very modern girl star in such an Edwardian story in which the comedy was verbal rather than visual? Elinor learnt the answer as soon as production began. Her screenplay was abandoned and the small part she had written in for herself was scrapped. All the studio wanted of her was her name.

The original novel is dedicated to all those with red hair and it was this dedication that was used for the new title, *Red Hair*. Elinor's heroine Evangeline, a young orphan doing her best to make her way in the world without being seduced, is transformed into the red-haired manicurist, Bubbles McCoy. The extent to which the very nature of Elinor's novel had been transformed is indicated by a piece in *Variety* which claimed, 'Bow plus Glyn equals underwear'.

Elinor soon ceased to have any illusions about these films ostensibly made from her writing. Although she was well paid for them, she thought little of them. Although they had brought fame and money to Clara Bow, Elinor recognised that they had not advanced the young girl's career at all. The conclusions she reached are given in *Romantic Adventure*: Clara Bow, she said, should have been given 'particularly tragic parts, for which she had a far greater aptitude than for the comedy scenes which I had to make her act in my films'.

Sadly Elinor Glyn felt that she had not had the kind of influence on Clara Bow that she would have liked. But her contact with this 'flapper girl', the kind of young woman defined by F. Scott Fitzgerald as 'pretty, impudent, superbly assured, as worldly-wise, briefly clad and "hard boiled" as possible', made a lasting impression on her.

She was fascinated and disturbed by the difference in values and expectation she had encountered in Clara Bow and those of herself at that age. She thought about all the young women who, because of her films, took Clara Bow for a role model. The result of her close observation and her pondering was *The Flirt and the Flapper* published in 1930.

The piece might almost be a transcription, so accurately does she capture the specifics of the kind of slang Clara Bow used. Elinor's tactics in this piece are those she had used in her early satirical novels. The values of one part of society are questioned by someone who is innocent about the going rate and is, therefore, shocked. In this case a flapper girl is overheard by the portrait of her grandmother as a young woman. The portrait steps out of her frame in order to try to understand the speech and behaviour of her granddaughter who seems to her like a creature from another world. Through the comedy and raciness of this piece Elinor promotes values and standards she elsewhere urges more seriously.

The flapper does all the things that we know Elinor deplored. First of all she drinks too much bootleg alcohol. When she tries to make her grandmother understand what she means by 'hooch' she describes it as 'Re-distilled, denatured alcohol and – and a few flavourings'. In her innocence her grandmother responds, 'Dear me! What we called methylated spirits – that sounds very poisonous!'

Her grandmother cannot understand the activity she has seen the company engaged in after the alcohol has been drunk. When her granddaughter refers to 'snow' she is further puzzled. The flapper says impatiently, 'We sniff snow, we don't make balls of it.' The older woman cannot understand the flapper's attitude towards men, love, marriage and divorce. In her turn the flapper cannot understand why her grandmother is concerned about grammar, about self-respect and the notion of 'noblesse oblige'.

The grandmother's worst fears are realised when the flapper confesses that all her frantic activity has only two objectives, 'exhilaration or forgetfulness' and that she feels she is 'not obliged to do anything but kill time'.

In response to the flapper's defensive attitude towards what she feels is her grandmother's disapproval she replies, as Elinor herself would have done, 'I don't disapprove of you; I only fear you have no sense of values.'

The story ends the way Elinor would have liked to think all such stories ended. The flapper realises that she does have a serious side and that she does love and wish to marry someone and have children.

At the time *The Flirt and the Flapper* was published, if she had been the kind of girl who read books, Clara Bow would have laughed at Elinor's conclusion. But perhaps Elinor was wiser about Clara than the young girl would have acknowledged. Her life did become wilder and wilder and emptier and emptier. Part of her did long for a simpler life, marriage and children. And, for a while, to escape the dreadful scandals that brought her career to an end, she did live the 'simple life' with Rex Bell in Nevada.

All the excitement that had surrounded the making of the two films with Clara Bow had only delayed Elinor's decision to leave Hollywood. A further development taking place in the movie industry at the time seemed to her to confirm her view that there was no longer a place for her there. The 'talkie' was the new medium of the time. The kind of script that Elinor had been writing was definitely not what the studios were looking for to use with this technology. Elinor had a test for the 'talkies' but she never seriously considered appearing in them.

It is likely that working with Clara Bow had forced Elinor to recognise consciously the increasingly seedy side of Hollywood before she left and that is why she paints such a black picture of her time there in her autobiography: 'On looking back at it all I am staggered by my calm acceptance of many terrible happenings and my failure to appreciate or fear the dangers of the sinister atmosphere.'

When she re-read the diaries she had kept during her Hollywood years she found them terrible to contemplate. She felt that Hollywood represented the 'Lemurian Curse of the West Coast' which she describes in some detail.

> The early symptoms of the disease, which break out almost on arrival in Hollywood, are a sense of exaggerated self-importance and self-centredness, which naturally alienates all old friends. Next comes a desire for and belief in the importance of money above all else, a loss of the normal sense of humour and of proportion, and finally, in extreme cases, the abandonment of all previous standards of moral value.
>
> My natural character would I trust have saved me from reaching this final stage.

But it was difficult, if not impossible, for Elinor to exchange the 'hectic and abnormal' life of Hollywood for the quiet life in England that her family was urging upon her. As she later recognised, it would be some time yet before she 'could shake off the effects of the insidious poison of the atmosphere of Hollywood'. At sixty-three she was not ready to settle for the conventional life of a middle-aged woman.

Her thoughts turned to New York, that city 'filled with vitality'. It was far from Hollywood but had its own excitement. She resolved to try life there for a while, living in an apartment at the top of the newly constructed Ritz Tower.

29 THE CRASH

The formation of Elinor Glyn Limited had not really changed Elinor's way of thinking about money. She still assumed that there was always plenty on hand and that she could easily make more. For a while nothing happened to suggest that this was not so. While she lived at the Ritz in New York enjoying the extraordinary views from her suite she wrote pieces for the Hearst Press and her income seemed assured. Then her confidence that she could make plenty of money by writing was further bolstered when she unexpectedly sold her story 'Not Always' to be made into the film *Such Men Are Dangerous*. It was the first piece of hers to be used as the basis for a 'talkie', and for it she received six thousand dollars. She was sure that she could make more in the same way.

In the spring she made a brief visit to England. But even here she spent most of her time with Hollywood friends. Hearst had just bought another property, St Donat in Wales. She found that by now she was more at home in the company of Americans such as Marion Davies and William Randolph Hearst than with her English contemporaries. So, despite her family's pleas for her to stay, she found little to keep her in England and soon returned to the States. In the summer she was once more with Marion Davies, this time at Ocean House in Santa Monica.

It was staying with her rich friends in their various houses that gave Elinor the idea that she too, after all this time, would buy a house for herself. She decided that she would rather like to try living in Washington, DC. She was quite forthright about the fact that the large number of older, well-educated and wealthy men living there was a great attraction. She found what she considered to be a beautiful little house dating from 1790 in the Georgetown district. She looked forward to entertaining there but her first thought, inevitably, was how to redecorate the whole place and make it completely her own.

She had not yet moved into her new house when she learnt

from her daughters that Mrs Kennedy was ill. She was also troubled by a demand from the Inland Revenue Service for payment of taxes owed for many years. Because Elinor did not consider herself to be an American, she had somehow reasoned that she was exempt from American taxation. But the size of the bill that she was presented with and the threatening tone of the accompanying letter frightened her. She decided that these two matters together were sufficient reason for a visit to England. She could then see for herself how her mother was and she could consult the ever reliable and knowledgeable Rhys Rhys-Williams about her financial status.

When she arrived in England she found that she was expected to stay. Her daughters' determination was made clear when they took her to the large house, Wolsey's Spring near Kingston, which they had bought for her to live in. Margot had even had the house decorated throughout in colours and styles she thought would be pleasing to Elinor.

Because Mrs Kennedy had suffered a slight stroke, Margot and Juliet suggested that now that Elinor was back and had a home she could have her mother to live with her. And Rhys-Williams declared that unless Elinor had hidden away a great deal of money that he did not know about, she could not afford to return to the States and face the IRS.

Elinor was trapped.

Wolsey's Spring was a house that represented the kind of style Juliet and Margot felt to be appropriate for their mother at her age. But it was not at all to Elinor's taste. For a start it was far too large for her. She had always liked small places in which she could be alone. For much of her adult life she had lived in hotel rooms, able to come and go without the bother of organising cleaning and meals. Wolsey's Spring had servants and gardeners who needed her supervision and her instructions. And, although Margot had meant well by decorating the house, she had been insensitive to her mother's passion for doing this herself and for imprinting her own personality on wherever she lived. Above all Elinor did not like living in the country. She had turned her back firmly on that way of life when she had sold Lamberts, and since then she had always lived at the centre of activity and bustle. She tried to be grateful and to put a good face on the situation. But her daughters, and Margot in particular, knew that they had made a mistake.

Elinor did not regard taking care of a house as a real occupation and it was not in Elinor's nature to be without an occupation. She also wanted to make some money. Rhys-Williams had advised her to spend most of what she had brought from Hollywood on an annuity which would provide her with a regular income. She accepted the wisdom of this, but the income it would provide was not a large one and would certainly not support the extravagant style of living which Elinor had by now come to regard as her right.

Her book *The Flirt and The Flapper* which was published that year reminded her of her last days in Hollywood and of Clara Bow. She missed the pace of life in the States and, because she still believed that films were the best way of making large sums of money, she decided to take a bold step. She would recapture something of the life she had left behind her but she would no longer simply write scripts and then see them mangled and distorted by the production company. She would set up her own company and supervise the making of her films from start to finish.

It was a plausible and attractive proposition. Juliet's husband was sufficiently convinced by it to agree to invest in Elinor Glyn Productions Ltd. Juliet herself, who throughout her life had a remarkable gift for turning her hand to whatever needed doing at a given moment, was eager to help in the cutting room, putting to use what she had learned earlier in Hollywood. Elinor even managed to get her old acquaintance from her early days in Hollywood, Edward Knoblock, to join her enterprise. She rented studio space at Elstree Studios and employed a Production Manager and a Director of Photography of whom she had heard good reports from her friends. She negotiated with United Artists for a guaranteed release and an advance payment when the negative was delivered. All seemed set for Elinor to launch herself into a profitable business.

Unfortunately Elinor's lack of modesty about her ability to produce films made her enemies at Elstree from the start. She could not resist patronising British film making just as she had once scoffed at American lack of knowledge about European customs. She began to find the tyres of her car damaged when she wanted to get home after work. One day she even discovered that the wheel had been loosened and that she could have had a serious accident. But she tried to ignore such matters and concentrate on the job.

Rather than start from scratch on a new script, Elinor decided to use a story she had on hand, *Knowing Men*, originally intended for Clara Bow. Edward Knoblock wrote the screenplay and the film went into production. Juliet was excited to be working alongside her mother, and her enthusiasm prompted Margot to persuade her husband to invest in Elinor's company.

The actors and actresses to whom Elinor gave parts were very different from the young people she had been working with at the end of her time in Hollywood. Typical of her new protégés was the Honourable David Herbert, the younger son of the Earl of Pembroke. In his autobiography, *Second Son*, he claims that he was never too sure why Elinor had chosen him for a major part in her film as he had no previous experience. But, in fact, along with other young people including Cecil Beaton, he had been experimenting for some time with home-made films, revelling in dressing up and painting his face much to the consternation of his family.

He was, however, painfully conscious of having a very weak chin which he felt damaged his good looks. But Elinor was undeterred by this: she knew how to remedy such a defect. She insisted that he did regular facial exercises. He found them painful but Elinor convinced him that it was worth persisting. To his amazement and delight the exercises finally had the desired effect, his jaw clicked into place and the weak chin was gone for ever. But sadly this did not ensure that David Herbert would become a movie star.

When the film had its first showing in February 1930 at the Regal Cinema in Marble Arch, the reviews were terrible, condemning the film as amateurish. For although Elinor knew some aspects of producing a movie well, others she knew hardly at all and this was apparent to the reviewers. Even so, it was not remarkably worse than other films which did get distribution and which at least broke even.

All might yet have been well had not Edward Knoblock panicked. He was afraid for his reputation as a writer in being associated with a flop. He took the unusual and excessive step of applying for an injunction to prevent further showings of the film. He did not get a permanent injunction but even the temporary stay was sufficient to prevent the film being available for the contractual release date. This meant that the film could not make any money beyond the original advance. Edward Knoblock chose not to remember his part in this enterprise which he does not even mention in his autobiography, *Round The Room*.

Elinor in her sixty-sixth year could be forgiven for her subsequent depression and her sense of many aspects of her life coming to an end. Her film career now seemed to be completely over. And as if to emphasise the way the world was changing the news reached her that Lillie Langtry, that heroine of her youth, had died and been buried back in St Saviour in Jersey.

At this point most people would have given up and settled for a quiet retirement. But not Elinor. Her desire for vindication was stimulated by the encouragement of Joseph Schenk, the head of United Artists. Did this man really believe in Elinor's ability to see a production through to a profitable conclusion? Or was he hypnotised by Elinor's own confidence into telling her what she wanted to hear?

Unbelievably, Elinor started all over again. This time she had little money of her own to invest in the venture. She borrowed from her family, from the bank and from Lord Ilchester, the husband of her friend Birdie, who had become interested in films during a visit to the States. Somehow she managed to persuade all these people that they would not only see their money back but make a profit.

The script she chose this time was her earlier novel, *The Price of Things*. But in turning the novel into a screenplay she diminished it. Even so the film she made was technically and artistically an improvement on her first effort. Financially it was just as disastrous. Elinor with her lack of experience in seeing a film right through to distribution had not properly secured the necessary release. It was never shown to the general public.

Lord Ilchester appears to have borne no grudge about the loss of his money. But Elinor's family was thrown into turmoil by the repercussions of this second failure. First of all Wolsey's Spring had to be sold. If this had been all that was necessary, Elinor would not have been unhappy. She much prefered the small service flat in Hertford Street which became her next home.

But she was humiliated to find that she could neither give her mother a home any longer nor continue to support her financially. Mrs Kennedy moved to Miskin Manor, the family home in Glamorgan of Rhys Rhys-Williams, where she was given a suite of rooms for herself and her maid. Some of Elinor's furniture went with her as there was no room for it in Elinor's small flat.

For Mrs Kennedy and Elinor these were reasonably acceptable

changes. Margot, however, felt that she had come out of the whole business by far the worst off. She had lost so much money that she found it necessary to sell her house in St James's Square and move to Eaton Square. She blamed her mother; she blamed Juliet. Her rancour was, perhaps, made worse by jealousy. For years, as she had been growing up, she had felt herself to be her mother's favourite. She had, after all, been all over Europe with her mother while Juliet was at boarding school. But since Juliet's visit to Hollywood Elinor had grown closer to her second daughter, a bond which was strengthened by their shared interest in the occult and, until Elinor gave them up in disgust, by their excitement about the séances they attended together.

At family meetings increasingly Margot would display her hostility, blaming her mother not only for present difficulties but also recriminating with her about her neglect of her daughters as children, her callousness towards their father, her lack of interest in their marriages and her grandchildren. Above all, Margot expressed bitter resentment that Elinor had not shared with her family the affluence of her years in Hollywood.

When Juliet supported her sister in some of these accusations, Elinor was devastated. She wrote to Juliet expressing her intense unhappiness saying that she was afraid of Margot's vitriolic backhanders. She acknowledged that perhaps she could have been closer to the children when they were young and blamed her ignorance about how children should be brought up and how her absences might affect their development. She even admitted her thoughtlessness about money in the twenties saying, 'I thought you were both married and provided for and so in the rush of Hollywood I spent unjustified money on myself.'

But she claimed she had always loved her daughters and that she was especially grateful to Juliet for the way she had undertaken the support of Mrs Kennedy and worked hard for Elinor Glyn Productions without thinking of asking for a salary.

She concluded that her return to England had been a great mistake: 'I have had nearly two years of intense unhappiness here, and the undermining of all my self confidence, and joy of life.' She told Juliet that she had decided to leave England as soon as she could let her flat. Although she knew that she could not go back to America as she would really prefer, she could at least go to Versailles and be happier there than in England, for at least she would be away from the reproaches of her daughters.

In the event Elinor recovered from her depression when she was invited by Baron and Baroness Rubido-Zichy to visit Hungary to see if she could write something about the place. The prospect of travelling and seeing a new and unfamiliar place was still, as it always had been, a great stimulation to Elinor. And, of course, a new novel would bring in urgently needed income. She was predisposed to like Hungary because she had fond memories of the painter Lazlo and the stories he had told her about his country when she was sitting for her portrait.

Like all the other countries which had been involved in the war, Hungary had experienced great changes in recent years. It was now a republic and the aristocracy was much less wealthy than formerly. Although there were Hungarians who had always spent a great deal of time abroad, just like the Russians Elinor knew, she learnt that in Hungary there were many nobles who were unfamiliar with the larger world, who were intensely patriotic and who kept the old traditions and the language alive.

It was this group particularly who felt great bitterness about the treatment Hungary had received at the Treaty of Versailles. Elinor who had been present at the signing was sympathetic, and she allowed one of the characters in her novel, *Love's Hour*, to express the bitterness she heard all around her: ' "Romantic, chivalrous Hungary, that weary alien statesmen had carved up into pieces, and indifferently left bleeding – so tired they were at Versailles." '

On the whole, however, Hungary was far less different from England than Elinor had expected. If anything she found she preferred Hungary at that particular moment of disillusionment with her life in England. And so the novel which resulted from her time there is as much, if not more, a comment on England rather than Hungary.

The heroine, Aspasia, has many of Elinor's own characteristics. She is not a young woman; she too was born in October; she shares Elinor's view of the importance of Kharmic debts, and she loves cats. She recognises in herself a strain of cruelty and selfishness which she cannot always control successfully and she falls in love unwisely. But most of all she is bitter about what England has become since the war. One of the ways in which she feels it has deteriorated is in the fact that Englishmen have lost their attractiveness: 'There was no longer that innate sense of might, right and prerogative which they used to have, and so their compelling charm had gone. It was this factor, far more than the other effects of the War, which had made the great change in their fascination.'

The lack of respect for the past and for old things and the craze for whatever is new she finds deplorable. Perhaps Elinor's own new perspective on the kind of mother she had been is responsible for Aspasia's interest in the fact that in Hungary, unlike in England, in even the most aristocratic of households the nurseries always communicated with the rooms of the mother.

It was not only starting a new novel which restored some of Elinor's old confidence. An invitation to be a guest at the International Pen Congress in Budapest further strengthened her will to put all her efforts in future into her writing.

Back in England she became even more aware of this need to write and earn when, after the death of Cosmo in 1931, Lucy suddenly found herself very short of money. Elinor was luckier than her sister and never found herself in such a desperate situation largely because, throughout the next few years, with the practical help and encouragement of Juliet, she managed to continue to earn a reasonable living through journalism and writing short stories.

Although Elinor could not go to Hollywood, as she dearly wished, the next best thing was that Hollywood continued to come to her. Hearst and Marion Davies were frequently at St Donat and they always asked Elinor to visit them. Most of the other guests were young and unknown to Elinor. But that never worried her. When she had been in Hollywood almost everyone but herself had been young. She was gratified that many of them knew of her by reputation, since she had become something of a legend already in Hollywood and there were many anecdotes told about her time there. After the humiliations of the last two years this fame was delightful. And as her young friends tried, and failed, to shock Madame Glyn, she began again to see herself as *the* Elinor Glyn just as she had been depicted in *Show People*.

Gloria Swanson was in London in 1932 for the birth of the child of yet another marriage. She gave Elinor enormous pleasure when she showed her astonishment at how young Elinor still looked. She marvelled over her white, smooth skin and her slim upright figure. She wanted to know how Elinor had managed it and to be let in on her secret. So Elinor taught her how to do facial exercises and how to scrub her skin and told her what to eat and what to avoid. She advised her to read carefully the book she had published in 1927, *The Wrinkle Book*, in which she would find a complete guide to preserving her youthful skin. Gloria listened and learnt and did as the older woman advised. For both of them it was like being back in the days of their first meeting.

Clara Bow had made a brief return to movies in *Call Her Savage*. The film company, Fox, sent her on a publicity tour of Europe along with Rex Bell who was now her husband. She made a point of calling on Elinor when she was in London and she confessed to her that she now understood that a lot of what Elinor had told her and about which she had been scornful at the time had been good advice. She gave her a signed portrait with an inscription which both surprised and touched Elinor. It read: 'To Elinor Glyn, whom I respect and admire more than any woman in the world'.

Slowly Elinor was becoming reconciled to life in England. She had built up a circle of interesting friends by now. Elaborate weekends in English country houses were a thing of the past. But Elinor visited the Trees at Kelmarsh, the Pembrokes, parents of David Herbert who lived at Wilton, and, most frequently, the Ilchesters at Melbury. Birdie, Lady Ilchester, the daughter of Lady Londonderry, she regarded as her closest friend. She was full of admiration for Giles, Lord Ilchester, who shared her interest in history and tradition and who had published several books about his family and Holland House. She was entertained by his passion to maintain in good order that great phallic symbol the Cerne Giant, under the auspices of the Society for the Preservation of Ancient Erections.

She enjoyed her grandchildren, taking great pleasure in the promise they showed. She had, soon after the birth of her grandsons, invested money to help pay for their education. She was determined that they should go to Eton and was delighted when they did so. To encourage them she gave presents such as the works of Plato and to the four-year-old Geoffrey Davson, who was to become the writer Anthony Glyn, a typewriter. When they did show an aptitude for writing she told her friends about it with pride and did her best to help them get their early efforts published. But just as her own grandmother had done she insisted on her grandchildren dressing and behaving correctly and being able to converse rather than simply chatter. In their case she made no concessions to new ideas of informality and greater freedom for children. So that, although the children always found being taken out by their grandmother exciting and stimulating, they also found such excursions something of an ordeal.

Then there were visits to Mrs Kennedy in Glamorgan. Although her mother had lost her short-term memory and although she had blotted out of her mind whole periods of her life including all the years she had been the wife of David Kennedy, she loved to talk about the days of her marriage to Douglas Sutherland. And so at this late stage in her life Elinor came to know better the father she had never seen.

Other events in the past were brought into her mind when she visited Lucy at her flat in Rossetti Studios. Lucy was also trying to make some money by writing and was working on her autobiography which was published in 1932 as *Discretions and Indiscretions*. The sisters felt more kindly towards each other now as they shared their common past, and Lucy's portrait of Elinor in her book is an admiring one.

Elinor's own books continued to sell well, especially in the cheap edition, so that she was gradually able to pay off the overdraft she had incurred at the time of her venture into the film industry and was even able to offer some money to Lucy.

By 1934 Elinor felt able to express her new affluence by moving into a large flat in Connaught Place in Bayswater where she had a view of Hyde Park. She decorated her elegant living room in blue and gold and brought out of storage those pieces of French furniture, pictures and hangings for which there had not been room in Hertford Street. Once again she was able to have the company of her five tiger skins and she acquired two spectacular Persian cats which she named Candide and Zadig. She was satisfied that once again she had created an ambience suitable for Elinor Glyn, romantic novelist.

In her new, more spacious home she began to entertain. Her parties were a mixture of young and old, famous and aspiring. She took particular interest in young men and women, and loved to advise them and introduce them to the right person in a way she had not done, and perhaps was not able to do, with her own daughters. She enjoyed, as she had done in Hollywood, the role of the older, wiser woman, Madame Glyn.

That these same young people were having an influence on her in their turn is shown by *Did She?*, the novel she published in 1934. The language is quite different from all her earlier works, except perhaps that of *The Flirt and The Flapper* which had been influenced by Clara Bow. Again there is a great deal of slang used, though always with an awareness of how ephemeral it is.

But it is not only the language which is different in this novel, it is the whole perspective on society. In all Elinor's previous novels the greatest aspiration of the heroine was to marry into the nobility. This is true of such widely different characters as the young naive Elizabeth and that most self-assured and clear-sighted of heroines, Katherine Bush. The heroine of *Did She?*, Bernadine, is already of the nobility and is not proud of that fact. Her father is on the one hand obsessed with restoring his family to what he considers to be its true position and on the other hand completely irresponsible about money. He thinks nothing of drinking '87 port and wearing two pleated cambric shirts a day. His daughter feels 'how differently I considered gentle blood should manifest itself – responsibility, courage in adversity, consideration to those who are giving loving service'.

It is left to Bernadine to restore the family fortunes. Since she cannot do so by simply earning a wage – as a woman she cannot earn enough – she strikes a bargain both similar and yet utterly different from that which many others had done before her. Rather than marrying a rich man of her own class simply for the standard of living he can provide her with, she guarantees to spend three months with her employer doing exactly what he wishes and wearing only clothes of his choice. But one condition she establishes is that she will not be required to be his mistress. In exchange for her three months in this role of quasi-wife she will receive the ten thousand pounds she needs to clear her father's debts but she will not have tied herself up for life to do so.

Of course, this novel based on *Beauty and the Beast* ends happily. But the 'Beast' is not a prince in disguise. At the end of the novel he is still a forty-year-old rich man of good taste, a patron of the arts, a business man and, most importantly, not an effete aristocrat. For one of the principle complaints of the novel is the failure of upper-class men to be true males.

In this novel Elinor was trying to write the kind of book she felt was rarely encountered any more. She did not want to write an old-fashioned romance in which 'the girls were all thinking of love and dreaming of romance', nor a 'modern' one in which 'there is crude reality and sex, which is often so ugly that I am nauseated'. *Did She?* was Elinor's attempt to write a modern romance which was relevant to changed social conditions.

In 1934 Elinor visited Daisy Warwick at Easton Lodge. After their long estrangement, the result of their very different political views and their different ways of life, the two elderly women were reconciled. They had much to talk about, but their lives had led them into such different directions that they could never again be close. In fact each of them secretly rather disapproved of what the other had become. When Elinor left her friend she could not help thinking about how much the world had changed in the last years. All the glamour of Easton Lodge and Warwick Castle was now gone and her aristocratic friend, who had once been so rich, so influential and so sought after by men, was now a very heavy, far from beautiful, elderly woman living a rather lonely life in straitened circumstances.

Then there were Lucy's troubles. She too was desperately short of money. She had tried to economise, she had given up her car and no longer held parties. Her life too was much less than it had been.

These two examples of drastically changed circumstances worried Elinor. She began to wonder exactly how she stood for money. She wondered if it was for good reason that for some time both Margot and Juliet had been urging her to cut back on entertaining and had done their best to discourage her from embarking on an ambitious scheme for redecorating her flat. The letters she received from her accountant puzzled and worried her. Only one thing was clear to her and that was that she seemed to have less money than she had thought.

Towards the end of the year Lucy began to feel ill complaining of severe rheumatism in her knee. But as time went by and she grew steadily worse it became clear that her illness was more severe than anyone had at first thought. In fact she had cancer. As her illness progressed she needed more and more care but there was no money to pay a nurse or to put her into a private nursing home. Fortunately one of her old friends came to the rescue and paid for her to go into a nursing home in Putney so that the last month of her life was made as comfortable as possible. On 14 April 1935 Lucy died.

Elinor did not tell Mrs Kennedy that Lucy was dead. Instead she continued to write letters to her in which she pretended that

Lucy was still alive but in too much pain from rheumatism to either write letters or visit Glamorgan.

Disaster seemed to follow on disaster. Elinor fell ill and needed to have an operation. Her worry about money increased, so that when her daughters suggested a new financial arrangement she was only too happy to accept it. She could not bear the thought of the indignity of ending her days penniless and dependent as Lucy had done.

Juliet had realised at last that, as long as Elinor could write cheques, she would spend money without thinking about what there was in the bank to cover them. She had lived that way ever since her marriage and it was too late for her to change. So she took over Elinor's cheque book and arranged to pay on Elinor's behalf all the regular bills for rent and utilities. What was left of Elinor's monthly income she gave to her in cash. She could then see for herself exactly what she had to spend each month.

It was not easy for a woman of her age who had once had vast sums of money at her disposal to accept such restrictions. But she was sufficiently haunted by the spectre of being totally without means of her own that she did so. Did she know and relish the irony that her old rival Grace Duggan was similarly short of money by then? The woman who had once been so wealthy no longer owned Hackwood or any of the country houses that Curzon had bought or leased. She was in fact reduced to approaching the Earl of Crawford to help her negotiate the lease of Montacute House from the National Trust. He recorded their conversation in his diary entry of 5 December.

> And now Grace Abounding wants to return to this beautiful manor in the West Country – she has all the necessary furniture – in fact the equipment of the place itself, much of which she told me with real amusement was chosen by Elinor Glyn with whom dear George had a passage (before his second marriage according to his widow) and she, Lady Curzon, says the rooms furnished by the Glyn woman were exactly what are described in *Three Weeks* . . .

There was a further irony and another connection with that unhappy time in Elinor's life when she decided to rent a cottage near Taplow, the home of another old enemy, Lady Desborough. She had never forgiven this member of the Souls for turning Curzon against her. When she now met her again she found her as 'odious' as ever.

Just two years after Lucy's death Mrs Kennedy died in April 1937 at Miskin without ever having known that her daughter had predeceased her. She was ninety-six years old and so her death was no great surprise. But Elinor felt her loss keenly.

As so often before she dealt with grief and upset by moving. She took a modern flat in Curzon House at Saltdean near Brighton. The irony of the name did not escape her. She then set about decorating this modest home in the style of Louis XV.

The Elinor Glyn legend continued to grow. When a young journalist, Charles Graves, met her at a party he was somewhat alarmed by her. He had heard that she was quite capable of putting the evil eye on anyone she did not like. As a precaution he put his hand in his pocket and crossed his fingers tightly. He suffered no ill effects from the encounter but two young models he later introduced to her were less fortunate in her reaction to them. She greatly embarrassed them by rebuking them soundly in public for plucking their eyebrows and telling them that they had no character left in their faces as a result.

Then she was sought out one day by a Mrs Norman Taylor who turned out to be the wife of her cousin who was a Professor at the University of Toronto. Elinor liked her unexpected guest and admired her rather American chic and even talked vaguely of visiting her old home and her family in Canada.

Then in October the *Daily Herald* enquired about serialising an abridged version of *Three Weeks*. But Duckworth decided instead to re-issue the book in December. Once again the tiger-skin rhyme was in circulation and comedians once again made jokes about Nell Glyn; this time Elinor did not mind the publicity at all.

She was now frequently approached by newspapers for articles. She was asked to write something about the sinking of the *Titanic*. *The Winnipeg Free Press* published a long article by her and the *Toronto Star* approached her for material. New options were sold on *His Hour* and *Three Weeks*.

For a while it seemed as if everything was conspiring to make Elinor look to the past. But in October she broke new ground when she published an article entitled 'We – The Women'. It was perhaps the first time that a woman writer associated with glamour and romance had chosen to write about women over fifty.

The wheel had almost turned full circle when in February 1938 she was invited to return to Jersey to be the guest of the Governor and to stay at Government House. She was delighted and moved by the warmth of her reception. She visited all her old haunts but found that Colomberie which had once been her home was gone, and she failed to find the house where she had been born. And at dinner that night, where everything was far more informal than Elinor considered fitting, she remembered that occasion all those years ago when Lillie Langtry had been given just such a reception and when she, a small girl, a nobody, had been thrilled to speak to the famous beauty. Now Lillie Langtry was back for good, buried at St Saviour's.

Elinor remembered how Lucy had told her that Lillie Langtry had hated being old. In *Discretions and Indiscretions* Lucy had recorded a meeting with Lillie Langtry in Monte Carlo when the famous beauty had said: 'There is enough punishment for every sin we have ever committed in our lives in the penalty of growing old.'

Thinking about Lillie Langtry's words Elinor found that she did not agree. She knew she was still beautiful. Young people still admired her as she had recently discovered from Cecil Beaton the photographer and Beverly Nichols a young and aspiring journalist. She did not feel that life was over. She still wanted to write.

Despite being fêted everywhere she went on the island, Elinor was almost as glad to leave Jersey and go to France as she had been when she was a young woman. She found the island oppressive, limiting, full of gossip and backbiting. She was glad that it had not been her fate to stay there.

Back home again she was invited to a literary luncheon at the Dorchester. She astounded the company and consciously added to her image as an unusual and exotic woman by wearing her cat, Candide, draped on her shoulder instead of a more conventional fur.

But even a big luncheon party held at the Berkeley to celebrate her seventy-fifth birthday did not make her forget that once again England was at war with Germany. She remembered the signing of the Peace at Versailles and her premonition that the Germans would be back to fight again. Despite all the horrors she had witnessed in the First World War, she was entirely supportive of this second war against what she considered to be the forces of evil.

Always restless, she moved from Saltdean back to London and a small flat in Carrington House at Shepherd's Market. She did not feel afraid of the bombing which brought back vivid memories of her time in Paris in the First World War, but she did hate the blackout. She fell and hurt her knee once more, and was in pain and more or less immobilised for some time. But she had lots of visitors to cheer her up. One of them, Sir Paul Dukes, entertained her with stories of his time in Intelligence. She was especially interested in what he had to tell her about Russia after the revolution. In return she told him what it had been like before the Czar was deposed.

She went on writing. She began a review of her life and started a new novel. She might have been seventy-five but she was not too old to try a new genre. Her next novel was to be a thriller, unlike anything she had written before.

For the first time she became afraid of old age when her daughters decided that she was not safe in London and took her to Miskin in Glamorgan. This move depressed her greatly. Here she was living in the house where her mother had spent her last days and where she had died. Elinor was not ready to be put aside and be treated as someone helpless and dependent. She proved to herself that she had her old power to charm men. When an RAMC major came to inspect Miskin to see if it was suitable for requisitioning, she insisted on reading aloud to him from *Three Weeks*. He never did see the house. But this was a minor satisfaction only. Elinor continued to find life at Miskin lonely and uncongenial and finally she rebelled. She would not spend her last days in exile apart from her family, seeing them only at holiday time. She returned to her flat in London and in September was back in the social swing attending a literary lunch at Foyles.

She felt truly back at the centre when her old friend William Randolph Hearst asked her to write some articles for his press just as she had done in the First World War. Elinor agreed with alacrity. She set off in great excitement to Downing Street to interview that notorious womaniser, now Minister of Aircraft Production, the former Max Aitken, Lord Beaverbrook. The interview went well and Elinor was most flattered when Beaverbrook said that he remembered meeting her thirty years earlier at a lunch with Ralph Blumenfeld. Evidently she had impressed him more than he had her for she did not recall the occasion at all.

But this high moment was unusual. The war dragged on and touched Elinor's own life more closely. She was proud of her two grandsons in uniform fighting for their country. But, like the rest of the family, she was devastated when the older one was killed. This blow marked a turning point in her life and she was distressed to find that despite all her precautions she was beginning to feel old and slower both physically and mentally. Everything was more effort. When she fell ill, her recovery took longer and was less complete.

One of her remaining pleasures was the company of young people. David Herbert visited her regularly and brought his friend Michael Duff. They came to say goodbye to her just before they set off for the front and Elinor showed them that she still had psychic powers. She told them solemnly that they would return from the war safely but that they were seeing her for the last time. In six months, she told them, she would be dead.

She was right on both counts. The young men did return unharmed but on 23 September 1943 Elinor died in the hospital to which she had been admitted the previous week.

In the States Clara Bow was told of her friend's death. She wept and said she 'felt the world had lost a truly great person'.

30 SUMMING UP

Prompted by Lucy's *Discretions and Indiscretions* and by her sister's death the previous year, in 1936 Elinor decided to review her life and to write her own autobiography. She was as aware of the difference between her public image and the reality of her life as was Beverley Nichols when he wrote in *The Sunday Chronicle*:

> I looked again at the beautiful woman who was still beautiful because of her strict and almost Spartan respect for her body and her looks. It was Elinor Glyn. Reputations are curious things. I suppose if you had asked the average young man on the street what sort of woman Elinor Glyn was, he would tell you that she spent most of her time on a tiger skin, smoking scented cigarettes, writing passionate passages with a purple pen and occasionally sipping a liqueur.
>
> This is so exactly the opposite from her normal mode of life that it is worth noting.
>
> Elinor Glyn does not loll about on tiger skins, nor on anything else. She sits bolt upright on a hard chair. Hence she has the shoulders of a young girl although she is a grandmother. She does not drink liqueurs. She drinks water – lots of it.
>
> Discipline – discipline – discipline – that is the rhythm of Elinor Glyn's life. Mental discipline as well as physical – because she is one of the few women I know who goes daily to the fresh stream of the classics for her inspiration.
>
> And yet in the popular imagination, she is a whirlwind of eroticism.

Romantic Adventure is Elinor's own attempt to redress the balance in the public perception of her life.

She had no scarcity of material and documentation for an autobiography. She had kept a diary since the days when she was Miss Nellie Sutherland on Jersey. The trick would be to select from all those years of outpourings and craft the distillation into a structure more coherent than any life could be.

There are parts of *Romantic Adventure* which are copied straight from the diaries. When this is the case Elinor always alerts the reader to what she is doing. Such passages are mostly descriptions of what she saw and felt at the Front in France during the First World War. The writing is already so economical and vivid and immediate that there was no advantage to be gained in making changes.

But when it comes to the pages and pages of emotional overflowings of intense love, anguish and anger, Elinor uses the discipline of which Nichols speaks and none of this intemperate language finds its way into her autobiography.

Little of her disappointment in her marriage is revealed. Her comments on Clayton are kindly if rueful. She mentions her financial troubles but without revealing the nightmarish proportions they assumed. Her dislike of the Souls is never mentioned. Grace Duggan is not even referred to. It is as if in the process of writing her novels she had purged herself of her negative feelings about many things that had happened to her and many people she had known so that she did not need to dwell on them in her autobiography.

As she looked back it seemed to Elinor that the event which had most shaped her life had been the publication of *Three Weeks*. It was to this book that she owed her exile from society, her fame in Europe and the United States. It was because of that book that she had been invited to Russia, to Spain, to Hungary, to Scandinavia and to Hollywood. Even her passionate affair with George Nathaniel Curzon had begun with his interest in her as the author of that notorious novel.

And so she shapes her autobiography around the publication of *Three Weeks*. Right at the heart of the book is the declaration, 'The book meant everything to me.' Suddenly the reader becomes aware that *Three Weeks* has been woven into the story from the start and that what we are reading could just about be described as an apologia for that book. The passage which begins with the sentence above is a striking and powerful passage with good pace and memorable images such as 'the iron mask of self respect and self control . . . locked round my throat'. The heightened quality of the writing underlines the centrality of this book to Elinor's life.

It was the response to *Three Weeks* that opened Elinor's eyes to her society and affected her judgement of all that happened to her in her subsequent adventures.

At the time that she was writing her autobiography there was a revival of interest in *Three Weeks*. The attitude of English readers to the book in 1936 as opposed to that of the 1908 readers was an indication to Elinor of just how much England had changed during that period. She saw that it had been the war which had been largely responsible for that change. When she had written her novel it had been almost unthinkable that a woman should lead a man in a sexual relationship. But in 1936 women no longer always necessarily took a subordinate role, in sexual matters, in the family, or in the workplace. They even had the vote. It was no longer outrageous to discuss sex and there was less hypocrisy about relationships between men and women.

But it was not only society in general that had changed. All that had happened to her after the publication of *Three Weeks* had changed Elinor herself. Her own participation in the war had changed many of her opinions. She could look back on the extreme Conservative, hierarchical, imperialist views of her youth and early middle age and admit that she had been wrong.

In Hollywood she had seen class barriers broken down still further, but in retrospect she saw that there money had replaced class and that no longer seemed right to her either.

There is another, more personal reason why *Three Weeks* is at the centre of Elinor's autobiography. One of the most important relationships in her life had been with Lord Curzon. It was he who had given her most joy and been responsible for most despair. Yet the reader of *Romantic Adventure* would never know this. In the book he is described as if he were simply a good friend whom Elinor greatly admired for his qualities as a statesman. The joys and despairs brought about by *Three Weeks* echo and substitute for those of the real love affair.

Apparently Elinor was not alone in seeing the publication of *Three Weeks* as the central event of her life. For it is an irony, which would have greatly amused Elinor and confirmed her view of her life, that, when in 1974 an exhibition was mounted at the Ferrers Gallery to commemorate the 'Life and Times of Elinor Glyn', it was not her autobiography, *Romantic Adventure*, that was reissued to mark the occasion. It was *Three Weeks*. What would have pleased her greatly about this was that at this late date the book received good reviews. She would have appreciated being described by Peter Levi in *The Observer* as 'psychologically very accurate', and she would have welcomed his recognition that 'what must have shocked the world is that the fantasy is entirely female'. At long last her own view of herself and her novel was vindicated.

So what was it about Elinor Glyn that made her such a figure in her own day and that allows her work to continue to inspire readers? The question is best answered by a comment made by Peter Keating in *The Times Literary Supplement* in November 1974, a comment which describes what attracted so many people to Elinor herself in her lifetime, despite her self-confessed faults of vanity, snobbishness and extravagance. It is a quality which shines through her work even after her death. She was, above all, a woman who possessed 'magnificent vitality'.

NOTES

Three: First Impressions

1. Elinor Glyn, *Romantic Adventure* (New York, Dutton, 1937), p.4. Unless otherwise indicated all other quotations are from this autobiography.
2. Anthony Glyn, *Elinor Glyn: A Biography* (London, Hutchinson 1955), p.8. All future quotations attributed to this author are from the biography.
3. *idem*
   The house has undergone many changes since Elinor lived there. Twelve rooms at the back were moved to form a separate establishment on the estate. Later the estate itself was subdivided but the trees which surrounded the house in the 1860s are still there.
4. Edith Wharton, *A Backward Glance* (New York, Appleton Century, 1934), p.330.

Four: A Suitor

1. Lady Duff Gordon, *Discretions and Indiscretions* (London, Jarrolds, 1932), p.21.

Five: The New Life

1. Anthony Glyn, p.36.

Seven: La Belle Tigresse

1. Quoted by Arthur Gold and Robert Fizdale, *The Divine Sarah* (New York, Knopf, 1991), p.190.
2. Ruth Brandon, *Being Divine* (London, Secker & Warburg, 1991), p.330.

Ten: Marriage

1. Quoted by Keith Alldritt, *Churchill The Writer: His Life as a Man of Letters* (London, Hutchinson, 1992), pp.164–165.
2. Frances, Countess of Warwick, *Afterthoughts* (London, Cassell, 1931), p.158.
3. *idem*
4. *idem*

Eleven: Disillusionment

1. Quoted by R.W.B. Lewis, *Edith Wharton* (New York, Harper &

Row, 1975), p.437.
2. Anthony Glyn, p.79.

Twelve: A New Lease of Life

1. Anthony Glyn, p.82.
2. Frances, Countess of Warwick, p.159.
3. Anthony Glyn, p.82.

Thirteen: Financial Troubles

1. Consuelo Vanderbilt Balsan, *The Glitter and the Gold* (New York, Harper & Brothers, 1952), p.28.
2. Harold Nicolson, *Small Talk* (New York, Harcourt Brace, 1937), p.76.
3. Quoted by Peter Mansfield, *The British in Egypt* (London, Weidenfeld & Nicolson, 1971), p.318.

Fourteen: The First Tiger Skin

1. Theo Aronson, *The King in Love* (London, John Murray, 1988), p.180.
2. Axel Munthe, *The Story of San Michele* (London, John Murray, 1929), p.32.

Fifteen: A Changing World

1. R.D. Blumenfeld, *R.D.B.'s Diary* (London, Heinemann 1930), p.72.
2. Theo Aronson, p.218.
3. Quoted by Daphne Bennett, *Margot* (London, Gollancz, 1984), p.101.

Eighteen: Passion

1. Winston S. Churchill, *Great Contemporaries* (London, Thornton Butterworth, 1932), p.176.
2. Anthony Glyn, p.177.

Nineteen: Russia

1. Quoted by Dennis Stuart, *Dear Duchess: Millicent Duchess of Sutherland 1867–1955* (London, Gollancz, 1982), p.99.

Twenty-One: A Challenge to the Souls

1. Ruth Brandon, *The Dollar Princesses* (London, Weidenfeld & Nicolson, 1980), p.118.
2. Lady Duff Gordon, p.207.
3. R.W.B. Lewis, p.355.
4. Edith Wharton, *A Backward Glance*, p.336.

NOTES

Twenty-Two: Sharp Practice

1. Quoted by Nigel Nicolson, *Mary Curzon* (London, Weidenfeld & Nicolson, 1977), pp.126–7.
2. Anthony Glyn, p.226.
3. Quoted by Leonard Mosley, *The Glorious Fault* (New York, Harcourt Brace, 1960), p.159.
4. Humphrey Lewis was kind enough to draw my attention to the details of this case.

Twenty-Four: Interim

1. Quoted by Meredith Etherington-Smith and Jeremy Pilcher, *The It Girls* (London, Hamish Hamilton, 1986), p.194.
2. A.J.P. Taylor, ed., *Lloyd George: A Diary by Frances Stevenson* (London, Hutchinson, 1971), p.185.
3. Lady Angela Forbes, *Fore and Aft* (London, Hutchinson, undated), p.15.
4. This information was kindly supplied by James R. Mellow.
   The letter from Gertrude Stein to Ernest Hemingway in the Hemingway Collection, John F. Kennedy Library, Boston, is dated 11 July 1924.

Twenty-Five: Hollywood Adventure

1. Philip French, *The Movie Moguls* (Chicago, Regnery, 1969), p.47.
2. Gloria Swanson, *Swanson on Swanson: An Autobiography* (New York, Random House, 1970), p.160.
3. Samuel Goldwyn, *Behind the Screen* (New York, Doran Company, 1923), pp.236–7.
4. *ibid.* p.239.
5. *ibid.* p.248.

Twenty-Six: New Friends

1. Charles Chaplin, *My Autobiography* (New York, Simon & Schuster, 1964), p.202.
2. Quoted in *The It Girls*, p.220.
3. Charles Chaplin, p.309.
4. Anita Loos, *A Girl Like I* (New York, Viking, 1966), p.119.
5. Gloria Swanson, p.173.

Twenty-Seven: A Hectic and Abnormal Life

1. Anita Loos, p.120.
2. Raymond Durgnat and Scott Simmon, *King Vidor, American* (Berkeley, University of California, 1988), p.53.

3. *ibid.* p.54.
4. Leonard Mosley, p.257.
5. Charles Chaplin, p.318.

Twenty-Eight: The It Girl

1. David Stenn, *Clara Bow Runnin' Wild* (New York, Doubleday, 1988), p.5.
2. *ibid.* pp.100–101.
3. *ibid.* p.2.

SELECT BIBLIOGRAPHY

Abdy, Jane & Gere, Charlotte, *The Souls: An Elite in English Society* (London, Sidgwick & Jackson, 1984).
Alldritt, Keith, *Churchill The Writer: His Life As A Man Of Letters* (London, Hutchinson, 1992).
Aronson, Theo, *The King in Love* (London, John Murray, 1988).
Balsan, Consuelo Vanderbilt, *The Glitter and the Gold* (New York, Harper, 1952).
Beaumann, Nicola, *Cynthia Asquith* (London, Hamish Hamilton, 1987).
Bennett, Daphne, *Margot* (London, Gollancz, 1984).
Benson, E.F., *Dodo* (London, Methuen, 1894).
Blumenfeld, R.D., *R.D.B.'s Diary* (London, Heinemann, 1930).
Blunden, Margaret, *The Countess of Warwick* (London, Cassell, 1967).
Brandon, Ruth, *The Dollar Princesses* (London, Weidenfeld & Nicolson, 1980).
Brandon, Ruth, *Being Divine* (London, Secker & Warburg, 1991).
Brownlow, Kevin, *The Parade's Gone By* (New York, Knopf, 1968).
Chaney, L. & Cieply, M. *The Hearst Family and Empire – The Later Years* (New York, Simon and Schuster, 1981).
Chaplin, Charles, *My Autobiography* (New York, Simon and Schuster, 1964).
Churchill, Winston S., *Great Contemporaries* (London, Thornton Butterworth, 1932).
Cronin, Vincent, *Louis XIV* (London, Collins, 1964).
Curzon of Kedleston, The Marchioness, *Reminiscences* (London, Hutchinson, 1955).
De Wolfe, Elsie, *After All* (New York, Harper & Bros., 1935).
Duff Gordon, Lady Lucy, *Discretions and Indiscretions* (London, Jarrolds, 1932).
Durgnat, R. & Simmon, S., *King Vidor, American* (Berkeley, University of California Press, 1988).
Egremont, Max, *The Cousins* (London, Collins, 1977).
Erskine, Lady Angela St. Clair, *Fore and Aft* (London, Jarrolds, 1932).
Etherington-Smith, M. & Pilcher, J., *The It Girls* (London, Hamish Hamilton, 1986).
Fine, Richard, *Hollywood and the Profession of Authorship, 1928–1940* (Ann Arbor, UMI Press, 1985).
Forbes, Lady Angela, *Memories and Base Details* (London, Hutchinson, undated).
French, Philip, *The Movie Moguls* (Chicago, Regnery, 1969).
Gelman, Barbara (ed.), *Photoplay Treasury* (New York, Crown, 1972).
Glyn, Anthony, *Elinor Glyn: A Biography* (London, Hutchinson, 1955).
Gold, Arthur and Fizdale, Robert, *The Divine Sarah* (New York, Knopf, 1991).
Goldwyn, Samuel, *Behind The Screen* (New York, Doran Company, 1923).
Guiles, Fred Lawrence, *Marion Davies* (New York, McGraw Hill, 1972).

Hamilton, Ian, *Writers In Hollywood* (London, William Heinemann, 1990).
Herbert, David, *Second Son: An Autobiography* (London, Peter Owen, 1972).
Herndon, Booton, *Mary Pickford and Douglas Fairbanks* (New York, Norton, 1977).
Ingalese, Richard, *The History and Power of Mind* (New York, Dodd Mead, 1924).
James, Robert Rhodes ed., *Chips: The Diaries of Sir Henry Channon* (London, Weidenfeld & Nicolson, 1967).
Johnson, Leo A., *The History of Guelph 1827–1927* (Guelph, Guelph Historical Society, 1977).
Judd, Dennis, *The Life and Times of George V* (London, Weidenfeld & Nicolson, 1973).
Katkov, George, *Russia 1917: The February Revolution* (New York, Harper & Row, 1967).
Knoblock, Edward, *Round The Room: An Autobiography* (London, Chapman Hall, 1939).
Kobal, John, *Hollywood The Years of Innocence* (London, Thames and Hudson, 1985).
Leslie, Anita, *Edwardians in Love* (London, Hutchinson, 1972).
Lewis, R.W.B., *Edith Wharton* (New York, Harper & Row, 1975).
Loos, Anita, *A Girl Like I* (New York, Viking, 1966).
Mansfield, Peter, *The British in Egypt* (London, Weidenfeld & Nicolson, 1971).
Massie, Robert K., *Nicholas and Alexandra* (New York, Atheneum, 1967).
Mellow, James R., *Charmed Circle: Gertrude Stein & Company* (New York, Praeger, 1974).
Mellow, James R., *Hemingway: A Life Without Consequences* (London, Hodder & Stoughton, 1993).
Middleboe, Penelope, *Edith Olivier from her Journals 1924–48* (London, Weidenfeld & Nicolson, 1989).
Minney, R.J., *The Edwardian Age* (London, Cassell, 1964).
Morley, Sheridan, *Tales From The Hollywood Raj* (London, Weidenfeld & Nicolson, 1983).
Mosley, Leonard, *The Glorious Fault: The Life of Lord Curzon* (New York, Harcourt Brace, 1960).
Mosley, Nicholas, *Rules of the Game: Sir Oswald and Lady Cynthia Mosley* (London, Secker & Warburg, 1982).
Munthe, Axel, *The Story of San Michele* (London, John Murray, 1929).
Nicolson, Harold, *Small Talk* (New York, Harcourt Brace, 1937).
Nicolson, Nigel, *Mary Curzon* (London, Weidenfeld & Nicolson, 1977).
Norton, Lucy (ed. and trans), *Historical Memoirs of the Duc de Saint-Simon* (London, Hamish Hamilton, 1967).
Pickford, Mary, *Sunshine and Shadow* (New York, Doubleday & Co. Inc., 1955).
Pound, Reginald, *The Lost Generation* (London, Constable, 1964).
Priestley, J.B., *The Edwardians* (London, Heinemann, 1970).

Richardson, Joanna, *Sarah Bernhardt* (New York, Max Reinhardt, 1959).
Riddell, Lord, *Intimate Diary of the Peace Conference and After 1918–1919* (London, Gollancz, 1933).
Robinson, David, *Chaplin: His Life and Art* (London, Collins, 1985).
Robinson, David, *Hollywood in the Twenties* (New York, Tantivy Press, 1968).
Rose, Kenneth, *Superior Person* (London, Weidenfeld & Nicolson, 1969).
Rosslyn, The Earl of, *My Gamble With Life* (New York, J.H. Sears & Co., 1928).
Sackville-West, Victoria, *The Edwardians* (London, The Hogarth Press, 1930).
Salisbury, Harrison E., *Black Night, White Snow: Russia's Revolutions 1905–1917* (New York, Doubleday & Co. Inc., 1978).
Stenn, David, *Clara Bow Runnin' Wild* (New York, Doubleday, 1988).
Stuart, Dennis, *Dear Duchess: Millicent Duchess of Sutherland 1867–1955* (London, Gollancz, 1982).
Swanson, Gloria, *Swanson on Swanson: An Autobiography* (New York, Random House, 1980).
Taylor, A.J.P. (ed.), *Lloyd George: A Diary by Frances Stevenson* (London, Hutchinson, 1971).
Tweedsmuir, Lady Susan, *The Edwardian Lady* (London, Duckworth, 1966).
Vincent, John (ed.), *The Crawford Papers* (Manchester, Manchester University Press, 1984).
Walker, Alexander, *Rudolph Valentino* (Harmondsworth, Penguin, 1977).
Warwick, Frances Countess of, *Afterthoughts* (London, Cassell, 1931).
Wharton, Edith, *A Backward Glance* (New York, Appleton Century, 1934).
Wharton, Edith, *Fighting France from Dunkerque to Belfort* (New York, Scribners' Sons, 1915).
Wharton, Edith, *French Ways and Their Meaning* (New York, D. Appleton & Co., 1919).
Wharton, Edith, *The Marne* (New York, Appleton and Company, 1918).
Wrench, John Evelyn, *Alfred Lord Milner: The Man of No Illusions 1854–1925* (London, Eyre and Spottiswoode, 1958).

INDEX